Arthur Latham Perry

Introduction to political Economy

Arthur Latham Perry

Introduction to political Economy

ISBN/EAN: 9783337076320

Printed in Europe, USA, Canada, Australia, Japan

Cover: Foto ©ninafisch / pixelio.de

More available books at **www.hansebooks.com**

INTRODUCTION

TO

POLITICAL ECONOMY

· BY

ARTHUR LATHAM PERRY, LL.D.,

Orrin Sage Professor of History and Political Economy in Williams College.

A market for products is products in market.

NEW YORK:

CHARLES SCRIBNER'S SONS,

743 AND 745 BROADWAY.

1883.

TO

My Only Brother,

BAXTER EDWARDS PERRY,

AND TO

My Nephew, the Blind Pianist,

EDWARD BAXTER PERRY.

PREFACE.

I **HAVE** endeavored in this book so to lay the foundations of Political Economy in their whole circuit,
that they will never need to be disturbed afterwards by
persons resorting to it for their early instruction, however long and however far these persons may pursue
their studies in this science. It seems to me of no
advantage, but quite the reverse, for any young person
to gain a conception of a science that will have to be
discarded afterwards for a better one, or to lay in the
interest of ease and quickness temporary foundations
that will have to be relaid before any solid and extended
superstructure can be built upon them.

I have endeavored at the same time to make the
sense of every sentence as clear as language can make
it, and to connect the limitations of all general principles with the statement of the principles themselves.
Political Economy has to deal throughout with the
idea of Value, which is not only an abstract but also a
relative idea; and it is a task of some difficulty to
combine with a scientific exactness of treatment a
plain and easy way of putting the points before young
minds. I dare not hope that I have succeeded completely in this task; for I appreciate thoroughly what

is involved in the fact that two desires and two efforts of two persons, and these in constant action and re-action on each other, must be borne in mind throughout in each and every transaction involving Value; but I have aimed constantly at simplicity in connection with accuracy, and at making the discussions as lively and interesting as the subject-matter will allow.

I have also tried to make the discussions bear directly upon questions of current interest, such as the disputed points in relation to Money, Trade and Taxation; and the illustrations of principles have been drawn almost entirely from recent facts and events in this country and in Europe; so that there is reason to hope that the book may prove acceptable to general readers of all ages in life, while its more special aim is to become a text-book in high schools, academies and colleges. It is believed both by author and publishers that young persons of ordinary intelligence and training, who have reached the age of fourteen years, will find no difficulty in mastering every point in these pages; and it is also believed that many colleges, which feel compelled to allot too short a time to this science for the mastery of a more copious treatise, will find this compact presentation of economical facts and principles just adapted to their wants.

It is now fifteen years since my larger book on Political Economy was given to the public. I am deeply grateful to teachers and others, whose kindly appreciation of that book has already carried it to its seventeenth edition. The present volume is not designed in any sense to take the place of that: because, while that is copious, this is condensed; while that is comprehensive in fifteen chapters, this is restrictive in six; and while that is considerably historical even in form, this recurs to history solely for scientific illustration. Still the present volume is not at all a mere compend of that, but is throughout a new book, very few sentences having been transferred from one book to the other, and fresh illustrations having been employed for the most part. The same scientific divisions and doctrines are of course maintained in them both; and the same profound convictions — the result of thirty years' study and teaching — are expressed and argued in them both. If the public shall continue to accord its favor to the older book, it is my firm purpose to continue to keep it, by revision and amendment, fully abreast of the times so long as it promises to be useful. And, if the public shall approve of this second pains-taking attempt at once to systematize and popularize Political Economy, I shall spare no future pains to make it as perfect in substance and in form as my abilities may permit it to become.

The readers of these books have certainly not found in either of them the Scotch Economy of Adam Smith, the English Economy of John Stuart Mill, or the American Economy of any of my predecessors in this country; that is to say, my main point of view, and the consequent scientific outlines of the whole subject, are quite different from theirs: not that I sought for novelties, but I sought for a point of view that would yield *a distinct province* for the science, — a province that could be circumscribed by an exact definition, and then scientifically subdivided in accordance with an actual state of things. I found that province to be described by the terms Buying and Selling, and the subdivisions of things bought and sold to be Commodities,

Services, and Claims; and accordingly I defined Political Economy to be the Science of Sales, and proceeded to elaborate (very imperfectly indeed at first) the whole subject from that single point of view, and was delighted to find that every thing fell orderly into its proper place under that view, that the gain over the old Economy was great in point of simplicity and exactness and certainty, and that *here* indeed was a science " clear as the sun and beautiful as the moon." The Frenchmen Condillac and Bastiat, the Englishmen Whately and Macleod, and several others also, had labored in these precise directions before me; but with the exception of Bastiat's, to which I am always most glad to acknowledge my obligations, their work was wholly unknown to me when I published my first book in 1866; and I do not know that any one of them all ever carried out before that time into all its parts this fundamental conception of Political Economy.

I have long been, and am still, ambitious that these books of mine may become the horn-books of my countrymen in the study of this fascinating science. Unless indeed these may already be said to be such, there are certainly none such at present; and it is a pleasure to think that only *better* books than these can ever displace them from their hold already gained on the public.

As the motto on the title-page of this volume has been in certain quarters referred to as a proverb, I deem it proper to state that the expression is my own, and that it may be found in the first edition of the book already referred to.

A. L. Perry.

Williams College, Aug. 16, 1880.

TABLE OF CONTENTS.

POLITICAL ECONOMY.

CHAPTER I.

THE first thing to learn in the study of Political Economy is the answer to the question, "*What is it about?*" The adjective "Political" set before the noun "Economy" leads some people to suppose that the subject is somehow related to Politics, which is only true in a remote and incidental way; and thus this *name*, under which the science has mostly gone since Antoine de Montchristien issued his book with this title at Rouen, in France, in 1613, has been some hinderance to the proper unfolding and understanding of the subject; especially as Aristotle, a great thinker among the Greeks, first used this name in a different and political sense, although he threw out many sound thoughts upon the real subject-matter of our science more than three hundred years before Christ.

To remove this hinderance out of the way, sev-

eral other names for the science have been sug
gested from time to time; for example, "Catalac-
tics," from the Greek verb *to exchange*, suggested
by Archbishop Whately in 1831, and "Economics,"
suggested more recently by Mr. Macleod. The
last, which is perhaps the best, drops the usual
adjective, but retains with a changed ending the
noun, which comes from two Greek words meaning *the law of the estate.* Stern usage, however,
seems already to have fixed the old name beyond
the likelihood of any general adoption of a new
one; and there is a certain reason, which will
appear by and by, why even the adjective "Political" is not wholly at fault in this connection.

What is it about? Let one stand for an hour
upon London Bridge, — perhaps the busiest bit of
street in the world, — and watch the passers-by
and whatever else can be seen from that stand-
point, and he will soon satisfy himself that the
most of the bustling activity in view is the activity
of *buyers and sellers.* Goods of every description
are being carried back and forth; artisans of
every name are going and coming; merchants of
many nationalities step within the field of view,
porters and servants and errand-boys are moving
to and fro; vast warehouses, built in the interest
of trade, lift their roofs towards heaven; the river
above and the "Pool" below are alive with boats
and ships; and nearly the whole of all this, and
of much more than all this, is in direct reference to
buying and selling. Doubtless some few persons,

like our observer himself, may be there for mere
pleasure or instruction; but, for the most part, the
persons, the things, the buildings, even the bridge
itself, are there in the interest of *Sales* of some
sort. What is thus true of a single part of London is true of every other part of London, of
every part of New York, and of Chicago, and, in
its measure, of every other city, village, and ham-
let in the whole world. Wherever there is a
street there is trade, wherever there is a market
there are buyers and sellers.

One cannot live long in the world without see-
ing and continuing to see that by much the largest
part of the visible activities of men is employed in
some form of buying and selling. To get something ready to sell, and then to sell it, is the principal work of all civilized people. The farm, the
shop, the store, the street, the bank, the office, the
market, the school, the church, — all are places for
buying and selling. One soon sees, too, that each
buyer is at the same time a seller, and each seller
at the same moment a buyer. The buyer must
pay for what he buys by selling that which he
pays with, and the seller take pay for what he
sells by buying that with which he is paid. Indeed, no man can buy without selling, or sell
without buying. Our observer perceives also
after a while, that as the world gets older and
more civilized, and as any society of men anywhere becomes more advanced, these relations
between individuals as buyers and sellers become

more numerous and intricate, and the *actions* put forth by them all in reference to sales of some kind become more apparent, more absorbing, and more cosmopolitan. ˙*Precisely these actions in their motive, operation, and result, are the subject of Political Economy.* Our science has to do with nothing on earth but Sales.

Can there be a strict *Science* of Sales? Certainly. There *is* such a science already, although it has been largely built up under a narrow and imperfect nomenclature. It has usually been called, in England and America, the Science of Wealth; but the word "Wealth" is at the same time too vague and too narrow for the purposes of this science, and has been the main reason of its relatively slow progress, and of its still too slight public recognition. This word is entirely needless as well as always confusing, and has now at length been discarded as a scientific term, to the great advantage of the science in point of breadth, clearness, and certainty. While deeply indebted to Aristotle, to Quesnay, to Adam Smith, to Bastiat, and to many more, who have used this word, or some equally concrete equivalent, the science can be under no obligation to continue to use the poor tools of its founders when every way better ones offer themselves to its later laborers.

To show that Political Economy fulfils every condition of a strict science, it becomes necessary to define that word. *A Science is the body of exact definitions and sound principles educed from and*

applied to a single class of facts or phenomena.
Sales, or, what has precisely the same economic
meaning, Exchanges, are the class of facts with
which our science has to do. They *are* a class of
facts distinct by themselves, — never confounded
with gifts, and never confounded with thefts, —
and that is the first condition of a science. Then
they are open to observation and analysis, to all
the processes of Induction and Deduction, consequently to "exact definitions" and the educing
and testing of "principles," — and that is the
second condition of a strict science. Moreover,
these facts are universal: everybody takes part
in them more or less, — and thus the science has
the advantage of everybody's introspection and
experience, since everybody knows something of
the motive, the operation, and the result of those
actions peculiarly human, which we call sales or
exchanges. And, lastly, these actions are of such
a nature that all the parts of them may be orderly
arranged into a "body;" all the definitions and
principles, the proofs and illustrations, may be
grouped in one harmonious whole.

In developing this science thus shown to be
possible and actual, we shall find that sales in all
their kinds, extent, and gainfulness, are influenced
and determined by three things only, to which, as
the sources whence all the points and principles
of the science are drawn, we shall constantly need
to have our attention directed : namely, — first,
those invariable attributes of *human nature* which

have always led men, and always will lead them,
to buy and sell; second, those arrangements of
Providence in the physical earth and the structure
of society, by which his design is manifest that
men should promote their welfare by buying and
selling; and, third, those *laws and usages devised
by men* to facilitate on the one hand, or to impede
on the other hand, the privilege of buying and
selling. To avoid monotony of expression, we
shall use interchangeably the synonymous terms,
" Sales " and " Exchanges," to denote those actions
of men, which are the direct subject of our study.
These actions are not done in a corner : the earli
est dawn of History shows us men already engaged
in them ; and the welfare and progress of mankind
have always been promoted by them.

The one peculiarity of the actions referred to,
that brings them under the view of this science,
is, *that one person renders something to another for
the sake of receiving back from that person something in return.* The milkman, for example, delivers to the baker a quart of milk, and receives in
pay a loaf of bread. This is a simple instance
of exchange, and contains, in substance, the points
of the whole matter. Let us analyze this instance.

First, there are two persons, the milkman and
the baker. Second, there are two things, the quart
of milk and the loaf of bread. Third, there are
two desires, the desire of the milkman for bread
and the desire of the baker for milk. Fourth,
there are two efforts involved, the effort of the

milkman to procure the milk and the effort of the baker to procure the loaf. Fifth, there are two estimates implied, the estimate of the milkman by which he prefers the loaf to the milk, and the estimate of the baker by which he prefers the milk to the loaf. Sixth, there are two actions, the action, namely, of each party passing over to the other the ownership in something for the sake of receiving from the other the ownership in something else. Seventh, there are two satisfactions, for the sake of which the transaction was had, and in which the transaction ends, namely, the satisfaction of the milkman in the possession of the loaf of bread and the satisfaction of the baker in the possession of the quart of milk. It is with such transactions as this, and only with such, every one of which has the peculiarity defined above, and every one of which can be analyzed with the same results as this, that our science of Political Economy has to do.

In this instance of the exchange of the milk for the bread, or, what is exactly the same thing, the bread for the milk, the things exchanged are material, visible, tangible things, such as are called in Political Economy *Commodities*. This is the first class of things exchanged, and they must be carefully noted. Originally, the word *commodity* was an abstract noun, and meant nearly the same as *utility*. Gradually it took on a concrete sense, and came to mean the things that afford the utility rather than the utility itself, such as goods, wares, merchandise, the produce of land and man· ufactures. About two hundred years ago, Locke said, " Commodities are movables, valuable by money, the common measure." Although the notion of movableness was long attached, and is still attached more or less, to the term Commodi· ties, the legal distinction between Real Estate and Movables is quite different from the economical distinction between commodities and the other two classes of exchangeable things.

The distinctive feature of commodities is the fact that they are material rather than movable, and, as material, may be possessed, employed, and sold by individuals. The ownership always, and the com- modity itself usually, pass over at the time of the sale into the hands of the buyer. For example, a barrel of flour, a bale of cotton, a bushel of corn, a bag of coffee, are commodities. All such salable things from the jewel to a top are commodities. Horses and cattle are commodities. Ships are com- modities. Houses and lands, provided an absolute title to the whole of them can be given by one per- son to another, are commodities also. A railroad might be a commodity under the definition, but is commonly bought and sold by means of *Shares* so-called, which belong to a different class of salable things, as we shall see. When, in 1867, the United States Government purchased of the Russian empire for $7,200,000 the territory called Alaska, both the sale and purchase were acts of sovereignty, and acts of sovereignty are very

different from acts of ordinary sale, and conse
quently, Alaska could not properly be called a
commodity. Governments often buy and sell
commodities proper, but in this case they are acting commercially, as individuals act, and not in
their capacity as sovereignties. It is only with
sales in a purely commercial sense that our science
has any thing to do.

The exchanges in the market-place, the trade of
the shops, the commerce of the world, are largely
in commodities. But it would be a serious mistake to suppose that nothing is ever bought or
sold excepting things of this character. Over
against commodities, and yet having perfectly the
peculiarity already mentioned, stands a second
class of salable things, what are called in this
science *Personal Services.*

For example, a physician is called to prescribe
for a patient in a case of fever. He renders to
that patient no material thing, not even medicine.
He writes a prescription merely. But he renders
something nevertheless; something, too, which the
patient, or his friends, prefer to that which he or
they must render in return ; the physician renders
the intangible result of his medical skill, and the
patient, if he gets well, or his representative, if he
does not, in due time renders a five-dollar gold-piece
in pay. This is a commercial transaction. It is a
sale. The physician sells the result of his skill,
which was acquired for that very purpose. He
sells a personal service, and takes in this case a

commodity for pay. He might sell his personal service, and take in pay the personal service of somebody else, as, for example, the lawyer's service, who collects for him his bills. The domestic servant, the dramatic actor, the skilful singer, the eloquent advocate, the patient teacher, the faithful preacher, and a thousand more, sell their personal services, that is, render an immaterial, intangible something to others for the sake of receiving from them something else in return, and thus come completely under the view of Political Economy. No inconsiderable part of the exchanges of the world are in things of this second sort.

But there is still one other class of exchangeable things. A little way back, a reference was made to railroad shares. These may illustrate the nature of the third and only remaining class of things that are ever bought and sold. A railroad share does not give a title to a specific part of the railroad, still less to the railroad itself, as a deed does to real estate, or a bill of sale to personal property, it is a *claim* or *right* merely. It gives the owner a claim to a certain proportion of the net earnings of the railroad. It gives him a right to participate in a certain way in the management of the road. It is property, because it was bought and may again be sold. It is not a title to any specific thing whatever, as a bill of lading is a title to a parcel of goods, but a general claim, or a right to demand something of somebody under specified conditions.

A railroad bond is similar to a railroad share in its nature as a claim, though the specified conditions of the right to demand something in virtue of it are different. A bond of the United States vests in the owner a right to demand of the government a certain sum as interest and another certain sum as principal at certain specified times. A United States treasury note, commonly called a greenback, is a printed promise of the government to pay to the bearer a certain number of dollars. Dollars are a commodity, but these promises are a claim. Bank bills, bank checks, all notes of hand, charges in a trader's book, copyrights, leases, and many more such things, belong to this third class of salable things. I shall generally call them *claims*. In some connections, the word *credits* best expresses their nature, in other connections, the word *rights*, — meaning always, of course, commercial rights. The amount of transactions throughout the world in this class of things is something amazing: the daily average exchanges of checks and bills at the London Bankers' Clearing House is about $100,000,000; at the New York Clearing House at present, a little less than $75,000,000. In 1872, the clearings at New York were over $32,000,000,000 for the year. These immense sums represent but a small fraction of the amount of the world's annual transactions in claims of all sorts, including international bills of exchange.

If any one of my readers is disposed to question the accuracy of this analysis, and to think that

there are more than three classes of purchasable
things, the exercise of his ingenuity in trying to
discover a fourth class is likely to convince him in
a little time that there is here a true trinity, as so
often elsewhere in Nature. The interchanges of
friendship, the gifts and self-denials of love, the
bestowments of benevolence, as well as all frauds,
thefts and robberies, are clearly out of the question here. These fall into the sphere of morals, not
into the sphere of economy. The renderings of
charity are free — *they* look not for a return; the
impulses of Duty are quite distinct from the impulses of trade; and stealing, to which all fraud is
assimilated, is a function of force, and not of mutual
consent. The economical rendering is always voluntary, is always made in view of a return and for
the sake of a return, and this gives a pretty sharp
line of difference between economy and morals.

If, then, there are only three classes of things
commercially exchangeable, it follows that there
are only six cases of exchange possible; — namely,
(1) a commodity for a commodity, as the milk for
the bread; (2) a commodity for a personal service,
as the half-eagle for the doctor's prescription; (3)
a commodity for a claim, as a house for ten railroad shares; (4) a personal service for a personal
service, as, the physician's exchange with the
lawyer, already mentioned; (5) a personal service
for a claim, as a month's work for a fifty-dollar
bill; and (6) a claim for a claim, as a lease of a
hotel for a bond of the United States. I believe

that every commercial transaction, that ever was made or ever will be made, falls under one or other of these six cases.

The field of our science is now pretty definitely before us. We are to inquire after the terms, the definitions, the principles and their proofs, that are concerned with all these exchanges. It is obvious from all the old records of our race that such exchanges have been very numerous from the beginnings of history; it is open to observation and record that these exchanges are constantly becoming more numerous, delicate and complicated; the thoughts and efforts of most men are constantly employed in making exchanges, or in preparing to make them; the continued existence, the increased comforts, the moral progress of mankind are largely dependent upon the ease and multiplication of exchanges; and while many men have always given their minds to devise means to make exchanges easy, it is also true that some men have given, and are still giving, their minds to devise expedients to make exchanges difficult. The practical importance, accordingly, of this subject is very great. It would be impossible to overstate its importance. The French economist Say has shown that most of the European wars of the seventeenth and eighteenth centuries grew out of false principles relating to this subject. Very lately Gov. Musgrave has said,[1] "I suppose that the teachers of

[1] Studies in Political Economy. London, 1875.

no science have so much human misery to answer
for, or have assisted at so much fraud, as the
doctors of Political Economy." The late Mr.
Buckle affirmed on the other hand that "Adam
Smith contributed more, by the publication of his
Wealth of Nations, towards the happiness of man,
than has been effected by the united abilities of
all the statesmen and legislators of whom history
has preserved an authentic account." It is, therefore, to questions of vital consequence to the welfare and progress of society that the attention of
the students of this science is called.

Now we are ready for a technical definition of
political economy. It is the *Science of Exchanges.*
It was the French writer Condillac, in 1776, the
same year in which Adam Smith's "Wealth of
Nations" appeared, who first gave this definition
to the science. The popularity of the latter
book overshadowed the definition for a long time
until it was re-proposed by Whately in 1831, and
adopted by the Scotch economist Macleod in
1858, and by the present writer in the first edition of his larger book in 1866. It may now be
said to have become the leading definition in all
countries, and it is certain ultimately to dislodge
all others, because only this expression or some
equivalent one defines perfectly the subject-matter of the science. The German writer Kiehl [1]
gives as his more exact definition of the subject
an equivalent phrase which we shall consider a

[1] Anfangsgründe der Volkswirthschaft. Berlin, 1875.

little further on. Just so far as the word
" wealth " appears in the definition and scientific
discussions of the subject, cloudiness in it a⁻d
distrust of it appear also, because 'that worδ is
not broad enough and definite enough for the use
proposed, and because indefiniteness at the beginning carries indefiniteness throughout the discussion. On the other hand, the term " Exchanges " circumscribes the field of economical
inquiries simply and exactly.

But we are not yet through with our prelimi-
naries. Another piece of analysis must conduct
us through the word " exchanges " to a word still
more important than that, — to the word which is
the title of this our opening chapter. In any one
of the six cases of possible exchanges, already
exemplified, we need a term to express the *power*
of either of the things exchanged to procure the
other. Take again, for example, the loaf of bread
and the quart of milk. There is something in
the loaf then and there, — not indeed in itself
considered, but considered in reference to the
quart of milk, and to the desires and estimates
of the owners of each, — that enables its owner
to procure by means of it the quart of milk.
Precisely the same sort of power in the same circumstances enables the owner of the milk to procure the bread. It goes almost without saying,
that *persons* are more important in Political
Economy than *things;* that the buyer is of more
consequence *economically* as well as morally than

that which he buys, and the seller than that which he sells. The power consequently is not *in* either commodity looked at by itself, but it is in each looked at in relation to the other, and to the *wants* of the two *owners* respectively. The one commodity has this power in the same sense as the other, and the degree of it in each is measured in the terms of the other. How much purchasing-power has the loaf? Enough to buy the milk. How much corresponding power has the milk? Enough to buy the bread. Each accordingly is measured in the terms of the other. So of all exchanges whatsoever.

This power of any exchangeable thing in any one of the three classes, to buy in the way just indicated any other exchangeable thing in any one of the three classes, is what is called in our science *Value*. Thus we have reached the foundation-word in Political Economy. The meaning of it must be caught at the beginning, and held to the end of our studies. It is not accidental that this word stands as the title of the first chapter of the book before us; because to unfold it in its scientific sense is the first main thing that confronts economists, and because by over-mastering the difficulties presented by its meaning all after economical inquiries become comparatively easy. The word itself is derived from the Latin verb *valere*, which means *to pass for, to be worth,* so that the comparison or relation that is always involved in sales is present in the original meaning of the word. Value accordingly is a consequence of sales, and is never realized except by means of them. We can never say with certainty that any thing has value until an actual sale of it has determined just how much the value is. Value may be *expected* from a future sale of something, and there may be an *estimate* as to its amount; but value never *comes into being* until the sale has taken place, and then the amount of the value is the thing received in exchange, and even then it is not certain that a second sale of the first thing will bring in the same amount of the second thing. Value, though of vast importance in human affairs, is transient in its nature. It comes and goes. It appears and reappears. As always a consequent of exchanges, it is always consequently changeable. For example, the baker may have expected to exchange his loaf with the milkman for a quart of milk, but it is never safe for him to announce that his loaf is *worth* that until it has actually been exchanged for that. The views of the milkman are liable to change in regard to bread in general, and especially in regard to that particular loaf; and even the baker himself may not desire at the decisive moment that particular quart of milk so much as he expected. If they trade, the loaf is worth the milk, and the milk is worth the loaf; and value thus created passes out of being in this case by the probably immediate eating-up of the two articles.

All this shows us the need of one other technical word before we can give the final definition
to Value. This word is *Services*. In order to
define Value, and at the same time to throw a
clear light upon the inmost nature of its facts,
Political Economy finds it necessary to use the
word Services in a broad sense, including both
what we have called personal services, and also
every other economical rendering. To the bril-
liant French writer Bastiat, who died in 1850, we
owe the introduction of this scientifically admirable word. A service in this broad sense, which is
in no danger of being confused with the specific
sense already explained, *is the rendering of any
thing for something in return.* In this sense, the
man who sells me a ton of hay, the second man
who sells me ten shares of bank-stock, and my
gardener who sets and tends the celery, all alike
do me a *service*, and, in paying them, I do each of
them a *service* in return. Buying and selling is
nothing in the world but the rendering of mutual
services; and the beauty of the term "services"
consists in this, that it always implies, (1) two
persons, each of whom is reciprocally serving and
served ; (2) two efforts, the effort of each person
serving ; (3) two desires, the desire of each person served ; (4) two things, the thing rendered
by each person ; (5) two estimates, the estimate
by which each prefers the thing offered by the
other to his own thing offered ; and (6) two satisfactions, the satisfaction of each in the thing
received.

Having now this term "Services," with its definite economical meaning, we are able to define ultimately, and with precision, the term Value. It will require, however, beyond the definition, a good deal of further elucidation. Since exchanges are the rendering of mutual services by two persons, *Value is the relation of mutual purchase established between two services by their exchange.* It will be seen at once from this definition, how indifferent it is, so far as the deeper meaning is concerned, whether we define Political Economy the Science of Exchanges or the Science of Value. At bottom the two mean the same. There can be no exchanges without value, and no value without exchanges. We have already intimated that Kiehl defines Political Economy as the Science of Values.[1] There is a fair reason, nevertheless, why the former definition is technically to be preferred, because exchanges or sales are concrete and are easily grasped by the mind, while their consequent — value — is more abstract, and is, as the definition puts it, a "relation." A relation is not so easily seized and held as is an outward fact or an attribute of matter. Still we cannot get along at all without the term Value. That which this term covers is central in all economical inquiries. It is the kernel under the external husk of sales. Buyers and sellers are often not so much interested in the *number* of sales of a given thing as in the *rate* at which they

[1] "Die Lehre von den Werthen."

are taking place, and at which they suppose them likely to take place in the near future. Rate is value. We shall see pretty soon that market rate often affects the number of sales of a given article, and also that the number of sales often affects the market-rate. The men of the market accordingly feed on value, and grow fat or lean according to the rate at which sales are taking place.

Besides this indispensable word Value taken in its strict scientific sense, as just defined, it is convenient, and perhaps necessary, to have a looser general term to cover the mass of salable things of the three kinds in the hands of an individual, in the State, in the Nation, and in the whole World. Let that word be *Property*. In its original Latin the sense of this word was wider and less definite than its present economical sense; which is, *either a part or the aggregate of things esteemed salable, whether they be actually sold or not.* Value is only reached and registered by a sale. Property may be reached and registered by estimation. It is in the way of estimation, aided in many cases by actual sales, that the tax-assessors and the census-takers proceed. They intend to include nothing that cannot be sold, and nothing at a rate beyond which it may be sold; but their results, in the nature of the case, lack the accuracy reached only by the sale-test. Property, then, may be used in a sufficiently scientific sense, to denote parcels or masses of sala'le things. The adjectives *valuable* and *sala-ble* may be used as synonymous, although the nouns Value and Property are not synonymous, but the two nouns together, each with its definite meaning, relieve us completely from any need to use technically the old and poor word " wealth."

It is indeed true, that the word value is often used in another than the economical sense, as when we speak of the value of a good example, or the value of practical religion to any community. In such connections, the word is used in a moral sense, which is not likely to be confounded with its scientific sense. Political economy has no occasion whatever to use the word in any other than the scientific sense, and so no confusion from this source need be apprehended. Adam Smith, who himself calls attention to the distinction between " value in use and value in exchange," in fact confuses the two senses, as has almost everybody else who has tried to use the word " wealth " in a technical sense; but there is no need of this, since our science has nothing to do with " value in use," except to distinguish it sharply from value proper, that is, " value in exchange."

If language were rich enough to give a separate word for each separate sense, a complaint might justly be raised against the economists for taking as their foundation-word a word susceptible of another meaning than theirs; but, fortunately, the poverty of language is accompanied by no practical difficulty in this case; for, if any one gains a firm conception of what value is .in the strict sense, he will not be troubled at all by the fact that some people use the word in a loose sense, any more than the banker is troubled in his use of the word "redemption" by the fact that the clergyman uses the same word in a very different sense. In this book, only one kind of value will be recognized or spoken of. If there be occasion, as there will be, to refer to what Smith calls "value in use," the word *utility* will always be employed to designate that. Even the adjective "intrinsic," that is sometimes applied to the value of the precious metals, will be avoided as unnecessary and confusing. Value is value, and there is only one kind of it, and we must now get a clear and sharp conception, which we shall never need to alter, of what it is, how it arises, and the causes that vary it.

We have already seen, that, in every case of exchange, two desires of two persons are met by means of the exchange. But some of our desires are met without the necessity of making any exchange. Some very desirable things come to us freely. We pay nothing for them. For example, the air we breathe costs us nothing, though nothing can be more desirable to us. So the sunlight comes to us freely. The water we drink from the spring or brook is followed by no demand for a return, except a return of gratitude to God, which is not an economical rendering. For the most part, the enjoyment of natural objects, such as landscapes, mountains, lakes, and ocean, comes to us freely. The songs of the birds and the blooms of the spring-time, which afford a very high pleasure to many, are gifts. All such things as these, which are capable of satisfying human desires, but which do not need to be paid for, are possessed of *utility*, but *value* does not attach to them. Many *useful* things can be had for nothing, but a *valuable* thing can never be had for nothing, otherwise it would not be *valuable*, that is, poised over against something else as a return for it. *Utility is simple capacity to gratify any human desire whatsoever.* Considered by itself, and separate from all human efforts, it is always free. It is God's gift to man. Value, on the other hand, is always connected with human efforts, and hence is never free.

So far, the distinction between utility and value is plain enough; but there is a further point in the matter that requires insight and carefulness. Utility is one thing, and value is a different thing, but utility is always present in every case of value also; that is to say, in each service rendered, whether it be a commodity, a personal service, or a claim, nature's gifts play some part, as well men's exertions. Take the public singer, as an example. Take Mr. Whitney, who sang so well the solos at the opening of the Centennial Exhibition at Philadelphia. He sings in concerts, and is paid roundly for his service. It is true, that he

has spent time, and money, and hard labor, in preparing himself to be a public singer, but then,
also, nature gave him a superb bass voice. His
efforts have been combined with original gifts,
and, as the result of the two, he offers to society
a service of great *value*, that is, a service for which
he receives large pay. Utility, which is nature's
contribution, is always an element in services, as
well as effort, which is man's contribution.

Take a bushel of wheat. Man has labored to
produce it, and he now sells it, but of himself
alone he never could have made it. He availed
himself by a series of efforts of the provisions of
nature, and has wheat to sell. So of all commodities. Furniture is man's handiwork, but who
furnished the oak out of which it is made? So
too of all claims. New England railroad shares
would scarcely be valuable at present, if the
rivers and brooks had not been for ages wearing
passages up to, and even over, the water-sheds.
Mining stocks would be worthless if nature had
not deposited the metals. Banks are the birth of
business, and business is the outgrowth of natural
advantages, and natural advantages are made use
of by far-sighted and laborious men. Thus utility
is the basis on which man works for the creation
of value. The two become, as it were, commingled. All will allow at once that utility by
itself is gratuitous: does it cease to be gratuitous
after it has been united with the onerous efforts of
men? Does the maker of the oaken chair, for

example, charge so much for the efforts of the men, who felled the tree, sawed the plank, carved the wood, finished the chair, and *so much addi- tional* for the original qualities of the oak?

This is a nice question. Political Economy asks and answers no more delicate and difficult question than this. The example of the oak chair will answer, perhaps, as well as any other to dis- play the principle that underlies all such cases. If there were but one oak tree, or a few, and if the durable and other excellent qualities of oak were well known, and oak chairs consequently were strongly desired in the community, I know of no economical force that would prevent the maker from realizing on his chairs a value out of all proportion to the onerous efforts involved in simply making them and bringing them to market. He might claim and gain something on the strength of what nature had done for the oak wood. There would be no competitor to offer chairs like his for a fair reward of the onerous human efforts involved. His offered service is unique. There are no other chairs like his. In that case, and in all similar cases, no market-rate is possible. Competition, which is the offer of a similar service, has no play. The return service demanded and received may be such as to imply both compensation for the human effort and for an original gift of nature. It is true that the qualities of the oak cost nothing to the maker of the chair, but he has become pro- prietor of those qualities, and there is nothing to hinder him from asking something, and, so far as I can see, nothing to hinder him from getting something, on the ground of these gratuitous qualities.

So it may be with a horse of very extraordinary speed, which it has cost no more to rear and train than other horses, which will fetch much less on sale. So it may be with any other *unique* products, that happen to be in strong demand. The only practical limit on the return service rendered for such products is the willingness of the purchaser to pay, rather than forego the possession of the product. The principle is that of the auction-room rather than that of the market-place. Such products virtually go to the highest bidder, without any nice inquiries as to cost, or whether a free gift of nature is not influencing that which should only be influenced by the efforts of men.

It is very plain, however, that such cases are relatively few and exceptional. As a matter of fact, there are a good many oak trees in a good many countries, and the unreasonable demand of any vender of oak chairs is met at once by the assertion that similar chairs can be had elsewhere of other venders for a less return. As a matter of fact, competition has play in respect to the great mass of all things bought and sold, and tends constantly and effectually to crowd down the value of all things sold to the point at which a fair compensation is given for all human efforts expended, *and nothing more.* It is evident, that

God never intended that His free gifts to mankind should be peddled out by chance proprietors for a personal reward. He has ordered it so through the very liberality of His bounty, that men cannot sell His gifts. The cupidity of one anxious to do this is thwarted by the readiness of others to dispose of a similar product for a reasonable compensation, that is, a compensation graduated to the actual human efforts expended on it. As a rule, therefore, while the utility of nature is always present as a part of that combined utility by which a service offered is fitted to meet some desire of the purchaser, and to call out from him a return service, it does not influence that return service to make it greater. It is eliminated by the action of competition from all effect upon value.

This is a point of much importance, as we shall see more fully when we come to the value of land and of its products. The reason why that portion of the utility of any service that is due to the efforts of men cannot be eliminated from influence on value is, that the efforts are onerous, they will not be put forth except in view of a reward, and if a suitable reward does not come, the efforts themselves will cease. Value, then, as a general rule, and almost universally, has its origin, not in what God has done, but in what men have done; and the value tends perpetually to be proportioned to the onerous efforts that have been put forth in connection with any service, provided only there

be a constant desire for such a service accompanied by an ability to remunerate it. .

There is another reason less effective than competition, yet co-operating with it, why value hesi-
tates to rise above the point that just offers
compensation for the onerous elements in it, leav-
ing no margin for the gratuitous elements, and
that is, that the demand for any service is apt to
slacken when a larger return is demanded, and
is apt to quicken when a smaller return is demanded ; so that, self-interest, a desire to dispose
of one's services in a brisk market, leads him to
disregard in his demand what has cost *him* nothing,
that so he may the more readily get his pay for
what has been onerous in the premises. We conclude, then, in answer to the main question, that
very little *additional* return is likely to be secured
on the strength of original and gratuitous qualities.

I believe that it is already growing clear to my
readers, even before I have formally broached the
point, *that value is not a quality of any one thing,
but a relation subsisting between two things.* It is,
as the definition gives it, *a relation of mutual purchase.* Just before beginning to write this paragraph, some ten minutes ago, I bought a bunch of
tacks and paid eight cents for them. The tacks
have certain qualities of their own, that any one
can ascertain by merely examining them. Their
material is iron, they are about half an inch long,
they are pointed at one end and flattened at the

other, and they are so made as to drive easily through a carpet into a floor, holding down the carpet above and inhering in the floor below. These qualities of the tacks, and many more, may be learned by a simple observation of them . but the *valie* of the tacks cannot be learned by an observation of them, for the reason that the value is not a *quality* of the tacks. No amount of study put upon the tacks themselves, no analysis of them, not even a complete account of their transformations and travels from the ore to the store, could ever reach the *value* of those tacks. Before it could be asserted that the tacks are worth eight cents, somebody must not only have made and transported them in the hope of getting something for them, but somebody else must also have desired the tacks, have estimated them in his own mind relatively to eight cents and preferred the tacks to the cents, and have given the cents for the tacks, the merchant meantime preferring the cents to the tacks and accepting them in pay for the tacks. Then, and not before, when somebody has *given* eight cents for the tacks, can the tacks be said to be worth *eight cents.* The merchant may have reckoned them at that, may have expected that they would fetch that, but could not say that they were *worth* that till the exchange was consummated.

Value, strictly speaking, begins and ends in a mutual *action* of two persons, not in their mutual desires alone, nor in their mutual efforts alone as represented in their respective services, though all these play a part preparatory to the realization of value. Value and the amount of value are the same thing. The value of any service is that other service that has just been exchanged for it. What is the value of the tacks? Eight cents. What is the value of eight cents in this case? The bunch of tacks. It is just as true, and just as important, to say that the cents are worth the tacks, as to say that the tacks are worth the cents. In every case of value, one service *purchases* the other service ; and the only proper expression of the value of any thing is the other thing that is exchanged against it.   As Mr. Macleod has well said, " The value of any economic quantity is some other economic quantity for which the first will exchange."   The value of any specific service whatever is that other specific service whatever which the first will buy.   But we need a scientific answer to the question, What is value? as well as to the question, What is the value of any *specific* service?   To this question, the definition of value already given is the right answer.   I believe that it is a perfect answer.   I think it is the only answer ever given, that is at the same time simple and scientifically complete.   VALUE IS THE RELATION OF MUTUAL PURCHASE ESTABLISHED BETWEEN TWO SERVICES BY THEIR EXCHANGE.

I hope that my readers will not be discouraged at all, because they find this one difficulty at the outset of this science, namely, that they must always in all discussions about value think of two things, and two things in·a relation with each other. Things in relation are not so easily conceived of and held in the mind as things by themselves. One thing, as a horse, is easily thought of, and its qualities easily discovered and discussed. But value has no existence in connection with one thing, or one person; and hence, it is a little hard ·at first to accustom the mind to hold steadily before it two things, two services, in a relation of mutual purchase, especially when one or both of the services are changing in their desirability, or difficulty of attainment. This obstacle is inherent in the very nature of the subject. It never can be obviated, of course. But the mind can be gradually led up to it, can be enabled to see completely around it, and in a little time can become so accustomed to it, that it shall cease to be any practical difficulty at all. Whoever will take pains to overmaster this at the beginning, to gain clearly and hold firmly the fundamental idea of *value*, will thereafter take positive pleasure in all economical ·discussions however elaborate; and no one must be allowed to suppose that value is the only subject that begins and ends with a relation. Marriage is a relation. A pastorate is a relation. Government itself is a relation. All attempts to study value comprehensively, that have regarded it as a *quality* of *objects*, rather than a *relation* of *services*, have partially and necessarily failed.

It follows from all that has been said, that value is not an attribute of matter, or of any form of matter. When commodities are offered for sale, it is indeed some material thing that is proposed to be rendered; and as the commerce of the world is largely in commodities, men came naturally to think that value somehow inheres in matter, that value resides in material forms as material. This is a great mistake, as I will proceed to show. I notice in the paper to-day, that silver is quoted in the London market as selling at 51⅜ pence per ounce. Silver usually sells in that market at about 60 pence per ounce. But an ounce of pure silver, so far as matter is concerned, is the same thing year in and year out, century in and century out. Its weight is the same, its specific gravity is the same, all its chemical and visible properties are the same. If then, value be an attribute of matter, the value of silver ought to be constantly the same. But it is not the same, either as compared with gold, as in the given case, or as compared with other things. Just now, silver is very cheap all over the world, owing partly to the fertility of the mines, and partly to the fact that some leading nations have changed their money-standard from silver to gold, and have consequently silver to sell, which lowers the value of silver in accordance with a principle soon to be explained. Circumstances may be easily supposed, and have often occurred, under which an ounce of silver would fetch nothing at all. During the plague in

London, in 1665, according to the description of Daniel Defoe, it would go hard to sell an ounce of silver, or even things ordinarily much more valuable than that.

What is true of silver, is just as true of gold, and still more true of most other material commodities. A sudden change in the fashion, for example, will frequently take away at a stroke one-half the value of goods, that were fashionable but are so no longer. The matter is all there, and the form of the matter is all there, but the value is one-half escaped. If value be so loosely connected with matter even in commodities, which always have a basis of matter, how almost independent of matter must it be in the second and third classes of salable things, namely, in personal services and claims, which are only remotely related to matter, or not at all! Concert tickets, for example, for which five dollars apiece are eagerly paid, or the good-will of a business, which is something still more intangible, have little or nothing to do with matter, and show that persons with their various capacities and changing choices are quite as much a factor in economical discussions as dead matter and its forms.

We must now trace the rise of value as it comes before us practically in every-day life. Animals do not exchange; there is no evidence that angels do; but men have always been exchangers, are now, and always will be; and we can see that value has its birthplace in the DESIRES of MEN.

Some of the natural and acquired desires of all persons are satisfied through the bounty of Nature, and others of them are satisfied through the gifts of friends, but there are still others of them that can only be satisfied through exchanges. It is the desire that first points to the exchange. Clearly, if a person does not desire something, he will not buy it, that is, render something else in exchange for it. If his desire for it be feeble, he will be willing to render but little in exchange for it; if his desire for it be strong, and not counterbalanced by the desire for something incompatible with his obtaining it, he will be willing to render much in exchange for it; if his desire for it cease, the exchange will certainly not take place. This play of human desires, out of which value takes its rise in every case, makes it needful to one, who would be successful in offering his services to society, to study human nature well, to observe the current of desires in the line of his trade, to anticipate so far as possible the changes in these desires, and to adapt his services, whether they be mediated through commodities or not, both to the present and to the prospective desires of his customers.

Exchange affords abundant opportunity for the exercise of intellectual powers. It is no dead level of sluggish uniformity. It is a sea with currents and tides and waves. Observation, adaptation, invention, caution, enterprise, and many other high qualities, have room and verge enough in the attempt to meet at the right timo and in the right measure these varying desires of various men. Some classes of desires, such as those for food,, for houses, for the education of one's children, are steadier, and hence can bo better calculated upon, than other classes of desires, such, for example, as those of clothing, of ornamentation of all kinds, of equipage, and so on. As society advances, the desires of men that can be met through exchange become more numerous and delicate, and ten thousand services are now offered and accepted that were never thought of in the days of old. Moreover, the desires of men are of such a nature — so capable of increase in number and degree — that there never can be a general glut of services offered, because all the desires of all men never can be fully met. Exchanges, therefore, can go on without ever a fear that the ultimate goal will be reached. A partial glut of services there may be, that is to say, certain services of a certain kind may be offered at a certain time and place more than sufficient to meet the desires of the men then and there for such services. This often happens.

The offer of print-goods in this country at present is more than sufficient to meet the desires of our people for this class of goods, at least, more than sufficient to call out from them in return remunerative services; but a vent for our prints is found in foreign countries nevertheless. A miscalculation upon desires is possible; but an over-

supply for all the desires of all men everywhere is
impossible ; and consequently, value, which has its
starting-place in these desires, great as is the part
it plays at present, is destined to play a greater
and still greater part in the future. Wherever,
and so long as, there is a desire in a human breast
that can be met through some exchange with another person, there, and so long, value is possible,
and is likely to be realized.

It will not be realized, however, unless somebody
puts forth an EFFORT to gratify that desire. Mere
effort in itself, mere work, mere exertion of muscle
or mind, will not issue in value, any more than
the mere indulgence of desires will issue in value.
" If wishes were horses, beggars might ride." It
is the effort adapted to satisfy the desire of another person, the effort put forth for that purpose,
and accepted to that end by that person by his
rendering to the first a corresponding effort
adopted to gratify *his* desire, that issues in value.
Value is the offspring of the marriage of certain
efforts with certain desires. A great many efforts
of all men, just as a great many desires of all
men, come forth without any reference to the
desires of others in the one case, or to the efforts
of others in the other case. Many efforts are put
forth for personal gratification merely, as when a
musician plays for his own amusement, or that of
his friends. Other efforts are constantly put
forth, that were expected to issue in value, but
do not, because there was a miscalculation upon

the desires to be gratified through such efforts. For example, some railroads are built that pay no dividends, because there is less freight and less travel than was expected.

Still, when one looks out upon society, the mos* striking thing about it is, the assidrity and success with which efforts of all sorts are put forth by each sort of people to meet the desires and exchange against the efforts of other sorts of people. Society is one hive of buyers and sellers. Almost everybody, paupers and prisoners excepted, brings something to the market, and carries something off. To be successful, efforts must be skilful; in order to become skilful, persons must devote themselves to one employment, or at least to very few; hence, the diversity of avocations, what is called "the division of labor;" hence, also, by concentration of attention and constant practice, men come to be able to offer skilled services, each along his own line; these services come to be desired by those, whose attention and practice have been called in other directions, and who consequently can be better served in these matters than they can serve themselves, and who, in turn, in consequence of their own training, can render better services to the first in other matters; so that, through skilled efforts, all adapted to gratify the desires of somebody, exchanges are multiplied, value is realized, and the happiness of mankind unmeasurably augmented.

It will now be plain to my readers, — and the

point is very important, — that all value, through mutual desires and mutual efforts, *proceeds upon a diversity of advantage as between different men in different respects.* For example, there are at this moment three men engaged in painting the exterior of my house, and I am to pay them for their service out of the proceeds of my service as a public teacher. If they could teach as well as I can, and I could paint as well as they can, it is perfectly certain that they would not now be painting for me. I have an advantage over them as a teacher, because I have devoted myself for many years to that art, have in consequence acquired a certain skill in it, and am able to demand for my services a reasonable salary; on the other hand, they have an advantage over me as painters, because it is their trade. They can paint better than I can; and, therefore, I hire them to paint my house; and I rely upon another exchange, namely, the one I make with my employers, to obtain the means of completing this exchange, that is, to pay my painters. The success of one exchange is always a path to other successful exchanges. Now, it is no disadvantage to me that they have an advantage over me as painters, and it is no disadvantage to them that I have an advantage over them as a teacher; on the contrary, the more they surpass me as painters, the better for me, — I get a better service; and the more I surpass them as a teacher, the better for them, — I am more likely to exchange with them, because I am thereby better able to pay them for their service. From this example, which is a sample in this respect of all exchanges, we get this principle: — *The greater the diversity of relative advantage as between the parties, the more profitable do exchanges become.*

This principle may be illustrated arithmetically. Suppose a shoemaker has an efficiency in his own trade which we will call 6, which has not heretofore been increased, because he has also made his own and his children's clothes, having an efficiency in that subordinate trade which we will call 5. Suppose also in the same community a tailor, who can make clothes with an efficiency of 6, but who, instead of exchanging with the shoemaker, has thus far made his own and his children's shoes with an ability of 5. As shoemaker and tailor, there is a diversity of advantage between them of 2, sufficient perhaps to justify an exchange, while it is certain that there could be no exchange except for this diversity, such as it is. Suppose now, that each, under the encouragement of prospective exchanges, devotes himself wholly to his own trade, and, by concentrated attention and constant practice and possible inventions, carries up his efficiency to 15, the ability of each in the trade of the other remaining, as before, at 5. Now, when they come to exchange, the diversity of advantage between them is 20 instead of 2. The motives for an exchange, and the gains of an exchange, are ten times greater than they were before. Not only can they serve each other a great deal better than before, but they are now in position, owing to their increased skill, and the new rapidity with which they can turn off work, to offer their services to many more parties than before, who will now share in the benefit, and who, if, in the mean time, they have been acting similarly, will in turn confer a new benefit upon these.

The result of a greater diversity of relative advantage as between exchangers, accordingly, is, that the quality of the services is improved, and also, that the number of possible services is multiplied. In the light of this principle, how petty is the jealousy that pines over the superior eminence of any individual in his industrial or intellectual pursuits! The higher he has carried his proficiency in his own art, the better and the more services he can proffer, and all who come into relations of exchange with him share in the profit of his superiority; and, if they will only be stimulated by his success to carry their own advantage over him in their art to the highest point, the profit then becomes mutual and the highest possible. Exchange rejoices in all excellence in any direction, and especially in excellence in all direc tions, because thereby its gains become larger and more universal.

Even if others in the community stupidly hold on to old methods, when improvements might be made, they are nevertheless benefited by the enterprise of any one who pushes on improvements in

his own craft, unless, indeed, he practises the
same occupation with themselves, in which case
he will draw away some of their business from
them, and, so far, harm them. Nobody can justly
pity them, however; their loss results from their
own want of spirit. Our former supposition a
little modified will show just how the principle
works in practice. The shoemaker, not encouraged by a corresponding vigor on the part of the
tailor, nevertheless carries up his own efficiency
to 10, his ability in making clothes and the tailor's
ability in both trades remaining as before. If the
two exchange, there is now an aggregate advantage of 6 to be divided between them. The
exchange is three times as profitable as it was at
first, owing to the progress of only one of the
parties. The other should have kept up. If he
had to the same degree, the exchange would have
been five times as profitable as at first. The practical inference from this is, that everybody, who
improves his capacity in his own avocation, benefits his fellow-men, as well as himself; although
the highest possible benefits of exchange are conditioned upon improvements going on among *all* the
exchangers. If there is no diversity of relative
advantage, there is no motive for any exchange,
and of course no exchange; if there is great
diversity, there can be a very profitable exchange;
and, therefore, each man may as rationally rejoice
over the superiority of his neighbors to him in
their business, as over his superiority to them in

his cwn. The time has now gone by, the world has grown too intelligent, to tolerate the animosities and restrictions that used to spring up in view of the enterprise and progress of others. Values grow big just in proportion as individuals and nations mutually surpass each other at different industrial points.

Having established this principle, to which we shall have to recur further on, we pass next to look at the mutual ESTIMATES, which men always make before they trade with each other. Of course, the ground on which they trade is *self-interest*. No other motive than self-interest is appropriate in the premises: Men often *give* from the impulse of duty — they never *trade* except from self-interest. In the sphere of morals, "It is more blessed to give than to receive." In the sphere of exchange, It is more blessed to receive than to give! It is no gain for morality to disguise the truth that men trade for their own advantage, or to try to mingle things so distinct and incompatible as charity and commerce. God is indeed the author of economical laws just as much as of the moral laws, although they are less a matter of express legislation, because they are in a lower sphere and less *essential* to men's welfare. It is necessary for men to be good, but it is not necessary for them to be rich. Besides, it is more *natural* for men to trade, than to fulfil their moral obligations. Both sets of laws, the moral and the economical, work together for the

benefit of mankind, only they work in quite different ways. Men are to be good, and to do good,
because they *ought* to do this: men are to trade
because it is for their *advantage* to do so. No man
was ever yet under a moral *obligation* to make an
exchange, because, by the very definition of an
exchange, it is made with a view to the *economical*
return. As exchangers, men are under the moral
laws, because they are *men*, not because they are
exchangers. Men must be honest in all things,
including exchanges, if they make them, because
this is *right*, but it is wholly a matter of their own
choice, to be decided in view of self-interest,
whether they make them, or not. Exchange is a
sphere, all whose operations are under the sur-
veillance of conscience of course, but it is not,
and never was designed to be, a sphere of benevolence. It is a sphere of gain only. The popular
notions concerning this point are so loose, that it
is worth while to clear it up once more, although
even the apostle Paul draws a sharp distinction
between the "spiritual things" and the "carnal
things."

Now, the estimate that each person puts upon
what he receives in an exchange is greater than
the estimate he puts upon what he renders, otherwise he would not render it. He may be mistaken in the utility to himself of what he receives,
and he may be mistaken in what would be the
utility to himself of what he renders in case he
retained it, — exchanges are sometimes disappoint-

ing to one or both parties owing to misapprehen sions or miscalculations — but generally they are not. The mutual estimates prove to be correct; and the difference between the estimate of what is rendered and the estimate of what is received is the measure of the gain of the exchange.

These estimates are mental processes. The minds of most men derive their chief development in connection with the necessity and the habit of making these estimates. Mercantile sagacity consists largely in the ability to make these estimates quickly and accurately; and in times of general depression of business, like 1873–1879, when the current gains of exchanges are small, and when it is the question with many whether or not to continue their industrial enterprises, this ability is what makes the difference between a continuous success and an abrupt failure. Shall I buy it at' all? What grade shall I buy? What quantity shall I buy? What price can I afford to give? What price am I likely to get for my own product, the proceeds of which must pay for this product? These questions, and questions like these, enter in as elements into the estimates that invariably precede exchanges. The necessity of asking and answering them keeps the minds of men on the alert, obliges them to consult sources of information, induces them to read, compels them to reflect, stimulates conversation, and in various other ways helps to educate individuals, and to keep society from stagnation. To know when *not*

to buy, as well as when and where and how to
buy; to learn to know the present, and as far as
possible to anticipate the prospective, purchasing-
power both of one's own product about to be
parted with and of another's product about to be
received; to come into an apparent or real colli-
sion of interests with other men, and hold one's
own of temper, of judgment, and of property, in
the struggle; — all this is a part of the good disci-
pline that Exchange offers to almost all men.

It is true, that many men fail in this matter of
making proper estimations, and, consequently,
they "fail" in business, or fall into hopeless
debts; but it is nevertheless true, that the meth
ods of exchange are in their nature not random
but rational; they imply in their groundwork the
intelligence of God, and in their practical working
the intelligence of men; and no exchanges are
properly made except those preceded by the delib-
erative action of two minds, each of which concludes, on grounds of rational probability, that
what is about to be received is of more consequence'to the recipient than what is about to be
rendered. This is enough for the present about
estimates.

The last element in this series, and the one
pleasantest to discuss, is the resulting SATISFAC-
TIONS. These lie in the region of the Sensibility,
as the estimations lie in the region of the Intellect.
Desires are followed by efforts, and efforts by estimations, and estimations by an exchange, and the

exchange by satisfactions ; and thus tne Sensibility, that gives rise to the desires, becomes also the
seat of the ultimate satisfactions. The Intellect
and the Will intervene in their action between
the original desire and the subsequent satisfaction.
Thus all the parts of our nature are involved in a
single act of exchange ; and Political Economy,
which is a science by itself, recognizes and rejoices
in all the other sciences, and particularly in those
sciences, which, like itself, find their culmination
in man. In the first detailed commercial transaction on record, which was the purchase by Abraham [1] from the sons of Heth of the field and cave
of Machpelah for four hundred shekels of silver,
any one skilled to read between the lines may
easily discover the evidence of the satisfaction of
the patriarch through the copiousness and itera-
tion of the details, when it is said, " the field and
the cave which was therein, and all the trees that
were in the field, that were in all the borders
round about, were made sure unto Abraham for a
possession, in the presence of the sons of Heth,
before all that went in at the gate of his city."
A little after, as if loath to leave them, the main
features of the bargain are repeated ; — " And the
field, and the cave that is therein, were made sure
unto Abraham for a possession of a burying-place,
by the sons of Heth." Some of the circumstances of this purchase were of the saddening
sort, — it was the purchase of a tomb and its envi

[1] See Gen. xxiii. 3-20.

rons as a last earthly resting-place for himself and for his family, — but his satisfaction in the purchase is most evident, a satisfaction that has justified itself in the probably inviolate sacredness of the tomb from that day to this,[1] and in the veneration with which Israelite, Mussulman, and Christian alike,.even now draw near to the mosque at Hebron.

This incidental reference to Abraham makes natural an additional word or two respecting the alleged fondness of the Jews for bargains of all sorts. If they be fonder than other people are of a good trade, something may perhaps be said in the way of explanation of it. The national trait, if it be one, certainly goes back to the founder of the nation. Long before the transaction just mentioned, Abraham, though a double exile, is said to have departed out of Egypt " very rich in cattle, in silver, and in gold." Isaac, though his life was quieter, was obviously not less an accumulator; for he " sowed in that land, and received the same year a hundred-fold, and the Lord blessed him, and the man waxed great, and went forward, and grew until he became very great, for he had possession of flocks and possession of. herds and great store of servants, and the Philistines envied him." Jacob also, the third in the line, was a consummate trafficker, not to say trickster, in his bargains; and thus the *pitch* seems to have been

- See Dean Stanley's Lectures on the Jewish Church. Appendix.

given by the patriarchs to the song sung by the
Jews ever since. They have come honestly, that
is, through inheritance, by their tendencies to
traffic. Moreover, the disabilities they have been
.put under by the laws of most European countries,
such as those forbidding Jews to hold landed
estates, and so on, (even Magna Charta forbids
the debts due by wards to Jews to bear any interest,) may have driven them more to become
peddlers, merchants and bankers, and thus to
exhibit their mercenary spirit in a more conspicu-
ous way.

But it may be questioned, after all, whether the
Jews take more satisfaction in exchanges than
other people. Everybody likes to trade. The
satisfaction from a fair bargain is legitimate and
universal. An intelligent exchange is in every
case the gratification of two human desires. The
boy with his new top, and Vanderbilt with his
new steamship, present the same phenomenon;
and the satisfaction of the shopman who sold the
top, and of the contractor who furnished the ship,
is just as real as theirs. Neither party to an exchange is more recipient than the other, since
they are both reciprocally recipient; and neither
has a better right to a satisfaction than the other,
since both have parted with something reciprocally
less esteemed for the sake of receiving something
reciprocally more esteemed. Thus the happiness
of the world, — the satisfaction of the world's
innumerable desires, — not to speak of the power

of the world, and the progress of the world, all which are indeed the same thing in different aspects of it, is constantly and increasingly ministered unto by means of exchanges. The satisfaction is that for the sake of which the exchange is had, for the sake of which it was prepared for perhaps years aback, and in the realization of which it finds its sole purpose and end. The present exchange is for the present satisfaction, though to make ready for the present exchange many men may have long been toiling. As Whittier sings to the shoemakers : —

"For you, along the Spanish main
    A hundred keels are ploughing;
For you, the Indian on the plain
    His lasso-coil is throwing;
For you, deep glens with hemlock dark
    The woodman's fire is lighting;
For you, upon the oak's gray bark,
    The woodman's axe is smiting.
For you, from Carolina's pine
    The rosin-gum is stealing;
For you, the dark-eyed Florentine
    Her silken skein is reeling;
For you, the dizzy goatherd roams
    His rugged Alpine ledges;
For you, round all her shepherd homes
    Bloom England's thorny hedges."

There is one important inference to be drawn, in passing, from the general point last established. If satisfactions are the goal of exchanges, then, to try to stop exchanges is to try to destroy satisfactions. The only motive that leads men to trade is to better their condition, is to increase the sum of their happiness, and if governments, under a mistaken notion of their functions, undertake to prohibit trade, or to burden it by throwing arti ficial obstacles across its path, the effect is and must be from the nature of the case to lessen human happiness, to weaken human power, to retard human progress. He is an enemy to the human race, and flings himself into the face of Providence, who, for ends of his own, undertakes, by means of the action of government, to prevent exchanges which would otherwise take place. He thereby undertakes to annihilate satisfactions which would otherwise take place.

The exceptions to the noble principle of free exchanges are so few and petty that one is almost ashamed to put them down alongside of the principle itself. The father, for example, may properly enough restrain his boy in his eagerness to engage in boyish traffic until his mind is sufficiently trained to make relatively just estimates respecting the things to be bought and sold; though a wise father will give his boy considerable liberty in his tentative trials of skill in bargaining, since he will learn skill through his own mistakes and losses. Governments may properly enough re-strain exchanges whenever it becomes needful to do so in the interest, first, of public health; second, of public morals; and third, of public revenue. Health, morals, and revenue; — these are all higher considerations than the gains of individuals, and the latter must give way to the former. The law may prohibit the selling of tainted meat for health's sake, of obscene publications for morals' sake, and of " crooked " whiskey for revenue's sake ; but all these, and all such as these, are but as a drop in the bucket to the mass of things purely and properly commercial. I do not think of any other exceptions to the right of free exchange in time of peace. If governments go beyond this, and try to give *commercial* reasons for interfering with *commerce*, they go beyond their depth, and go to the bottom. This point will be taken up again in the chapter following the next. It is enough to say at present, that, as exchanges find their only aim in human satisfactions, the exchanges themselves, with the slight exceptions noted, should be everywhere untrammelled.

We have now gained a general idea of what VALUE is, and of the circumstances under which it arises. It is clear, that there is no inherent quality called value in any thing, any more than there is an inherent quality called size in any thing. Value, like size, is relative, is the result of a comparison. Can value, like size, be measured ? Is there any external standard, by means of which the value of purchasable things in general may be ascertained, just as the dimensions of physical things may be ascertained by an external standard like the French metre ? It has often been sup-

posed that there must be such an external standard, and economists have expended a great deal
of ingenuity in trying to find out what it is. Mr
Ricardo contended that the value of any thing is
measured by and constituted of the quantity of
labor necessary to produce or obtain it. Mr. Malthus contended on the other hand that value consists in and is measured by the quantity of labor
that the thing can *command* as an article of exchange. Adam Smith, though not always consistent with himself, seems to think that *corn* is a
better measure of general exchange value than
labor, or even coin. Mr. Mill, and many others,
regards the *cost of their production* as the best
gauge of the value of valuable things. Mr. Carey
thinks that he makes a great advance upon this,
when he affirms, that it is the prospective *cost of
their reproduction* that is the measure of the value
of salable things.

All of these opinions imply more or less of misapprehension as to the nature of value, both in
supposing that tangible things alone have value,
and that value is somehow or other a quality
wrapped up in these commodities. Indeed, it is
difficult, or impossible, to use language that is free
from all implications of this sort. Language is
formed for popular, not scientific, use; and every
writer is obliged more or less to employ words
that have already acquired significations, or at
least, implications, adverse to a strict scientific
conception. It is not strictly accurate, for exam-

ple, to say that any thing *has* value, for that implies that value is a quality of the thing itself,
whereas it is only a transient relation which that
thing holds to other things which it will buy, and
which at the same time will buy it. So, also, we
sometimes speak of `value as *purchasing-power* re-
siding in this or that. Such language is illusory,
though we cannot, perhaps, always avoid using
it. I promise my readers, however, that, if they
will be both careful and patient, I will give them,
by means of the best words our language affords
for our use, not only a clear conception of what
value is, but also a clear conception of the only
sense in which it can be said that there is a *measure* of value.

As the measure of lengths must itself have the
attribute of length, (the metre is 39.37079 inches
long,) and the measure of capacities be itself possessed of capacity, (the litre contains 61.02705
cubic inches,) so; clearly, if there be a measure of
values, it must be some *valuable* thing. If value
is a relation of mutual purchase, then the measure of values must be capable of standing in a
relation of mutual purchase with all other purchasable things. If it pretend to be a universal
measure of values, then it must be universally
acceptable in an exchange for other things. But
the *value* of the measure of values must in any
case arise just as all other value arises, namely, it
must be the object of desires, the subject of
efforts, the target of estimates, the cause of satis-

factions. From the very nature of value itself it is impossible that there should be a perfect measure of values, inasmuch as the measure, which must be valuable, is subject to the causes which vary more or less all other values. There is nothing, men's desires for which are always uniform, efforts to procure which are always equally onerous, estimates in relation to which are always the same, and satisfactions arising from the possession of which are always equally great. Therefore, a perfect measure of values is impossible to be found, and would never have been sought after, had the nature of value been fully understood.

Much can be said in favor of each of the above-alleged measures as a kind of index to the probable value of many salable things; that is to say, if it be known, how much of labor a thing has cost or will now command, how much of corn or coin it will now buy, what its cost of production has been in money, or what will be in money the cost of the reproduction of similar things, a sort of rough guide is thus obtained to the power of that thing to purchase things in general. It is in this sense only that there can be any such thing as a measure of value.

In the chapter on Money we shall have occasion to ascertain the important fact, that gold is the best attainable measure of value in the sense already explained, because there is nothing else so generally *desired* by men, nothing else secured at all times by such approximately equal *efforts*,

consequently nothing else so likely to be uniformly *estimated* as over against other things, and
consequently also nothing else so likely to give
satisfaction in its possession through its command
over other satisfactions. To say that gold is the
best attainable measure of value is only to say
that its own value is steadiest. Whenever any
service is sold for money, the amount of money
obtained for it is called its Price. Value and
Price must be carefully distinguished in the mind
of every student of Political Economy. The
value of any service is its power to command, that
is, to buy, all other services; the *price* of any service is its power to command, that is, to buy,
money. There can be no general rise or fall of
values, because, if some services rise in value, that
means that other services for which these exchange have fallen in value. To say, for example,
that horses have risen in value, is only to say that
they will buy more of other things than formerly,
which is only to say that those other things will
buy fewer of horses than formerly, so that, if
horses rise, other things fall as compared with
horses, and accordingly a general rise in value of
all things is a contradiction in terms. Some
things may rise in value, but if they do, some
other things must correspondingly fall in value.
A fall in value of certain things implies of course
that certain other things will buy more of the first
than before, that is, have risen in value.

Value is not only a relative term implying a

comparison, but is also a general term implying a
comparison with all other valuable things. The
value of a watch, for instance, never can be completely stated, because that would require a comparison of the watch with all other salable things
whatsoever, and a statement in the terms of those
things how many of them or what part of them
the watch will buy. This inconvenience, which
always exists under the form of trade called Barter, is removed by reducing value to price. *Price
is the value of any thing expressed in money.* By
knowing how much *money* any service will fetch,
it is easy to compare all other services with that.
Money becomes the standard of value, to which all
purchasable things are referred, and by means of
which they are brought into easy numerical relations with each other. So soon as it is ascertained
that the watch is worth $100, its relations of value
to all other things whose price has also been ascertained become simple enough. Price is indeed
only a case under the class Values, but practically
it becomes a very important thing in Political
Economy, because the value of almost all exchangeable things is determined through price.
So far as commodities, personal services, and
claims are exchanged against each other directly,
without the intervention of money or the use of
the denominations of money, price plays no part
though value does, but these cases are few and in-
significant as compared with the whole.

It is hardly necessary to add, that price, though

relative, is specific and not general, and consequently that there may be a general rise or fall of
prices. If the money of a country become relatively more abundant than before, general prices
will rise in that country for reasons already made
apparent; and when the money becomes less
abundant, prices will fall for corresponding reasons. In this country, since 1862, the general
range of prices has been high, at times very
high, mainly on account of the state of the national money. Things have exchanged against each
other about as before — *values* have not risen — but
as exchanged against money, owing to the quantity
and quality of that, *prices* have been high. After
1873 prices fell, partly because of the panic of
that year, and partly because paper money became
better in quality; in 1879–1880, prices rose again,
partly because business confidence was restored,
and partly because the volume of money was
slowly but steadily enlarged. The subject of
prices will be better understood in the light of our
subsequent discussions of Money, but we must
now conclude the direct discussion of Value by
unfolding the great law that underlies it. ·

This law is commonly and properly called the
Law of Demand and Supply. It is the most comprehensive and beautiful law in Political Economy. We must first define our terms. *Demand is
the desire of purchasing something coupled with the
power of purchasing it.* The demand for any service is usually expressed by the offer of money

wherewith to pay for it, or by the promise express or implied to pay the money at some future time, but a demand may be constituted by the offer of any other exchangeable thing besides money. Demand expresses the element of desire as measured by the effort involved in what is offered as pay. Mark Lane, London, is a great European market for grain. The demand in that market on any one day is constituted by what is virtually offered that day in pay for the grain then and there offered for sale. *Supply is any class of exchangeable things offered for sale against money, or other exchangeable thing.* In common commercial language, the money or its equivalent offered in the market for commodities, services, or claims, constitutes the demand for them, while the commodities, services, and claims are a supply in reference to that demand; but it must always be remembered, that, in reality, some commodities, services and claims are a demand in relation to others, which thereby become a supply in relation to them. In other words, a market for products is products in market. Money itself is always either a commodity or a claim; and whoever has salable things of whichever kind to dispose of, need have no fear but he can buy whatever he wants, either through the intervention of money, or without it.

Still, it is less confusing to unfold and to understand the law of supply and demand under the ordinary commercial terms, and afterwards at our leisure to give to the law its utmost possible generality. This method will lead us astray at no point. Let the article be wheat in the market of Milwaukee. There is much wheat in stock, and many buyers representing many cities and distant lands. Let us first follow the action of Demand as affecting the value of the wheat in stock with-out reference to any change in the Supply of wheat. The buyers want wheat, and have money to offer for it; the sellers want money, and have the wheat to give for it. What now will determine the price of wheat? The buyers have a desire for wheat, but it is not an unlimited desire. The money they must give for it represents an onerous effort already expended. They begin their estimates. Some of them may desire the wheat more than others, but there is a limit beyond which no one of them will go. Suppose that limit to be 80 cents a bushel. The price can by no possibility rise above that. The most sanguine buyer concludes that at 80+ he cannot dispose of his wheat with a profit, and 80+, therefore, becomes an impossible price. At 80, he may take some, if he cannot get it for less.

But the sellers have been making their estimates, too. Some are more anxious to sell than others, being in greater need of the money, but there is no one among them who will at present dispose of his wheat for less than 70 cents a bushel. He is bound to get as much more than that as he can, but lower than that he will not go.

The wheat represents to him an effort already expended, and 70 — does not in his judgment represent an effort equivalent to that, and 70 —, accordingly, becomes an impossible price in that market at that time. Between 70 and 80 the price may fluctuate, — what will determine the price ? The competition as between the buyers on the one hand, and the competition as between the sellers on the other hand, will determine it. . Suppose the first sale be at 72, a figure that the buyers regard as very favorable to them, and they show a readiness to buy largely at that rate. The sellers observe their quickness of offer, and are prompt to take advantage of it. They allege that 72 is a ruinous price for them, that the man who took that was under stress, that 74 is the least the market will bear.

In the mean time, a few eager buyers have actually given 73, and as the market is evidently rising, and there is still a fair margin of profit for the buyers, 74 is conceded by many, and there are large transactions at that rate. A strong demand has raised the price, and seems to hold it steady. Just then, come telegrams in cipher to some of the foreign buyers, that wheat has taken a sharp turn upward at Mark Lane. Now is a chance for extra profit even at 74. Demand increases. Sellers are keen to read the thoughts of buyers. The sellers get some telegrams, too; and the price goes up to 75. An increased demand caused by a larger number of purchasers, or by the same number for some reason made more eager, other things being equal, increases the price of any article or service; but it must be noted also, that the enhanced price in turn tends to lessen the demand by lessening the number of those who will purchase at the higher rate; so that, each rise of price from enhanced demand tends to check itself by cutting off demand. More men will purchase wheat in Milwaukee at 73 than at 75.

On the other hand, it must be noted, that a slackened demand tends to lower the price. If buyers become less eager than they were, sellers are apt to become more 'pliant than they were. When the sales at 75 become few and far between, it is for the interest of the sellers to tempt the market by offering wheat at 74, perhaps at 73, possibly at 72. A lower price, which is itself a consequence of slack demand, tends immediately to quicken demand by enlarging the circle of buyers, and this quicker demand tends to carry up the price again. Looking at demand only, within those outermost limits formed by mutual desires and efforts beyond which price will not go, there is a natural check that keeps price from rising to an extreme in the fact that high price from sharp demand cuts off demand and tends consequently to lower price again, and there is a natural check of the same kind that keeps price from falling to an extreme in the fact that low price from small demand is apt to call back demand and consequently to stiffen price again.

But this is only a part of the full beauty of the natural law that regulates values. We have observed the checks acting in either direction through changes in the demand; there are also checks acting in either direction through changes in the supply. There are three classes of services in respect to the law of their supply: first, those whose supply can be indefinitely increased at short notice; second, those whose supply can only be increased after a considerable lapse of time; and third, those whose supply cannot be increased at all, like the paintings of the old masters, and unique products generally. The line between the first and second of these classes is not a very sharp one, but still definite enough to lead to important practical consequences. Salt, for example, is a product whose supply in any market can be indefinitely increased at short notice.

Cotton, on the other hand, when once the crop of the year has been gathered, cannot be enlarged in quantity for a twelvemonth, though this quantity may be differently distributed under varying demand. The same remark applies to wheat, and other agricultural products, though cotton is a better example, because it is successfully raised at only few points, mostly in the United States, where 9,518,000 acres were planted to cotton in 1876. Now, in respect to the first two of these classes, and particularly the first one, whenever a brisk demand is carrying up the price in any market even before the rising price is checked

in the manner already indicated, it is apt to be
checked by an increase of the supply. A market
in which prices are rising is a good market to sell in.
The farmers and speculators within hailing distance
of Milwaukee find out that wheat is creeping up
towards 75, and the stock in that city is quickly
augmented through their action. Increased supply
tends to lower price, because there are now more
sellers, at least more stock to be sold, more motive
to trade at some price. Thus, in these classes of
things, there are two ever-present checks to a rising price, namely a falling-off of purchasers, and
an increased supply. Of course, in this discussion,
we take no account of changes in the quantity or
quality of money. We assume a fixed standard.

So also, there are two ever-present checks to an
extreme fall of price in respect to every thing of
which a market-rate can be predicated. There are
various unique' things, articles of *virtu*, things
whose price depends on fashion or caprice, in respect to which no useful principle can be laid
down beyond the most general ones already given.
They belong in the auction-room rather than in
the market. Their price is high or low according
to taste and circumstances. A portrait by Gains-
borough has just been sold in England for about
fifty times the sum of a previous sale. Such
things, though their changes in value are interesting and illustrate our fundamental propositions,
are of comparatively little account in Political
Economy, which interests itself mainly in things

that have a market-rate and in principles applicable to that. When a market is falling, there is,
as before, a double check that tends to prevent its
falling further. First, the enticement of new
purchasers through a low price, which tends
thereby to become higher; and second, the action,
through supply, of holders and speculators, who,
respectively, withdraw their stock for a better
market, and buy up now while the article is cheap
to store away till it shall be dearer. This acts on
supply to lessen it, which acts on price to raise it.
At this very time of writing, the woollen manufacturers of this county are buying California
wool far in excess of their immediate wants,
because wool is exceptionally cheap there at present, — because it can be bought for 11½ cents per
pound and brought round by the Horn for one
half cent per pound, with no heavy duties to be
paid on it, such as must be paid on foreign wool.
This prudent action of my Berkshire neighbors
affects the California wool market to prevent the
price there from falling so low as it would otherwise fall. At one and the same time it lessens the
supply and increases the demand there.

This law of Demand and Supply thus doubly
and harmoniously working, thus tending to keep
steady and calculable the prices of the great staples of human life and activity, while more obvious in its application within the field of material
commodities, nevertheless extends its operation
over the field of personal services, and the field of

commercial claims. It is all-comprehensive. The tendency of all economical forces is towards the equalization of demand and supply, that is to say, towards the disposal of each man's own product where it is most wanted, and the returning to him in lieu of it the product he most wants. The result may be called the EQUATION OF COMPETI-. TION. The mainspring of action in the economical world is self-interest. The practical regulator of values is competition. These words sound harsh, but the impulses underneath them work equally for the good of each and for the good of all. They work in a sphere prescribed for them. They work under limitations and checks that are marvellous to the mind that comprehends them. That they do not work perfectly is admitted. Sales are not always made at market-rates. There are sometimes, so to speak, more market-rates than one in the same market-town. Competition sometimes becomes unscrupulous and immoral, and combinations are made to prevent the play of wholesome competition. Sometimes even governments are persuaded to frame individual "mischief into a law," and to throw obstacles in the way of the free working of natural forces. But, after all, these forces vindicate themselves in the long-run; they punish the transgressors, even if they do not restore the individual sufferers; they emphasize the maxim by results, that, Honesty is the best policy; they exhibit a wisdom and scope and persistency in marked contrast to human industrial legislation; and they demand to be let alone to work out in freedom — under moral restrictions only — the economical progress of mankind.

Before closing the chapter, it may be well to remark, that, under this great law of value, which .will be further illumined in subsequent chapters, prices will be steadiest in that class of things whose supply can be soonest reached and is largest in amount; next steadiest in the second class of things, like farm products, whose supply is dependent on the seasons, and in which fluctuations in price and speculation are oftener observed than in the other class, although since the abolition of the Corn-Laws in England and the consequent opportunity for free importation from all countries, grain has approximated there in steadiness to the staples of the other class; and least steady in the third class of things whether material or other, whose price is more dependent upon demand, and less able to be regulated through supply.

Let us now put into a summary for review the principal points already made : —

1. *Political Economy has to do with men as* BUYERS AND SELLERS *only.*

2. *There is a Science of* SALES, *because these afford all the conditions under which other strict sciences are built up.*

3. *A Science is the* BODY *of exact definitions and sound principles educed from and applied to a single class of facts or phenomena.*

4. *The pre-arrangements of Providence, the attributes of human nature, and the laws and usages devised by men, are the* SOURCES *of economical truth.*

5. *Commodities, services, and claims are the three* KINDS *of salable things, — giving rise to six possible cases of sales.*

6. *The rendering of any thing for something in return is a* SERVICE.

7. *Value is the* RELATION *of mutual purchase established between two services by their exchange.*

8. *Utility is the simple* CAPACITY *to gratify a human desire, and so is quite different from Value.*

9. *Price is Value expressed in* MONEY.

10. *Value starts in desires, gives birth to efforts, proceeds by estimates, and ends in* SATISFACTIONS.

11. *The fundamental* LAW *of Political Economy is that of Demand and Supply.*

12. *There are three classes of valuable things in the law of their* SUPPLY.

CHAPTER II.

PRODUCTION.

I HAVE sought, in the previous chapter, to give a clear idea of what Value is, and of the important part it plays in the on-going of the world. Next to Virtue, Value is the most important thing for human happiness. It occupies the thoughts of men more than any thing else. It is itself the product of two minds estimating at one time two things in relation to each other, and, concluding them to be for certain purposes the equivalents of each other, accepting the one in the place of the other. Value has no existence outside the minds of men. The conditions for it indeed exist in the constitution of the physical earth, and in the structure of society, as well as in the nature of the individual man, but the determination of it, the calling of it into being, the pronouncing upon its reality and amount, is always the work of two minds. Value, accordingly, is always a result. It is the consummation of what has been prepared for. Things physical, things intellectual, things social, all play a part as preparatory to the realization of value. We must now attend to these *pro-cesses*, that lead up to this *result*. They may all be classed under the general name PRODUCTION.

The term Production is derived from the Latin word *producere*, which means, *to lead forth*, *to expose for sale*. Terence uses the expression, "*producere servos*," *to offer slaves for sale*. We must rid ourselves at the outset of the notion, that is apt to linger about this word, namely, that it is only properly applied to forms of *matter*, and that it only means to *make* something, or to *grow* something, or at least to *transform* something. Terence did not mean to say that the person of whom he was speaking brought the slaves into being, but only that he brought them out to sell. In common language, the growth of the farm is called *Produce*, but only when it is offered for sale, in which sense we speak of the *produce-market*. The fundamental meaning of the root-word both in Latin and English is *effort with reference to a sale ;* and this is the exact scientific sense in which I propose to use the word and its derivatives. I hope I am making at this point a slight contribution to a more exact nomenclature in Political Economy.

Production is always Effort, but it is not every kind of effort that is production. My boy is now playing the piano in the parlor; it is effort for him, — irksome effort, — but as he has no intention ever to sell his acquired skill upon that instrument, it cannot be called *productive* effort.

It is effort put forth for altogether other than commercial reasons. The effort of his music-teacher, however, who comes here to give him his lessons, is productive effort, inasmuch as it is put forth solely with reference to a sale. Efforts of all kinds that find their purpose and end in an exchange are Production: efforts put forth for amusement, for self-improvement, for benevolence, for personal or family gratification, are not Production. Political Economy has to do with processes simply as these are related to sales; and it makes no difference what kind of processes they are, if they have that design and issue. Some efforts, like those of the farmer, the miner, the wagon-maker, have to do with material things in the way of preparing them for sale, and Political Economy is interested in these efforts, inquires after their kinds and cost, as bearing on the sale that is to come; other efforts, like those of the banker, have to do with salable credits, and Political Economy inquires into all the processes of banking; while still other efforts, like those of the public singer, prepare for and are connected with the rendering of merely personal services, and Political Economy accordingly inquires into the conditions and law of wages. *Production, then, is effort in getting something ready to sell, and selling it.* A Producer is a person who does just this, without any reference to the kind of things he sells, whether they be commodities, services, or claims. *A product is any thing ready to be sold.*

The adjective *productive*, although it is often used as synonymous with fertile, finds its only proper economical sense in harmony with these definitions.

In current language, one hears *consumers* contrasted with *producers*, and *consumption* spoken of as the opposite of *production*. These words are correlative to each other in much the same way as supply and demand. One set of men are not the producers, and another set the consumers, but each producer is in another aspect a consumer, and each consumer is in another aspect a producer. As derived from the Latin *consumere*, which means *to use, to employ*, as well as, *to waste, to destroy*, the English derivatives have a little stronger taint of ambiguity about them than the derivatives of *producere*, which, as we have seen, have not wholly escaped ambiguity. In their economical sense, however, with which alone we have to do, *to consume means to take up, to use ; the consumer is the customer, the purchaser ; and consumption is simple purchase.* Many things purchased are destroyed as to form almost immediately, while many other things purchased are not thus destroyed, but both are equally " consumed " in the technical sense.

For example, a shoe manufacturer buys at the same time a stock of leather and a pegging-machine : the leather immediately disappears as leather, and re-appears in the form of shoes ; the pegging-machine for years and years " keeps pegging away; " but the manufacturer is equally the "consumer" in relation to them both. Whenever any producer exchanges his product for another, he becomes a consumer in relation to that product, while the other party is equally producer and consumer in relation to him. This illustrates the complexity and the harmony of interests in the economical world. The sooner any man's product is consumed the better for him and for everybody else.

We are now in position intelligibly to discuss the requisites and processes of Production. These requisites are only three: NATURAL AGENTS, LABOR, CAPITAL.

By Natural Agents is meant every thing, outside of man himself, furnished gratuitously by God to men, by means of which their productive operations may be sustained and facilitated. The chief of these are the Land, out of which comes our bread; the Materials on the earth and within it, like stone, timber, the metals, coal, petroleum, and salt; the Sea, which at once divides, unites, and enriches the nations; the various natural Forces, such as those of wind, water, steam, electricity, and so on; and what are called the domestic animals, the ox, the ass, the horse, and others. These are all gifts of God to men. Originally, and before any labor is expended in connection with them, all of them are wholly destitute of value. Some of them, like the salt and the spontaneous growths of the earth, may have utility, that is, capacity to gratify human desire,

but value they have not, and never get, except as
labor is expended on them or in some connection
with them. Wind blows, and water gravitates,
and steam puffs, and electricity darts, for nothing.
The Hollander builds his windmill with onerous
effort, and can doubtless sell the structure to his
neighbor, but the wind that fills its wings costs
neither of them any thing. Most of the factories
of New England are propelled by the weight of
falling water, but the water leaps to those wheels
of industry without pay. The United States exported in the first six months of 1876, 101,389,183
gallons of petroleum, but the *value* of it was due,
not to what had been done in the wonderful
laboratory of Nature, but wholly to what had
been done by men in boring the wells, in securing
the oil, and in transporting the product. Providence indicates its will that men should be producers by offering on every hand free materials to
be wrought upon, and free forces by means of
which production may be made easier. It is
proof complete that these materials and forces are
offered gratuitously, since no man has ever authenticated his claim to ask any thing for these things
in God's behalf.

If men have done any thing in the way of labor
to better these materials or to harness these forces,
they may ask pay for *that*, and get it; but if they
go beyond this, and ask something for what they
or their predecessors have done, and something
additional for what God has done, their cupidity

will be thwarted both by the competition of other
men, who will offer similar products for a fair
compensation for the human labor expended, and
especially by the fact, that there are other free
materials and forces not yet laid hold of by anybody, which can be put into just as good shape for
use as these, by no greater expenditure of labor
than has been put upon these. God is a Giver,
and not a Seller. The whole world of materials
and forces has been thrown open to men with such
liberality, and under such circumstances, that
they cannot first appropriate the gifts, and then
peddle them out for pay. There may seem to be
cases in which this has actually been done, but,
as I believe, they will mostly or wholly disappear
under a rigid analysis, and particularly so, when
it is remembered, that abstinence from use or
enjoyment, as well as actual labor bestowed, either
by a man himself or by those of whose labor
and abstinence he has rightly become proprietor,
entitles him to demand a return.

Vei, contrary to what has often been taught
even in books on Political Economy, these general
principles apply perfectly to Land. Land is the
most important natural agent. Its cultivation
employs the efforts of more than half of the
human race. In many countries its possession is
eagerly desired on account of social considerations
attaching to it. What, then, does its value depend
on? I answer, that it depends on precisely the
same considerations as the value of other things

depends on, namely, desires, efforts, and estimates. Until human efforts are put forth upon a piece of land, or in some immediate connection with it, that land is valueless of course, both for other good reasons, and because no one can lay any claim to it, or show any title to it whatever. God gave the earth to men on the condition that they "replenish and subdue it." Conquest and confiscation aside, the personal ownership of land has always virtually come in under the efforts implied in this word *subdue*. Whenever an individual, or a family, has expended labor upon a parcel of land, has improved it, has made it easier for another family to gain a living from it, then, wishing to leave it, he might properly enough offer to sell it to a new-comer. But *what* would he offer to sell? The inherent qualities of the soil? Those natural forces which he had not improved? No! He could only sell what he himself had contributed of betterment. He would not *think* of selling any thing else; and even if he did think of it, he would not succeed in doing it, for the reason, that no one would give him any thing for the original qualities of the soil. In the beginnings of societies and settlements there is always an abundance of land to be had for the mere occupation and subjugation of it; and it is contrary to the impulses of human nature to suppose that a later would give an earlier comer any thing more than a fair equivalent for what had been wrought of actual improvement. while other lands just as

feasible as that originally was are all open to him
" where to choose." It must be remembered that
estimates always precede value; and that men do
not, as a rule, give something for what they can
just as well have for nothing.

In older settled countries, in which the fee simple prevails, after all the good lands have been
taken up, men are always found willing to part
with land as with any thing else for about what it
has cost them of effort or money, and the action
of these tends to make a market-rate for lands,
and competition eliminates all the gratuitous elements involved from any action upon price, and
leaves the value of land to be determined as other
values are by the onerous elements involved.
This abstract view is confirmed by facts. It has
long been a maxim in our Western States, that
farms of the most fertile land are worth about the
present value of the improvements on them, and
no more; and it has been calculated at large by
Mr. Carey, that the lands in all countries are now
worth far less than it has actually cost to amelio-
rate them. I know from personal knowledge, that
farms in my native state of New Hampshire,
which, in my boyhood, supported large families,
have been abandoned by their late owners, and
are now growing up to forest again. They could
not sell them at any price, they have simply left
them to lapse into their primitive state, while they
and their families have migrated to the West.
All this does not look as if lands had value in

themselves separate from the endeavors of men.
Nothing has value in itself separate from the
endeavors of men.

On the other hand, it must not be supposed
that the value of different parcels of land is
always proportioned to the amount of efforts put
forth upon them ; the efforts may have been mis-
directed; the utility sought to be conferred by
labor may not have found the requisite utility
underneath; the desires calculated to be met may
have taken another turn; and so, there may be a
greater diversity in the value of lands than in the
amount of efforts expended upon them. Still, the
efforts are always the *basis* of the value, and not
the natural fertility of the lands. While it is not
denied that the varying natural fertility in lands
may within certain limits vary the prices of those
lands, it is confidently affirmed, that a high degree
of natural fertility has been scattered with so
bountiful a hand, and that lands naturally less fertile have such compensating advantages of another
sort, that, under a broad view, the degree of original fertility becomes a common factor cancelled in
price, according to principles already explained.

Let me remind my readers also, that lands are
often desired on other grounds than their fertility,
and that whatever goes to make them an object of
special desire becomes an element in their value.
Land in cities often becomes extremely valuable,
not at all on account of native fertility, not so
much on account of what has been done on or

concerning that particular patch, although the ex
penditure and abstinence of previous owners may
a good deal influence the price, as we shall better
understand when we come to study Capital, but
mainly on account of what has been done and is
being done all around it: — a busy city has grown
up around it, and that piece has become desirable
for business or other uses in consequence of the
action of others than the owner. It is thus that
social, municipal, and political movements win
their power to influence values by making some
things more *desirable* than they were, and other
things less desirable. Lands supposed to contain
rich mines, or holding an extraordinary water-
power, or containing a building site of unusual
beauty, frequently excite a strong desire in certain persons to possess them, and bear in consequence a high price. These lands are assimilated
in the law of their value to other unique products.
If there be no competition in the sale of such
things, and consequently no market-rate, the only
gauge of their value is the degree of service which
the owner can render the purchaser by means of
them. That portion of their utility that is the
free gift of Nature is commingled with the utility
that has been conferred by man, and there is not
the usual opportunity through competition to
throw out from its action on value the gratuitous
utility. These are comparatively unimportant
exceptions, and themselves come with precision
under our fundamental principles.

We can now see exactly how Natural Agents stand related to Production. They are a requisite of production. They assist and sustain the processes. They are not of equal rank in production with man and his efforts. Men make use of them to further and enlarge their designs of sale. Lands are subdued and cultivated and improved by men for the sake of more profitable harvests; but the lands demand back nothing for themselves; they are not an independent and co-ordinate contributor to production; if they are hired, as they often are, the rent paid for the use of them is not in virtue of the original qualities of the soil of which some chance grabber became proprietor, but in virtue of previous human toil and care, which must also be continued in the future, or else the lands will become valueless again as they were in the beginning. Moreover, liberally as lands respond to improvements in agriculture, there is ˙a limit to their power to respond. If I double the labor upon my turnip-field, I may possibly for a single year double my crop of turnips; but if I redouble the expense for the next year, I shall not redouble my crop; for, if that were the law of returns in agriculture, if increased effort upon a given area increased the produce in the same ratio, an acre were as good for productive purposes as 100 acres, and 100 acres were as good as a continent.

If it were not for this universal law of agriculture, namely, *that relatively diminishing returns accompany increasing expenditures upon land,* the surface of the earth would not now be occupied by husbandmen as it is occupied. The agricultu ral motive that leads men to pass from the first to the second acre, from the old farm to the new, from the mother-country to colonies, and from one country to another, is the fact, that, under any given conditions of agricultural skill, the limit of productiveness is soon reached, the law of diminishing returns comes into play, and it becomes profitable to migrate to "fresh fields and pastures new." Of course, all improvements in scientific and practical agriculture, the discovery of new methods like the rotation of crops, the invention of better implements, the application of new fertilizers, the light thrown upon farming by Chemistry, retard the law of diminishing returns, and tend to keep husbandmen as such in their old haunts. Providence has made use of this law in order to people the whole earth in accordance with the original direction that the earth be "replenished;" and in making man the lord of the earth, and giving him "dominion over the fish of the sea, and over the fowl of the air, and over every living thing that moveth upon the earth,"[1] there is unmistakably brought out the essential, though subordinate, relation of all natural agents to man.

Notwithstanding the law of diminishing returns in agriculture, which, as has been shown, has already had important effects in dispersing people

[1] Gen. ii. 28.

over the earth, the earth has never yet in any part of it yielded what it is capable of yielding for the sustenance of her children. Her produce cannot indeed be indefinitely increased in a geometrical ratio, but it may be immeasurably increased in an arithmetical ratio ; and while it is abstractly possible that population may increase in a geometrical ratio, that is, double itself in each generatior ; and while Mr. Malthus has given his name to a theory of fear lest population may one day trench on the possible means of sustenance ; yet it is undoubtedly true, as a matter of fact, that the population of the earth, increased as it is, was never as a whole so well fed and clothed and housed as it is to-day ; and it is undoubtedly true, as a matter of reasonable conclusion, that the earth is capable, under a proper development of all her food-sources of flesh, fish, fowl, cereals, and vegetables, of sustaining in comfort a population many thousand-fold greater than the present ; while it is also undoubtedly. true, whatever may be said of abstract possibilities, that legitimate checks to population, which come silently and effectually into play as men come more and more under the sway of reason and affection, may be rationally expected forever to prevent the Malthusian impinging of population upon food.

In respect to all the other natural agents, just as in respect to the earth itself, they are ready to slave in the service of man. What the earth does in producing wheat, or rice, or any other of her growths, enters as no element into their value; since the sun shines free, and the rain falls free, and the chemical actions in growth and maturing work free; and the more bountifully under more skilful culture the earth can be made to yield her increase, the lower, so far forth, will be the value of any specific part of that produce. Just so, the other natural agents are ready to work without money and without price. Ever since the Atlantic cable was laid, and a path was made for the lightning, electricity has done its part in ocean telegraphy for nothing. Did my readers ever think for what purpose men require the ·help of most of these natural agents? *It is simply to produce motion for them.* Indeed, in physical labor, all that man himself can do is to make a series of motions. His muscles are only adapted to do that. When he has moved things into right positions, the powers of nature will do the rest. At any rate, that is all *he* can do.

I have heard all the morning in the fields around my house the click of the mowing-machine. It is moved by two horses, a man riding on the machine, and guiding both the horses and the machine. All that the horses do is to draw the machine through the grass, and all that the man does is to guide the horses with one hand by pulling the reins, and guide the machine with the other by lifting or depressing a bar. The mowing is nothing but a series of motions animal and human. Formerly, men did all the mowing by

scythes drawn by hand. That was simple motion.
Now, they substitute horse-power, that is, they
use horses to make the motion that cuts the grass.
If the swath is spread by fork or tedder, it is
motion that spreads it, human or animal, as the
case may be. The tedder is superseding the fork
for that use. The hay is lifted to the cart, and
thence to the mow, by another series of motions,
in which some progress has already been made in
substituting power for muscle. Haying is motions.
So is ploughing, and harrowing, and sowing, and
reaping. So are all the operations of the farm
whatsoever. So is washing the sheep, shearing
the fleece, dyeing the wool, carding, spinning,
weaving, specking, gigging, finishing, packing, —
all the processes of manufacturing from beginning
to end. Think of it! Physical work is nothing
in the world but the contraction and relaxation
of muscle guided by an intelligent mind. But
this, repeated and continued, becomes wearisome;
and, probably, in the very beginnings of society,
certainly, very early, men looked around for helps
in this matter of making motions.

They first pressed the domestic animals into
this service; and it is worth noticing, that the ox,
the ass, the horse, are only desirable and valuable
as creators of motion for man. They greatly
relieve his muscles, and greatly enlarge the sphere
of his physical activities. Savages dig the earth
for planting with a hoe; civilized men plough and
harrow it by means of natural agents. After-

wards, men thought of some inanimate auxiliaries in making motion, and the water-wheel and wind mill were devised. Gravitation is a constant force in nature, asks for no rest, feels no weariness, and, throwing water upon a wheel, can move things equal to a thousand men. In flat countries, the force of wind moving upon a vertical or horizontal wheel fitted with a kind of wing or sail to catch the breeze is only a less efficient agent than the force of falling water.

Much later, steam was discovered as a motive-power; and later still, electricity. The piston-rod moves back and forth by a motion quite analogous to that of the human arm; and all that steam-engines are wanted for on land or sea, on mountain-top or in deep mines, is just to reduplicate the power of which a human arm is capable. Nature is so cunningly constructed, that materials only need to be *moved* aright, and objects of utility and value are the result. I lately observed at the International Exhibition at Philadelphia a little machine, belonging to the United States, and tended by a single girl, which, when fed by a pile of white paper, cuts out in outline a mass of letter envelopes, then picks them up one by one much faster than I can tell it, folds them properly, glutenizes the edge for sealing, stamps them with the postal legend of the United States, and drops them into a receptacle ready for packing. The great engine communicates its motion by a band to this little machine, which itself, by another series of motions, completes beautifully stamped envelopes good through the national Post-Office Steam, like the domestic animals, makes motions useful in production; but, no more than they, can it be left to work by itself. All natural agents need the supervision of human intelligence.

Electricity, too, whose action round the world is a never-ceasing marvel to every thoughtful human being, works all its wonders by a series of little motions, or interruptions to motion. The electric current may be compared to the contraction of muscle, the breaking of the current to its relaxation. As the motions of the hand through the pen jot down the thoughts of the writer, and as the motions of the press make a record of thoughts upon the printed page, so the minute twitches of an invisible current rushing upon a wire communicate by sound or mark the thoughts of men across the continents. Great is motion! Great is the adaptation of the materials of the world to be transformed into useful products by the forces of the world! Great are the forces of the world to run to and fro over the earth to do the bidding of man!

All this brings us to a most cheering law of Production, which is, that *production is constantly going forward under less and less onerous conditions.* The reason for this is now very apparent, namely, that men are able to throw off more and more of the burden of production, that is, of the effort needed to get things ready to sell, upon the ever-willing

shoulders of nature. Nature furnishes all raw
materials gratuitously; and what is more, furnishes
on every hand animate or inanimate *powers*, which
men may avail themselves of, which men are
availing themselves of more and more, in fashion-
ing these materials for the world's great market.
Almost any physical product, that my readers can
name, represents vastly less of irksome human
effort than a similar product represented one cen
tury ago, not to speak of the greater contrast with
many centuries ago. Take for instance, a barrel of
flour. The improvements in agricultural implements and methods involved in growing and har-
vesting the wheat, out of which the flour comes,
make the onerous elements small compared with
what they used to be. Wheat used to be sown,
and reaped, and threshed by hand; now all these
processes are done by machines propelled mainly
by horses. Ridley's reaper, which is used in South
Australia, and other places where no rain falls in
harvest-time, combines the threshing with the
reaping. By the action of this machine, the grain
is literally combed off the stalks, and falls clean
into a receptacle all ready for the sack, while the
stalks are left standing.[1] It only costs $2 gold an
acre thus to reap, thresh, winnow, and bag wheat
ready for market. Hand reaping, threshing, and
so on, as against this machine work, costs there
$5.35 gold per acre.

In this country, owing to the climate, we have

[1] Musgrave's Studies, &c., p. 108.

not got so far as Ridley's reaper, although the
immense threshing-machines with winnower attached, which I have seen in Iowa, propelled by
ten horses, and used by neighboring farmers in
combination and rotation, greatly reduce the cost
from the old hand-flail times. Then, too, the
grinding into flour by improved machinery costs
less than formerly; and the barrel staves and
heads are cut by machines, which used to be
shaped by the cooper's hand; and transportation
by steam over steel rails is but little in cost compared with the old "teaming" times. The average
cost of good wheat to the farmers of our Western
States cannot be far from 50 cents, gold, per
bushel; and the difference between this and the
cost to the farmers of New England one hundred
years ago, which could not have been less than
100 cents, is wholly due to the free forces that are
now more fully in play.

What is thus true of an agricultural product,
is still more true of manufactured products of all
kinds. Natural agents can never have so free a
play in cheapening the products of the farm as of
the factory, for three reasons; first, the division
of labor cannot be carried very far in agriculture; second, from the nature of the case, machinery can be less employed on the farm than in the
mill, since the latter deals with dead matter and
the former largely with living tissues; third, nothing can materially shorten the time during which
the fruits of the earth must mature, while all the

processes of manufacture may be hurried forward
without intermission. The wool on the sheep's
back to-day may be in the dye-house to-morrow,
carded the next day, spun the next, woven the
next, finished the next, and be under the tailor's
shears before the week is out. It is an important
corollary from this principle, *that a given amount
of farm products tends, under free exchange, to buy
more and more of manufactured products of all
kinds;* inasmuch as this great law of gratuitous
auxiliaries, which tends to cheapen all things
relatively to a fixed standard, applies less completely to the farmer than to the manufacturer.
I have called this elsewhere [1] " The Farmer's
Advantage " because the value of farm products
is more calculable in the present and future, is
less liable to fluctuations, and especially to sudden
decline, than the value of manufactured products
in general. The farmer naturally holds a more
secure and conservative position in the realm of
value than the manufacturer does; while both
should strive to avail themselves to the fullest
extent of all the helps that nature offers them in
their respective fields.

There is no branch of industry, whose operations are not becoming easier and more effective
in consequence of the increasing use of natural
agents. The various forms of physical production, that is to say, the bringing forward for sale
of *commodities*, are more facilitated in this way

[1] Agricultural Address at North Adams, 1870.

than the other kinds of production, because *motion* can be more directly applied to them in their preparation and transportation than to the others; and natural agents pre-eminently furnish their aid in the form of motion. We have already illus-trated the cases of the production of flour and cloth. There are no commodities, that I am aware of, the processes of whose production in civilized countries are not being made easier by new applications of gratuitous natural forces; and the selling of personal services, and of claims of all sorts, though less directly affected by these applications, is nevertheless indirectly greatly pro-moted by them. For example, laborers can go much further to their work from their homes, and thus be more sure of finding work, by means of the railroads; the lawyer in his office working up a case can bring needed evidence from a distance by means of the telegraph; and bankers, brokers, credit-dealers of every name, proceed more safely in their business under the modern opportunities of swift information and rapid action even as between distant countries. Other, and perhaps better, illustrations will occur to every reader.

Now, the effect of all this is to make a given amount of effort in any direction more prolific in utilities. More is *produced* on all hands. Ex-changes are multiplied, since there is more to be exchanged. If men do not work fewer hours under all these improvements, then they can render a great many more of their peculiar services; and the probability is, that, working fewer hours, and having more leisure for their families and for self-cultivation, the improvements will more than keep pace with their relaxation, and so a double blessing comes through God's free bounty in natural agents. The cheering element about this is, that, under natural laws uninterfered with by the wretched legislation of men, more wants of all men tend constantly to be satisfied without any more onerous exertion on their part. The masses are no longer content with food and clothes and shelter, and they should not be encouraged to be. God has ordered it so, that, without additional *work*, everybody may have additional *comforts*. The wants of all men are indefinite in number and degree, and, therefore, production may go forward indefinitely without ever a fear of finding a general glut of its products. There is something better under natural law for the toiling millions than "irretrievable helotism." That natural law is, *that production may go forward under ever lightening burdens to men with an ever increasing volume of products to be distributed by exchange among men.* Certainly, in order that men may enjoy the full benefits of this law, they themselves must be industrious, frugal, temperate, virtuous; and their governments must not overstep their legitimate functions in legislation; these, surely, should not be considered grievances by anybody. The law is embedded by divine wisdom in the constitution of things. Free forces are so offered to men, that, if they avail themselves fully of those, they cannot fail, the necessary moral conditions being supplied, to rise continually in the scale of comforts, in the power to command through exchange the satisfaction of their wants.

The personal motives, that lead men to avail themselves in a higher and higher degree through implements of the help of natural agents, are to be found, partly in a natural love of invention, and partly in considerations that grow out of *value*. Some men are born with a knack for contrivance; others seem to develop this later in life; and many are never so happy as when trying to invent something, or to improve upon some invention already made. In almost all cases, these efforts look towards the construction of some apparatus to use for productive puposes the natural force of wind, water, steam, electricity, gravitation, friction, or some other. Doubtless, in most cases, these persons think, if they are successful, there will be pecuniary profit coupled with their invention, although to secure that does not seem to be their main impulse. They work in the love of it. Many others work at inventions out of a desire to make them immediately profitable. This is particularly true of men engaged in the manufacturing of fabrics or of implements, who are subjected to intense competition, and who, if they can bring in a little more of free force into their processes, will have at least a temporary advantage over their rivals. This makes it necessary to explain how improvements act upon the value of those things produced by their help.

We have already seen how competition tends to throw down the value of every thing towards the level of the onerous elements concerned in its production, so that men cannot, as a rule and for any length of time, sell God's gifts; it is a consequence of this, that the value of every thing whose production is facilitated by improved processes and free forces tends ultimately to decline relative to the value of every thing whose production is not equally facilitated. In the light of this, it would seem at first sight, as if there would be no motive on the ground of value to strive for better processes. Nevertheless, there is a temporary state of things after an improvement has been introduced, say, into a cotton-mill, during which the old price may be obtained for a product, which now costs less of onerous effort. This is the motive to bring in the improvement. So soon as the improvement becomes general in cotton-mills, down will go the value of the product to a new level, and almost at once after the first introduction, there will be a motive to lower the price a little, so as to get a better market and undersell competitors, but so long as the process is confined to that mill by patent or otherwise, there will be some extra gains there, sufficient perhaps to reward the inventor for his time and toil, and to become an inducement to him and to others to continue to exercise their skill as inventors. The tendency of secret knowledge is to become known, of special processes to become general, of patent rights to expire and be infringed on ; and so, production, which is especially open by double motive to invention, becomes a kind of perpetual contest, the issue of which is always favorable to common rights and lower values.

If two articles, which formerly exchanged against each other, are now both produced through improved methods, they will exchange against each other still at the old rate, provided both improvements release an equal amount of onerous effort; and if they do not, then that one will buy less of the other, whose production has been most facilitated; while both will buy less of money, or other product, that has remained fixed in the conditions of its production. As a matter of fact, there is no such product, though, for reasons to be given hereafter, gold comes nearer to that description than any thing else. This concludes our direct discussion of Natural Agents.

The second requisite of production is LABOR. *Labor is any human exertion that demands something for itself in exchange.* Every person puts forth more or less of muscular and mental effort without any expectation of a return for it. This is not labor. Nothing is labor that does not look to a sale ; and we are excused by the definition from the old discussion about " productive " and " unproductive " labor. All labor is productive in fact or in intention. If I watch all night with a sick neighbor, I put forth an effort irksome in itself, but done in kindness with no thought of a return. That is not labor. I write for pay an article in the newspaper with half the expenditure of vital force of the night's watching: that is labor. The mistress employs her powers of body and mind for two hours in dressing herself for a party: that is not labor. Her servant-girl gives a languid inter-ost, and lends an occasional hand, to the process: that is labor. It is not the kind of exertion, it is not the degree of the exertion, it is not the length of time during which the exertion is put forth, that constitutes effort to be labor; but it is the *end* for which the effort is put forth. Labor, like every thing else in Political Economy, is tested by the criterion of a *sale*. The only seal used in this science is the seal of the market.

A large part of the labor of the world is what may be called physical labor, that is, the exertion is primarily muscular, and is, in fact, *the moving of materials or implements with reference to a certain result*. In all cases, some action of mind is required to do this successfully; probably the inferior animals could not be trained to do it at all, though dogs do sometimes churn under supervision; yet the main thing furnished by the laborer is muscular motion more or less regular and constantly repeated; and it is in consequence of this feature of it, that the substitution of machinery in its place has already gone so very far, and is destined to go much farther. Machinery can only be made to perform regular motions; and therefore it can only be made a substitute for labor in so far as that labor furnished a series of more or less regular motions. Horse-power now saws the wood at our railroad station, where Pat and Mike and Jim used to saw it, because all that is required in either case is motion to bring the saw in contact with the wood.

So it is in spinning and weaving and printing and drilling. Machinery can be made to do wonders, but it cannot be made to think. All machinery, the simplest and the most complex, requires human intelligence to guide it. So far as the work was a mere recurrence of motions, machinery may come in to relieve muscle; so far as it was adaptation to circumstances, adjustment in exigencies, the human mind must be there as before. The introduction of machinery has lessened the demand for the simplest form of labor, while it has doubtless increased the demand for labor in general. The cheapening of individual products through freer processes has enlarged the demand for them, has multiplied the number of them, has even increased the aggregate value of them, and while fewer laborers are needed at one point of the process, more are needed at other and more complex points of the process. I have never seen the point made before, but I will venture the assertion, that the whole tendency of things is to drive laborers into places requiring more and more of intelligence and skill. The lowest places,

where laborers have swarmed for ages, are being
occupied more and more by labor-saving appliances, and laborers are now wanted to tend these
machines, to market the goods, to watch and wait
and judge, in short, to render services requiring
intelligence and will, rather than those requiring a
succession of motions mainly.

For labor is of various grades, and is paid for
accordingly at very various rates. Mr. Hugh J.
Jewett received as president of the Erie Railway
$40,000 a year as stated salary. Few men can
bear the burdens that he bore in that capacity.
The French painter, Meissonier, received 150,000
francs in 1867 for a single picture, " A Charge of
Cavalry," now in a private gallery in Cincinnati ;
and, more recently, 300,000 francs for the " Battle
of Friedland." These are works of genius, but
they are also fruits of labor ; and in wondering at
their price, we must not lose sight of the years of
toil in preparing for and painting them, of the
money paid for costumes and accessories, and of
the hire of models, and so on. Before Meissonier
painted his picture of Napoleon III. at Solferino,
he made a journey to Italy expressly in the way
of preparation, and another to Vienna, to make
researches and get hints for his picture of the
meeting of the emperors Napoleon III. and Fran-
cis Joseph at Villafranca. The truth is, that the
studies and labors of one's whole life are a needed
preparation for any really great work, and the extraordinary compensation that sometimes awaits

the completion of such a work, whether of an inventor like Prof. Morse, of an engineer like De
Lesseps, of an artist like Horace Vernet, or of an
author like Charles Dickens, is really the reward
of a long series of otherwise unremunerated
efforts. From the lowest forms of manual labor,
as the stone-breaker's and the wood-sawyer's, to
the highest efforts of professional genius, as the
piano-playing of Liszt and the legal plea of
O'Conor, is indeed a long way, and the interval is
filled up full with every variety of personal services rendered for pay, but the extremes and the
means are all alike *labor*, and it is difficult to make
any classification in this case, because the attempted classes are sure to grade into each other.

A rude classification of labor may be made into
common, skilled, and professional labor. Common
labor is that which can be acceptably performed
by an ordinarily competent person after a little
instruction and practice without any thing corresponding to an *apprenticeship* as a preliminary.
Farm laborers, railroad laborers, 'longshoremen,
teamsters, porters, miners, and many more, belong
to this class. Wages, which are *the remuneration
of labor,* are the lowest and steadiest in this class,
because, owing to the ease with which the class
can be recruited at any time from growing boys
and immigrating foreigners, the supply is kept
constantly large relatively to the demand. It is
time to remind ourselves again, that values spring
out of Desires and Efforts. Wages are a form

of values, their peculiarity being that they are received for a personal service rendered, and not for a commodity or claim rendered. The personal service may be incorporated into a commodity, or it may not; that makes no difference so far as the labor and its wages are concerned; Meissonier received his commission from the emperor to paint the "Solferino," and his labor was embodied in a commodity that belonged to the emperor so soon as it was done, and what he was paid for was his personal service as a painter; on the other hand, Parepa Rosa was paid a large sum for an evening's singing, and her service had no connection with any commodity. All labor is offered over against some desires of other men, and wages are the response to that appeal. It is easy to point out the maximum of wages: it is the point at which the labor-takers will sooner forego the labor than give any more for it: It is easy also to point out the minimum of wages: it is the point at which the labor-givers will sooner forego wages altogether than take any less wages.

Between these extremes marked out by the intensity of the desires on both sides, the rate of wages will fluctuate back and forth according to circumstances. There are a great many persons in all countries who desire such services as common laborers can render, and are able to pay for them at a moderate rate only, since their desires are not intense nor their means very ample. There are everywhere common desires for comforts and ordinary gain, just as there are often intense desires for distinction and for extraordinary gains. Common laborers, being numerous for the reason already given, compete with each other to secure the wages thus offered by those who desire their services. In many cases, these services could be and would be dispensed with, if a high rate of wages was demanded. Under these circumstances, a general market-rate of wages for common labor is determined — an equalization of demand and supply is had — and the rate is always moderate, because the service of the labor-givers has few elements of scarcity or difficulty about it, and because the return service of the labor-takers is not proffered under the impulse of unusually strong desires. Of course, a market-rate thus established is liable to change from time to time, being higher in flush times and lower in dull times, but on the whole steadier than the wages-rates in the higher departments for reasons soon to be given. I know of no guiding principle, other than these general ones, which determines in any country the rate of wages of common labor. The number of the laborers is of course an element, the general prosperity and hopefulness of employers is another element, and the amount and productiveness of capital is still another element, but this has more immediately to do with the wages of the next class to be considered in a moment.

The wages of *skilled* laborers, namely, of those who have had to pass through something equivalent to an apprenticeship in order to be able to offer their services, offer some points of difference from those of common labor. In the first place, their numbers are fewer, because comparatively few parents can afford to give their children the time and the money needful for them to learn a trade, or to become skilful in any art requiring education; and, as a result of this, their wages will rule higher than common wages, because the press of competition will be less felt among them, and because, being more intelligent and consequently mobile, they can better insist on their claims, and can better distribute themselves to points where their services are in demand. In the second place, they are more likely to be subject to a strong demand than common laborers are, on account of the close connection of their labor with special accumulations of capital.

We must here anticipate the discussions of following paragraphs so far as to say, *that capital is the aggregate of all products reserved as a means for further production;* that accumulations of capital are in their very nature a standing demand for laborers; that buildings, machinery, raw materials, and all the appliances of manufactures of all sorts, are a special demand for skilled laborers, because they alone can run this machinery, work up these materials, and make these whole investments of capital profitable to their owners; that the more capital of all kinds invested in branches of industry requiring skilled laborers to carry them on, the stronger the motive of the owners to employ the laborers, inasmuch as no profit comes from idle investments, but rather a constant loss besides the loss of profit; and that, in consequence of all this, the rate of wages of skilled laborers is sure to be higher than that of common laborers, and, as capital increases and business is prosperous, is likely to become still higher and relatively constant. Many forms of capital are more immediately dependent upon skilled laborers than upon common, and there is often a competition among employers for such laborers, and in profitable times they occupy an enviable position, capital being dependent upon them for its profit and increase. At the same time, common laborers will share to a lower degree with skilled in the benefits of a prosperous ongoing of the various industries. They are adjuncts to all mills, factories, and enterprises. The more products created in the higher departments the more work to be done in the lower departments. Even domestic servants feel the influence in a rise of wages of a general and continued prosperity of capital. Still, it remains true, that such prosperity affects more immediately and largely the wages of skilled laborers. The interdependence of labor and capital, and the cordial relations that should always subsist between them, will be better displayed after we understand better the nature and forms of capital.

Professional labor is the highest form of personal services rendered for pay, because it involves the

most of time and expense in the way of preparation, because it is most often connected with high
natural abilities and genius, and because for these
reasons it receives the highest remuneration. It
is not pretended that a sharp line can be drawn
between professional and skilled labor, any more
than between skilled and common labor, and we
do not confine the adjective "professional" to
what used to be called the three learned professions, theology, medicine, and law. We mean by
professional labor the services of those who have
received a technical education (not an apprenticeship) expressly to fit them to render these services,
and who have the requisite character, talents, and
genius to enable them to succeed. Clergymen,
physicians, lawyers, literary men, artists, actors,
and many more, render professional services loosely
so called. The obstacles at the entrance to this
path, occasioned by the lack either (1) of appropriate natural gifts, or (2) of the requisite industry
and character, or (3) of the means of a suitable
education and training, practically exclude so
many persons, that the competition in the higher
walks of professional life is not such as to prevent
a large remuneration for services rendered. Comparatively few men reach a high point of excellence in their respective professions, and they
have in consequence what may be called a natural
monopoly in these fields of effort, and receive for
their labor a very high rate of wages.

The competition in the professions would be

less than it is, if men entered upon them solely
on economical grounds, and if the needed education had to be fully paid for as other things are
paid for; as it is, the respectability which attends
them, the desire of knowledge for its own sake
which is gained in connection with them, the
instruction wholly or in part gratuitously offered
to those in course of preparation for them, and the
desire to do good which actuates many who enter
upon them, all these increase more or less the competition in professional labor. It may be worth
while, just in passing, to note, that moral considerations mingle in with the economical much more
in the higher than in the lower walks of effort,
although we are concerned with the moral considerations merely as they bear upon the economical.
For example, we are concerned with the clergyman's salary, with the services he renders for *pay*,
but we may note the fact that there are more
clergymen than there would be, if the pay were
the only motive to enter the ministry, especially
as the moral motive influences in turn the amount
of the pay. So, too, the underlying *character* of
a man, except so far as it may affect the accept-
ableness of his paid-for services, is *economically* a
matter of indifference; but then there are some
services, like those of the preacher, the teacher,
the treasurer of corporations, and others involving
great trust, which depend so directly upon moral
character, that we are bound to observe the points
of contact, especially again as the comparatively

small number who have all the *other* requisites for such trusts is still further reduced by the employers insisting upon the *additional* quality of a character recognized to be good, which scruple undoubtedly enhances the pay of the few who have all the required qualities. Character, however, it must be insisted, though it has its points of contact with things to be sold, stands on ground very distinct from them. Skill, for instance, is acquired to sell; character, if genuine, is maintained for its own sake, and will never compromise itself for the sake of gain.

It must be added, in explanation of the high wages of professional labor, that the demand is often peculiarly intense, as well as the supply peculiarly limited. If great interests of property, of reputation, or of life are at stake, it is felt that the best men to secure these must be had at almost any price. Fees and rewards for services of great delicacy, of great difficulty, or great danger, are paid by individuals and corporations and nations without grudging. Persons able to confer an exquisite pleasure, particularly if the pleasure can be conveyed to a great many persons equally at the same time, by oratory, reading, singing, playing, acting, and so on, secure extraordinary returns for their efforts. Beecher, Dickens, Cushman, Lind, Rubenstein, Rachel, will occur to every one as illustrations.

Labor is effort put forth in the way of exchange, and is equally honorable whether common, skilled, or professional. Indeed, at bottom, there is but one class of laborers. Our superficial classification has been used for convenience merely. Political Economy makes no radical distinctions as between its toilers, offers a fair field for all according to their abilities, and has its " well-done " for the patient husbandman, the ingenious mechanic, and the eloquent advocate alike. Labor is blessed ; but let no exchanger trifle with private morals, with the public health, or with the revenues of his country. Even Science, while claiming all its own field, may deprecate infringements in its name upon the neighboring fields.

" God speed the ship ! — But let her bear
　　No merchandise of sin,
　　No groaning cargo of despair
　　Her roomy hold within.
　　No Lethean drug for Eastern lands,
　　Nor poison-draught for ours;
　　But honest fruits of toiling hands
　　And Nature's sun and showers."

This is the place to explain briefly what political economists mean by the Division of Labor. The phrase, which is the title of the first and most famous chapter in Adam Smith's Wealth of Nations, was not very aptly chosen, though it has become a settled phrase in our science, and its meaning is *the dividing up of a complex process or employment into particular parts in such a way that each person employed may devote himself wholly to*

one section of the process. The proposition is, that
by this division, the labor of each person becomes
more efficient and the production as a whole more
profitable. This must be so, because different
persons have varying aptitudes according to natural gifts and previous training. It is one of the
grand things about exchange in general, that it
gives room for every kind of talent, for every
degree of strength, for every variety of accom-
plishment the result of training, for every sort of
service which all sorts of men are able to render.
Nature speaks through all this variety of gifts and
opportunities, in as loud a voice as she can utter,
in favor of the freest possible exchanges among
men everywhere, since thus only can these remarkable diversities be fully utilized to their pos-
sessors and to the world.

The doctrine of the division of labor is only
a particular application of this general truth.
Within any single branch of production, there are
usually parts and possible divisions of the process.
If, now, different persons are put to these different parts of the work according to their strength,
ingenuity, acquired skill, and power to organize
and command, it is plain, that the work will be
far more cheaply, easily, and rapidly done, than if
the operatives had to pass from one part to another, and all try to learn all the parts. Under division of labor, the easier parts may be performed
by women and children, whose labor is less expensive; the ruder parts by ruder and cheaper

hands; and only the more difficult and delicate parts by the more skilful and expensive workmen. Adam Smith illustrates the division of labor by the manufacture of pins, as that was carried on in his day. One man draws out the wire, another straightens it, a third cuts it, a fourth sharpens the points, a fifth grinds it at the top for receiving the head; the making the heads consists of two or three distinct operations, each confided to a single person; the remaining processes are similarly divided up, and the result is, that in a single establishment, employing only ten persons, 48,000 pins are made in a day, while if each man went through all the processes himself, he could hardly make 20 pins a day, or 200 for the whole establishment. Of English watch-making by hand, there are said to be 102 distinct branches, to each of which a boy may be put apprentice, and when his time is out be unable to work at any other branch without further instruction, the watch-finisher being the only one able to work in other departments than his own. If my readers will take the opportunity to visit any factory working cotton, wool, wood, or metals, and observe for themselves the acquired skill, the rapidity of movement, the economy in tools, and the cheapness from classification, under the division of labor, they will be more impressed than any words of mine can impress them by its economical advantages.

A summary of these advantages may be put as follows;—

1. The improved dexterity, corporeal and intel ectual, acquired by the repetition of one simple operation, instead of many operations consecutively.

2. The saving of time lost in passing from one kind of work to another, and in the change of position and tools.

3. The invention of improved implements and processes, because a simple task is just what machinery can be made to perform, and just what an operative with his mind on it is likely to devise machinery for.

4. The saving of the waste of materials, partly as the result of the improved dexterity, and partly as the result of the shorter time required to finish up the product.

5. The more economical distribution of labor by classing the operatives according to their strength, tastes, skill, and costliness.

6. The saving in tools, which, being now in constant use and thus yielding a better return on their cost, can be afforded of a better quality.

7. The division of labor between the wholesale and retail trades brings producers and consumers into safer relations, through a better understanding of the local markets, and a consequently better control of the various streams that feed the wholesale reservoirs.

I think there are some disadvantages resulting from a division of labor : —

1. The work in some departments becomes

monotonous and irksome from its simplicity, while some diversity of employment would afford relief by calling out different muscles, or different faculties of the mind.

2. There is some tendency to dwarf the mental and corporeal powers, through exclusive attention to one part only of a complicated process.

3. A person has less power to adapt himself to a change of circumstances, and becomes more dependent on the continuance of the business in that form, after he has learned and long made the means of a livelihood a single part of a process, than if more versatility had been allowed him.

The degree to which the division of labor can be carried, depends (1) upon the extent of the market, and (2) upon the nature of the employment. For example, if the market will not take 48,000 pins a day, the division of labor cannot be carried so far, some of the ten persons must be discharged, or else they will remain idle a part of the time, some of the separate parts will be combined, and each pin will cost more than before from the limitation of the market. The other expedient sometimes adopted under a dull market, of working but half or three-quarters time and endeavoring to keep up full division of labor during the shortened hours, is apt to take on the other form or be combined with it, inasmuch as it is difficult to hold a full complement of hands to a considerable period of short hours. In either case, production becomes less efficient from the limitation of the market. Limitation of the market is itself usually caused either (1) by some miscalculation about the kind of goods the market will take at that time, or (2) by some artificial restrictions on trade shutting up a market otherwise open, or (3) by some use of an inferior money which never fails to bring in as a sequel commercial dulness and disaster. Under freedom, a universal limitation of the market is impossible; since the desires of men, which the efforts of other men can satisfy, are ever active and increasing; and since the efforts of men in production may find a scope and a market, until these desires of all men are all met, — which can never possibly happen. Production, accordingly, is most profitable when the market is broad enough to allow a full division of labor, and full employment during all the usual or legal hours of work; and, the market being presupposed, is more likely to be profitable in large establishments than in small, because, (1) the division of labor can be carried to a fuller extent; (2) more, and more perfect, machinery can be afforded; (3) relatively less superintendence is required; and (4) the scraps and ends of a large business may justify one or more subordinate branches in connection with the main business. On the other hand, there is a counter-working principle in favor of small establishments, that these are usually owned and managed by individuals instead of a company, and that the " zeal of limited owner ship " in its economy and painstaking fidelity is sometimes more than a match for the otherwise superior advantages of great corporations, which have to be served by hired agents exclusively. The nature of the employment also limits the degree to which the division of labor can be applied. Agriculture, for example, because its processes cannot be made simultaneous, can never allow of this division so much as most other forms of production. The farmer, more than most others, has to wait upon Nature. No effort of his can bring the reaping-time nearer to the sowing-time. He himself must learn to do all the parts of farm-work in succession. We have already learned the reason why machinery can never be applied in agriculture to the same extent as in manufacturing, much as that fact discredits the etymology of the word *manufacture;* and we have also learned that the law of diminishing returns applies to all agriculture everywhere. These three facts, taken together, furnish the ground for the important truth, that agricultural products tend constantly to rise in value as compared with other commodities.

The third and last requisite of production is CAPITAL. This word, which is derived from the Latin word *Caput, a head or source,* carries along with it always the meaning of its root. However otherwise defined, the word always implies that that denoted by it is *a source of further production.* The common word *cattle,* and the

law term *chattels*, are both derived from the same
root, though they do not hold so distinctly as
capital does the root-signification. I give, with
much confidence that it will be found to cover all
the cases, the following definition: — *Capital is
any valuable thing, outside of man himself, from
whose use springs a pecuniary increase or profit.*
Capital itself is always a *product*, and its nature
as capital is conferred on it by the determination
of its owner to use it for the sake of an *increase*
to come by means of it. Many products are
devoted to the gratification of present desires,
without any reference to the rendering of future
services by means of their help. Such products
are not capital. They are valuable, but capital
they are not. Capital is a smaller class under the
great class Values. Capital, too, must never be
confounded with personal powers, although the
boundary between the two is hopelessly confused
by the definitions of Mr. Carey and Mr. Macleod.
Personal powers are only brought into the world
of value through *Labor*, and the reward of labor
however skilful is *Wages*, and wages are a *return*
for the exercise of personal powers through labor,
and not an *increase* secured by means of them. The
primary notion of *capital* is lacking in any proper
view of personal powers, or their exercise for pay;
and hence, I do not hesitate to say, that capital is
always either a commodity or a claim, since these
alone can be reserved as a *source* of further production. Personal powers cannot be sold, because

they cannot be *parted with ;* their exercise through labor may be sold, and this is wages; but each renewed exercise of them through labor must be paid for independently, that is, fresh wages may be received, the labor is *worth* so much; but in all this, we do not get beyond the idea of a *return,* while it is essential to capital that it have the power of *increase.*

When it is said that a young man's integrity, or his acquired skill, is his *capital,* the word is used in a metaphorical, not in a scientific sense. The meaning is, that these qualities are *like* capital in some respects. Capital can always be parted with, and become fruitful in the hands of another, unless the owner prefer to retain it himself for further use in production. As an example of all this, take a steam-engine in a lumber-mill; the owner can sell it any day, if he choose, for $1,000; if he sell it, that $1,000 is a simple *return,* which indeed he may transform into *capital* by loaning it out at interest, or by buying another steam-engine with it for his own use; but if he choose to retain the first engine, it is because he expects something *additional* to the $1,000 from the use of it; he expects, perhaps, to gain $100 net for the use of it for a year, and then to be able to sell it for $1,000, or, if he wear it out by use, to get in consequence of its use not only his $1,000 back, but a yearly profit additional. This illustrates the nature of capital, and affords a correct definition of the term *profit.* *Profit is the increase from the use of capital.*

As capital is a *product* to start with, it cannot
be said to be, as labor is, an absolutely essential
requisite to *production*, but production can go on
but a very little way without capital in some form,
as we shall see shortly, and so it is proper to affirm
that the three requisites of production are natural
agents, labor, *and* capital. It is the intention of
the owner that transforms a simple product into
capital. As a product, he can sell it at will, use
the return for the gratification of the wants of
his family, or in gifts of benevolence; but if he
chooses instead to employ it as a help in further
production, if he *abstains* from the present enjoyment of it, or its proceeds, if he *saves* it for the
sake of a future increase of its value, he transforms it at once into capital. You cannot tell by
the looks of a thing whether it is capital or not:
that depends upon the use to which it is to be put.
The origin of all capital, accordingly, is in *abstinence;* and the reward of this abstinence is profit.
The amount of capital in any community depends
upon the foresight and frugality of the people, —
depends upon their willingness to forego the
present enjoyment of their values for the sake of
greater values to be had in the time to come. It
is a good thing for every man to lay by something,
if possible, in the form of capital, either to use
himself in his business, or to loan out to others on
interest; not only a good thing for him personally,
and for his family, but for the community as well,
since the economical progress of any community,

and especially the rate of wages paid to laborers within it, depend very much on the accumulations of capital there. The strength of the motives to abstinence will be the strongest where liberty of action, equality of privileges, and security of property are the greatest.

It will be profitable for us to go over the principal forms which capital assumes as an aid to further production. First, Implements. We have seen that there are obstacles in the way of the gratification of human desires in all directions, and that these obstacles are only overcome by human effort. When a man devotes himself to one class of these obstacles, with a view to surmount them, he will quickly discover that, if he had certain tools, his work would be easier. Man is not like the beaver, which gnaws down the tree with its teeth from generation to generation, but when he came to have occasion to fell trees, something of the nature of an axe suggested itself to his mind. Once thought of, he would try to invent, or induce others to invent, an axe. Whether of flint, or shell, or metal, so soon as any thing was devised that made easier the labor of felling a tree, capital made a beginning along that line of obstacles. The first axe was a product of labor and abstinence. The labor bestowed in making it might have been bestowed on objects of present gratification, but it was bestowed rather on something whose only use was to make easier future production. It was capital. Perhaps, among the more gilted races, progress in the way of tools was more rapid than we are wont to think it was, for we read that Tubal-cain, even in the times before the flood, " hammered all kinds of implements out of copper and iron." [1] The motive in inventing tools has always been the same, namely, to lessen some irksome effort which is the condition of a given satisfaction. This gives the key-note to the universal use and indefinite expansion of this form of capital. Natural agents, which are free, and whose power is indefinitely great, are made avail- able in production only through implements which are created by labor, and which, being retained as an aid to future labor, are capital.

Witness the plough, the axe, the water-wheel, the steam-engine, the electric-machine, and a thousand more. Every implement, from the tiniest needle to the most ponderous engine, avails itself of natural powers in order to make production easier, increases satisfactions relatively to efforts, is itself a product retained for the sake of an increase to its own value to come by means of it, in short, is capital. Since it takes tools to make tools, and the new tools assist in making others, and since the motive to lessen onerous human effort by the substitution of Nature's forces is universal, there is a tendency, which facts ex- emplify, to a rapid progress in the number and perfection of the implements and machinery of

[1] Gen. iv. 22. The rendering in King James's Bible is very imperfect.

production; and because capital in this form al· ways brings gratuitous natural forces into service, *the value of those things produced by the aid of much capital tends to decline as compared with the value of other things, in whose production capital less conspires.*

Second, Raw materials. These are accumulated with sole reference to their being wrought up by means of labor and machinery into more valuable forms. Production looks to an increase in their value by a change in their form. Wool is raw material to the woollen manufacturer, though it is completed product to the wool-grower; and cotton is raw material to the cotton-spinner, though it is completed product to the planter. Cloth is raw material to the tailor, and lumber to the cabinet-maker, and coal to all who use steam-engines in production. These materials, and many more, are destroyed as such, to re-appear directly or indirectly in higher forms of value.

Third, Buildings used for productive purposes. These are erected to facilitate the processes of production, and their cost is expected to re-appear with a profit in the value of the products to which they minister. They include factories, warehouses, stores, shops, offices, and so on. These do not stand in their own right, so to speak, they stand in the right of the commercial services rendered by means of their aid. They are strictly capital, as a man's dwelling-house is not, because he builds that to live in, not to trade in.

Fourth, Permanent improvements in land. Land originally costs nothing. It is a Natural Agent, the same as wind, or water. But permanent betterments in land are an investment made not simply in view of a return, but also in view of a permanent profit, which in the end, together with the improved land, shall be more in value than the investment. Owing to cheaper and better methods of subduing land constantly introduced, old investments of this kind do not generally yield a present profit, although they may; still, in intention and nature, they are capital.

Fifth, Investments in aid of locomotion, as in railroads, canals, ships, and every thing subsidiary to these. All such things as these are capital, if they are constructed with a view to pecuniary profit. The market-wagon, for instance, is capital, while the pleasure-yacht is not. The amount of capital invested in the United States in railroads alone, if it could be exactly ascertained, as it cannot be, would weary the very figures that expressed it, to say nothing of the minds that strove distinctly to conceive of it. Much of this capital has been at times "sleeping." According to "Poor's Railroad Manual" the bonded debts of the railroads of the United States, Jan. 1, 1875, were $2,000,000,000, of which, 40 per cent had been more or less in defaults after the panic of 1873. This statement takes no account of the original "stock," or other debts, of the roads. Notwithstanding these losses of profit, and, in many cases, of the entire investment, this form of capital is intimately associated with all commercial prosperity. Transportation is an essential part of production, since the value of things depends almost as much upon where they are, as upon what they are. 1880 was a great year for new railroads.

Sixth, Products on hand for sale and bought for resale, and products loaned or retained to loan. These require no explanation or remark.

Seventh, Most funds destined for wages. Some wages, as those of most domestic servants, for example, are paid with no reference to an ultimate profit, but most wages are paid out for the production of something, which is itself to be resold for an increase upon its cost. Such a product, whether made for sale or bought for resale, is always capital, and so, consequently, are the wages paid for producing it, as well as the raw materials entering into it.

Eighth, The national money. We have not yet learned the nature and forms of money, as we shall try to do hereafter with painstaking exactness, but we shall now assume what we shall then prove, that a nation's money is a product acquired just as other products are, that its value comes and goes under the same laws as theirs, and that it is an instrument absolutely necessary to any considerable development of exchanges. Because money is an instrument for making production easier, it is capital; because it is "a valuable thing, outside of man himself, from whose use springs a pecuniary increase," it comes exactly under our definition. Because, as we shall see, money measures values, and becomes a temporary store for them, as well as helps exchange them, it is able, as capital, to help production in a great many ways. It is a kind of *generalized* capital. A steam-engine can only work in one place, and a power-loom can only do one thing, and all other forms of capital are restricted in the possible help they can render to production; but money can make itself felt, anywhere, can work in all sorts of harness, can buy materials, pay wages, transport products, hold in itself values and gains till they are wanted, migrate anywhere, become all things to all men. The nation retains its money for all these profitable uses. To the nation at large, therefore, all its money is capital. In the hands of individuals, however, some money may be temporarily non-capital, because it may be spent for gratification merely. In the hands of the next man, it may become capital again. As a whole, in its relations to the nation and the world, money is the most active, the most versatile, the most profitable, and the most enduring, of all forms of capital; and no nation, consequently, can afford even for a day to have its money in respect of material, weight, or fineness, inferior to the best possible. The reasons that weigh in favor of the best possible machinery of all kinds, weigh with tenfold weight in favor of the best possible form of the most important implement in production — money.

We will now look at the distinction commonly made between Fixed and Circulating capital, and draw from it two or three points of considerable consequence. That part of the whole capital, *the returns for which are derived at once and once for all, is circulating capital;* while the rest and by much the larger part, *the returns for which come little by little from the use rather than sale of the product, is fixed capital.* Professor Bascom [1] gives a good illustration of the difference: "Tools in the hands of him who uses them are Fixed, in the hands of him who manufactures them, Circulating, Capital." Take another illustration: If we should go into a shoe-shop, among many other things we should see leather, thread, and pegs; we should also see lasts, hammers, and needles: the first three are only capable of one use in that form, and the returns for them accordingly as raw materials must wholly come from the sale of *those* shoes into which these materials have entered; while the second three are capable of repeated use, and the returns for them need only come in driblets from the sale of *all* the shoes in succession to whose make-up they have in turn contributed. If the reader will now turn back two or three pages, he will find a chance to apply this distinction to all of the eight forms of capital enumerated, and may thus familiarize himself with the difference between Fixed and Circulating capital.

As industry proceeds, and the aggregate of capi-

[1] Bascom's Political Economy, p. 71.

tal enlarges, there is a tendency to an increase of fixed capital relatively to circulating; and the older and more industrially developed countries show this disproportion strikingly in comparison with new countries, in which for a time the value of the circulating capital surpasses that of the fixed. Gradually, however, the terms are reversed, and Mr. Carey estimated that at the middle of the nineteenth century circulating stood to fixed in France as 1 to 8, and in the United States as 3 to 5. In advanced countries this growing disproportion between the two would become greater than it actually does become, were it not that almost all forms of fixed capital are subject to a rapid loss of value, due partly to wear and tear, and partly to the natural progress of improvements by which what is old soon becomes antiquated. In nothing, perhaps, is actual cost of production so useless a guide to present value as in machinery and other forms of fixed capital. Old machinery always sells low, and so usually do old factories, warehouses, and other buildings used for productive purposes.

Two points of practical caution grow out of all this: of which the first is, that industrial investors and operators should always inquire beforehand whether the sale of their *circulating* capital be likely to be able *to pay the interest on the fixed capital* at a given price or estimate, as well as all the expenses of current production, and a fair profit in addition. The second point is, that forms of *fixed* capital are sometimes pushed forward too rapidly for the general interests of production. For instance, the manufacturer must not put too much of his current income into new mills and machinery, for fear the residue will not be sufficient to buy raw materials with, and pay wages and taxes with. M:ltitudes of promising enterprises have foundered on this very rock. The circulating capital is the circulating blood of business bodies; and there must not be too many *bodies* as compared with the *blood* that gives them life and keeps them warm. Railroads, for example, are often built too fast and too far as compared with the business that alone can sustain them : and stockholders and even bondholders find that too much of their circulating capital has passed into presently unavailable forms. Fixed capital is good, and its healthful increase essential to the ongoing of exchanges ; but the maxim " Make haste slowly " is peculiarly applicable to it in comparison with the growth of circulating capital which ought to precede and justify it.

In passing we put in a plea for Peace by calling attention to the fact that the vast expenses of war are mainly a destruction of *capital.* War cannot be carried on for any length of time or to any great extent except by means of property existing in the form of capital. Savings previously loaned out, or otherwise used productively, are the sources whence war-supplies are drawn ; the capital as such is absolutely *destroyed* in the war ; the war-

debt remaining is only a memorial of this destruction, and an obligation resting upon somebody to
create new capital with which to replace the old.

Next we notice the wonderful power of capital in *reproduction.* Everybody knows how
soon even the ordinary interest of money, if
regularly compounded with the principal, will
double that principal. Capital breeds capital.
The rate of interest is usually reckoned by the
year, but the rate of profit may be reckoned by
the day, the week, the month, or by shorter irreg-
ular intervals. Mr. Samuel Hooper, a Massachusetts merchant, once shipped goods to China costing in Boston $8,000 : he sold these goods in the
port of destination for $50,000, and invested this
sum in goods there for shipment to the United
States; and this return cargo was sold in Boston
for $100,000. What was his rate of profit? Dis-
carding the other expenses of the voyages, and
supposing them to have occupied a year's time,
his rate of profit was 1250 per cent *per annum,*
that is, the ratio of his investment to his return
was 1 to 12.50.

Mr. Macleod mentions some interesting facts as
exhibited in the retail provision trade of Paris:
many years ago, the money lenders charged the
petty dealers two sous a week for the loan of three
francs : that is interest at the rate of 173 per cent
per annum : but if the dealer sold his three francs'
worth of victuals for three francs and a half every
day, as is likely, his profit, omitting Sundays,

would be at the rate of 5216 per cent *per annum :*
only a few years ago, a member of the Legislative
Assembly said in a speech, that a five-franc-piece
borrowed in the morning would buy provisions
that might be sold in the course of the day for
eight francs; that 25 centimes were paid in the
evening without complaint as the interest on the
money; and that is at the rate of 1800 per cent
per annum, while the rate of profit is 21,600 per
cent *per annum*, or twelve times the rate of interest.. All these instances are exceptional, but they
illustrate the better the nature of capital *to grow.*
Even at a very small ratio of profit to principal
on each transaction, a money capital turned rapidly over accumulates with a startling, almost
incredible rapidity. Hence the excellent maxim,
Quick sales and small profits.

Equally wonderful is the power of capital in
the form of machinery to hasten, facilitate, and
accumulate production. Even now, grain may be
loaded every day in the year at any one of the
interior railroad stations in the great North-west
of the Union, and be offered for sale in New York
within fifteen days, or, if the foreign market be
preferred, be offered in Liverpool in fifteen days
more. The saving of small sums for directly productive uses, or for loaning out to such uses, by
many persons at the same time, is the secret of
the increase of the national riches; and savings-
banks under secure conditions cannot be too
highly commended, which gather up the driblets

of capital, pay interest on them to the owners, and then loan out to productive operators on good security in considerable sums these savings of the people.

As countries become older and more prosperous, and capital in all its forms accumulates, there is a strong tendency in the rate of profit to decline. This is proved by experience, and might perhaps be inferred from the law of Supply and Demand. The rate of interest, which, though always less than the current rate of profit, is a correct gauge of that rate, has pretty steadily fallen for centuries in England and Holland, and has fallen already in the older parts of the United States as compared with the newer. The British government paid the Bank of England 8 per cent interest on a public loan less than two centuries ago : it now pays the same institution but 3 per cent. Some important consequences follow from this decline. One is, *that laborers as a class are more benefited by all increase of capital than are capitalists as a class.* As the rate of profit goes down as a result of the increase of capital, a smaller share of the proceeds of every hundred of capital invested goes to the capitalist, and a larger relative share to the laborer, since the two between them share the whole proceeds, taxes excepted. There is still a motive *to save*, aggregate profits are larger than before though the *rate* is less, capitalists as a class are better off than before ; but laborers as a class are relatively still better off than before, for if less goes to the capitalist and more to the laborer on every hundred and there are more hundreds than ever, of course relatively more goes to the laborers from the increase of capital than to the capitalists themselves! This is a lever, my readers will thankfully observe, that lifts on the masses of men! Another important consequence is, *that the value of things produced by the help of much capital will decline with the decline of the rate of profit relatively to things produced by the help of less capital and more labor.* That is to say, the creation of new capital, and the fall in the rate of profit, will make cheaper, relatively to a money standard, to agricultural products, to all other products in which capital less conspires, and especially to labor in which capital does not conspire at all, all those products produced by the help of more capital. Let it not escape the penetration of anybody, that the great underlying forces of production are no respecters of persons, but, like their Author, work unseen for the elevation of *all men.*

It will not take us long now to determine the elements of the COST OF PRODUCTION. This phrase is not relevant as applied to personal ser-vices merely, or to claims, but only to commodities produced by labor hired or estimated as hired and by conspiring capital. For example, a managing editor would not ask an editorial writer about the cost of production of his article, nor the buyer of a railroad bond inquire after the cost of production

of that bond, — the phrase would have no meaning
as applied to these, — but it would be very relevant as applied to a case of boots offered at wholesale, indeed, in most cases, it would be the element
determining the value. Now, natural agents are
free, and only labor and capital are paid agents in
production. Something, it is true, has to go in
the way of taxes, but these can be disregarded
for the present. The onerous elements in production are two, labor and capital, that is, effort
and abstinence, and both are irksome, and if we
can find out what the elements of these are as
bought, we shall know all the elements of the cost
of production, and this will be in all relevant
cases the exact measure of what we have called
the Effort in contradistinction from the Desire.
Sometimes two things, both of which have a true
cost of production, exchange against each other,
and very often all things exchange against metallic
money, which also has a true cost of production,
and, therefore, in determining the elements of
this, we go a good way into the very heart of
value.

Cost of labor is made up of three elements
always ; — (1) Efficiency of the labor, and (2)
The rate of nominal wages paid, and (3) The cost
to the employer of that in which the wages are
paid. To illustrate ; — If an employer hire two
men at the same wages, and one is twice as efficient
a laborer as the other, the cost of his labor is one-
half less than the cost of the other's labor ; or, if

the employer accustomed to pay one dollar per day is now obliged to pay one dollar and a half per day, the efficiency of the laborers being now considered the same, the cost of labor is increased in the ratio of 2 to 3 ; or, if, nominal wages and efficiency of labor remaining the same, the cost of that, whether money or other product, in which wages are paid, varies, the cost of labor varies of course. If nations unwisely, as the United States did in 1862–1879, use a depreciated paper money, that is, substitute for a true commodity a credit-claim because it is cheaper, then the rate of nominal wages ceases to be any correct indication of the cost of labor, and hence of the cost of production. The above analysis flings to the winds a host of conclusions drawn by superficial writers from differences as between different countries in the rate of wages. Rate of wages is not cost of labor. It is only one element in a cost of labor. There may be a very great difference in the rate of wages as between England and the United States, for example, and no difference at all in the cost of labor, or even the cost of labor may be the least in the country in which the rate of wages is the highest, on account of the superior efficiency of the labor there, or the cheapness of the medium in which wages are paid there. These three elements of the cost of labor must always be borne in mind in all discussions about wages, otherwise the arguments will be fallacious of course, the word " wages " in such discussions sometimes meaning "rate of wages" and sometimes "cost of labor," — two very different senses of the same word; and persons attempting productive enterprises of magnitude, particularly those coming into competition with similar enterprises abroad, cannot safely neglect this analysis, although the superior efficiency of labor in this country probably more than neutralizes the higher rate of wages so far as "cost of labor" is concerned.

Cost of capital is made up of three elements also; — (1) The rate per cent, and (2) The time for which the capital is advanced, and (3) The form of the capital as liable to wear out quickly or otherwise. To illustrate these elements in their order, let us suppose the rate per cent at Amsterdam to be 3, and the rate at New York to be 7, the cost of labor to be equal in the two cities, the time of advance one year, and no liability of the capital to wear out, then a commodity made at Amsterdam with an outlay of $100 can be sold without loss for $103, while a similar commodity made in New York cannot be sold for less than $107, — the rate per cent of capital being an important element in the cost of capital and hence in the cost of production; now, let the same suppositions be continued, except that the time of advance in New York be extended to four years, then the Dutch product will sell as before at $103, but the New York product for not less than $131, — the time of advance making a striking difference in the cost of capital, giving a sort of monopoly in enterprises requiring large capital and long periods before returns are realized to low-interest countries; lastly, suppose two establishments, in each of which is invested a capital of $11,000, in one of which is a machine costing $1000, which will be wholly worn out by one year's use, and in the other a machine costing the same, but lasting ten years, and suppose the rate per cent be 10, and the time one year, then, all other elements being equal, the commodity made in the first establishment must sell for $2100, while the commodity made in the second can sell without loss for $1200, — so important an element is durability in the cost of capital and hence in the cost of production. The durability of metallic money, as the most important form of capital, is one reason why countries which maintain it can undersell so far forth the countries which abandon it.

Cost of production, made up of these six factors, is a vital matter in all interchange of commodities; while it illustrates the necessity of forethought and great intelligence in order to successful commercial activity, that all these factors must be constantly attended to, and efforts be constantly made to lessen through one or more of these factors the cost of production in order to maintain a firm footing in competitive enterprises. The points at which efforts can be made with the most success to lessen the cost of the production of commodities are (1) to make the efficiency of labor greater by helping laborers to be more intel-

:igent, temperate, industrious, and frugal ; and (2) to lessen the time of advance in capital by improved methods of production and transportation, so as to make returns wait as quickly as possible upon investments.

It only remains in this elementary discussion of production, to call attention to a beautiful generalization, which gathers up and holds firmly most of the results to which we have already come, namely, *The value of finished commodities tends steadily to decline towards the value of the raw materials out of which they are formed.* This is owing to a constantly lessened cost of manufacture. The lessened cost of manufacture is owing to an increased use of capital in the form of improved machinery for transformation and transportation. The increased use of capital is owing to the habit ·of saving, and to the arts of invention, by means of which free powers of nature are more and more substituted for aching human muscle. The result is, that a pound of raw cotton, for example, is approximating the price of the cotton cloth that is made out of it, — less and less of the price of a commodity being due to the process of producing it from the raw material. This great tendency, which God has inwrought into the very framework of things, does not, in a large view, harm laborers as such, who have sometimes supposed themselves to be harmed thereby, because (1) labor is always required for the construction and repairs of all labor-saving appliances, and, so far forth, a new market for labor is opened up in place of any loss of market resulting from their introduction, and (2) the now cheaper products find a wider circle of consumers, and now labor is required to produce and distribute them, and (3) the commodities consumed by the laborers themselves are also cheapened by the new methods, and a given rate of wages secures for them a higher grade of comforts.

The following summary gathers up the principal propositions of the present chapter : —

1. *Value is a result, and the processes leading up to it are* PRODUCTION.

2. *Production is getting something ready to* SELL, *and selling it.*

. 3. *Consumption corresponds to Production, and consists in* BUYING *something.*

4. *Labor, Natural Agents, and Capital are the sole* REQUISITES *of Production.*

5. *The principal natural agent is* LAND, *whose value is due to the efforts of men.*

6. *Relatively diminishing* RETURNS *accompany increasing expenditures upon land.*

7. *People increase in number, and food in amount ; but the race will be* WON *by the latter.*

8. *The greatest physical thing in Production is* MOTION ; *and, as free natural agents are more used, production grows constantly easier to men.*

9. *Labor is any human exertion rendered for* PAY : *this pay is called Wages.*

10. *The higher the degree to which the* DIVISION

OF LABOR *is carried, the more profitable does the world's production become.*

11. *Any valuable thing reserved for future use in production is* CAPITAL; *and the increase that comes from that use is called Profit.*

12. *All capital is comprised under eight forms; and these are distributed into* FIXED *and* CIRCU- LATING *capital.*

13. *Capital breeds capital; and* LABORERS *as a class are more benefited by this than capitalists as a class.*

14. *Cost of commodities is made up of six factors; and production both demands and begets* INTELLI- GENCE.

15. *The value of commodities steadily declines towards the value of the* MATERIALS *out of which they are made.*

CHAPTER III.

COMMERCE.

It might seem as if the mutual benefit of exchanges were sufficiently demonstrated in the preceding chapters, which unfold their nature and processes. There are always two parties to every exchange, each of whom *has* something and *wants* something else, neither of whom is under any obligation whatever to part with what he has for what he wants, both of whom are in the very nature of the case the best judges both of what they have and of what they want, and it would certainly seem as if, so long as it is a matter of pure free-will and of personal advantage, and so long as the public morals, health, or revenue, are not infringed thereby, they might be allowed to make their exchange without let or hindrance on the part of anybody. The liberty to exchange does not compel anybody to exchange, does not recommend anybody to exchange, does not even bring any inducement of any kind to lead anybody to exchange; it simply permits those to exchange whose personal advantage in their best judgment would be promoted by an exchange. Common sense pronounces in favor of such liberty. Political Economy pronounces in favor of such liberty. But some governments, and notably the government of the United States at present, inter-fere with this liberty, practically deny the right of their people to exchange their own property for other forms of property in accordance with their own best judgment of their own advantage, and, putting up legal barriers across the path of exchange, announce pains and penalties for those who presume to part with what is their own for the sake of getting thereby what they want more. This action of governments, particularly of our own, makes it needful for us to examine more definitely still into the nature of *Commerce*, to investigate the alleged reasons for restraining it, and to vindicate for all Exchange, both domestic and foreign, its fair and natural *Opportunity*.

The English word Commerce is commonly applied to exchanges between citizens and foreign-ers, but there is nothing in the origin or meaning of the word that should so restrict its significa-tion. It is derived from a Latin word, which means *an exchange of goods*, and it is just as proper to speak of domestic commerce as of for-eign commerce, inasmuch as commerce, no matter who the parties to it are, is essentially one and the same everywhere. It is plain, that the motives to an exchange and the gains of an exchange are precisely the same, whether the parties to it belong to the same nationality or are of different nationalities. The accident of citizenship is a very important matter in ·certain relations, but it is a wholly indifferent matter when one comes to buying and selling. For example, I happen to live in the north-west corner town of Massachusetts: two miles west of my house is the line of New York, and two miles north of my house is the line of Vermont; now, does it make any difference with me in buying butter or maple sugar, whether I buy them of a New York neighbor, of a Vermont neighbor, or of a Massachusetts neighbor? Does the accident of state lines have any thing to do with the benefits of a *trade?*

I can assure my readers, that, as a matter of fact, nobody in this locality pays any attention at all to these lines in the way of business. Vermonters and New Yorkers come hither and go hence in traffic just as freely as Massachusetts men do, and exchange with them is just as profitable on both sides as if all lived in one state. " But all *do* live in one *nation,*" somebody interposes. Very true. But what has that to do with it? Shift the scene from the south end to the north end of Vermont, and there are neighbors on both sides of an imaginary line, who do *not* live in one nation. May not the Canadians and the Vermonters trade freely and advantageously across this imaginary line? The law thunders, No! I was reading in the paper this very day, that a Vermonter bought two quarts of rum across tho line to help him through his haying, and was intercepted on his return by the revenue-officer, who took away his rum, horse, and a brand-new wagon! I do not approve of the Vermonter's taste in buying rum, but I have a very definite opinion, and shall proceed to give the grounds of it, about a system that visits penalties, not in the interests of revenue, for trading across any imaginary line.

The Constitution of the United States goes a good way towards securing the benefits of a free commerce to all the people of this country. It forbids all taxation, by national as well as by state authority, of goods in passing from one state into another; and it secures the right of each citizen of a state to sell his personal services of every legal kind in all the other states of the Union. These two provisions secure a domestic commerce absolutely free; that is to say, no state can tax goods coming into it from another state, nor tax citizens of other states as such on the exercise of their trades within that state; and national taxes, if laid within the country, must be uniform throughout the United States, while the local taxes of the states may make no discriminations either as to persons or to goods found within their jurisdiction; so that, throughout the wide expanse of the country itself, containing great diversities of soil, climate, industries, and experience, there is a free interchange of commodities, services, and claims, possibly subject to a uniform

internal taxation by the nation, state, or munici
pality, which never has for its purpose to prevent
or lessen the exchanges, but only to draw a revenue out of their gains, which revenue is the larger
as the gains are the more numerous. All this is
just as it should be. Nobody complains that the
domestic commerce of the country is too free;
nobody desires that artificial barriers should be set
up, as between Louisiana and Massachusetts, for
example, because of any differences in age, industries, wages, rate of profit, or the like; consequently, the good sense of the people of the
country pronounces emphatically in favor of free
exchanges within the country itself. Can they
consistently do this, and at the same time be
opposed to free international exchanges?

Moreover, the Constitution of the United States
goes further in the direction of freedom. It expressly forbids any tax whatever upon articles
exported from any state. It thus guarantees not
only a free domestic commerce, subject only to
the claim of legitimate taxation, but also throws
the shield of its defence around foreign commerce, *so far as all exports are concerned.* The
people of the United States have had the privilege for a hundred years of carrying out of the
country without a tax any of their surplus products for which they could find a market anywhere
in the world. This little clause of the Constitution has contributed immensely to the commercial
prospr"ity of the country; and the other clauses,

already referred to, securing the right of free in‧
terchange at home, have contributed to this pros‧
perity still more; but all these have been more or
less neutralized by the abuse of another clause of
the Constitution giving Congress the power "to
lay imposts," that is, the power to tax goods
brought *into* the country from other countries.
The goods carried *out* of the country they are
forbidden to tax, but they have unlimited power
to tax at their discretion imported goods.

It is true, that the Constitution prescribes the
purposes for which these taxes must be laid,
namely, "to pay the debts, and provide for the
common defence and general welfare of the
United States;" it is true also, that this language
implies that these taxes are to be laid *in order to
get money* to fulfil these purposes; but it has been
held by all the co-ordinate branches of the govern‧
ment, and the view has unfortunately been car‧
ried out into practice, that this clause authorizes
Congress to lay such taxes on imports as shall
lessen and even prevent their introduction, thus
preventing the getting of money from these taxes,
which would seem to destroy the constitutional
purpose of them. I believe that the Constitution
of the United States, fairly interpreted, allows of no
taxes except such as are laid for the sake of bring‧
ing money into the treasury; but however that
point may be ultimately settled, I am prepared to
show that taxes laid with any other view than to
bring money into the treasury violate the funda‧

mental laws of Political Economy, and are followed necessarily by loss and disaster.

I shall assume now, that all my readers believe that free domestic exchanges are profitable, and should not be interfered with by anybody, and shall proceed to demonstrate that free foreign exchanges are profitable also, and should not be interfered with by anybody. A system that has been much praised in this and other countries under the name of "Protection to native industry," and that is still in full practical operation in this country at least, must be shown to be delusive in its name and nature, to be an obstacle in the way of natural laws, to be iniquitous in its motive, and to be calamitous in its results.

We have seen already, that all exchange proceeds on a diversity of relative advantage. One man must be able to render something easier and better than another, and the second able to render something else easier and better than the first, before they two will exchange services with each other; and when they have thus exchanged services, each has experienced a gain. So universally in the realm of exchange. The diversity that lies at the basis of the trade comes partly from nature and partly from practice. The cotton-planter of Mississippi has an advantage, both natural and acquired, in the raising of cotton, over his fellow-citizen of Maine ; and the cotton-manufacturer of Maine has an advantage, both natural and acquired, in the working up of cot-

ton, over the planter of Mississippi; and, accord
ingly, they exchange cotton for cloth to the
mutual advantage of both. Climate, soil, laborers used to the sun, and practice, conspire to
give his advantage to the planter: a mountain
stream leaping to his wheel with a song, and an
ingenuity and endurance common to him and
his neighbors from a colder clime and a harder
soil and a different training, conspire to give his
advantage to the manufacturer. These and other
irreducible differences exist for a wise reason even
within each single country, and make it certain that
profitable exchanges will prevail therein so long
as the world shall stand; while greater and more
irreducible differences as between different countries indicate unmistakably the will of God that
they shall continue to exchange with reciprocal
benefits so long as the world shall stand. Sometimes the ocean, sometimes a river, sometimes
mountains, and sometimes only an imaginary line,
divide the nations from each other; and these
barriers, wherever they exist, doubtless assist
somewhat in the forming and maintaining of the
differences on which trade depends, while the
barriers themselves make somewhat more difficult
the trade to which they indirectly minister; and
hence, how shallow and self-destructive is the
logic, which infers from the existence of natural
barriers, that some artificial barriers in addition
are needful, since these, if they could be permanently established, as they cannot, would only

serve to prevent the trade to which they might otherwise indirectly minister.

God made the world, and he made it wisely. He knew just what barriers to set up, considering all the ends that he had in view, some of which were doubtless more important than any interests of international trade. The applause of men certainly, not to say the favor of God, has always rested upon those who have been successful in overcoming these natural barriers for the sake of an easier traffic and a more extended intercourse. It would seem to be nothing less than presumptuous, in view of the natural and constant inducements to trade that spring out of the God-given diversities among the nations, and in view of the universal feeling that a Mt. Cenis tunnel or a Suez canal is a great blessing, for certain men to deem themselves wise enough to set up at will artificial barriers to trade, and then to undertake to defend their barriers as an economical blessing to the world! It would seem to be pretty clear beforehand, that such men must be mistaken in their supposed ability to improve on the world and to impose on the world!

These artificial barriers are brought into play by means of an instrument called a *Tariff*. The origin of the word will throw light upon the thing. The southernmost point of the Peninsula of Spain, which juts down into the Straits of Gibraltar, holds a town named Tarifa, so named from a Berber chief who crossed over from Africa to reconnoitre the country previous to its conquest by the Moors. After the Moorish conquest in 711, a castle was built on this spot, which commanded the straits, and vessels passing out of or into the Mediterranean were forcibly stopped, and compelled to pay " duties " on their cargoes at certain fixed rates. From this place and circumstance, the word "tariff" passed into the English and other European languages. The facts just recounted give illustration, however, of something more than the origin of the word; they illustrate the fundamental character of the thing; since a tariff, whether for Revenue, Protection, or what not, always demands something from somebody, and never offers to give any thing to anybody. It is always so much *taken out*. Its sign is minus, and not plus. In the given case, each ship that passed through the Straits was so much the *poorer* for all that was paid at Tarifa. It was not an exchange. It was robbery. It was black-mail. No one will try to defend the Moors for their act of extortion, but many, who try to defend a " protective tariff " so-called, forget its inmost nature, to which it is always true, namely, *that it takes but never gives*. Even a " revenue tariff " so-called, like that of England, from which has been eliminated every purpose but one of fair taxation, is still only a series of *demands*. *Thou shalt pay* is the only thing a tariff says, or can say. Some people have got it into their heads that a tariff is somehow or other a positively productive agent, a spur to the progress of industry, something indispensable to the ongoing of exchanges, while the fact is, that a tariff even in its best estate is only another name for *taxes*. A tariff in general may be thus defined; — *A schedule of taxes levied by a government upon imported goods.*

But, though all taxes are so much abstracted from the pockets of the payers, the purpose for which the taxes are levied makes a great difference practically in the character and effect of the taxes themselves. On a moment's reflection, my readers will perceive, that all taxes of whatever kind must come out of the gains of exchanges, since there is no other way, gifts and stealing aside, for any man to get the money with which to pay his taxes except through exchanges. Those tariff-taxes, therefore, that are not designed to discourage the buying and selling of foreign goods, that do not aim to prevent or lessen exchanges, but only to withdraw a fraction of their gains for the use of government, are far less objectionable every way than those whose design is to lessen or prevent altogether the buying of the foreign goods on which the taxes are laid. Their character is different, their relation to exchanges is different, and their effect is different. The difference between the two is just the difference between a revenue tariff properly so-called and a protective tariff properly *so-called*. *A revenue tariff is a schedule of taxes laid upon imported goods with an eye to just taxation only.* If such taxes are to bring in a good deal into the treasury (and that by the definition is their sole purpose) their rate must be low, so as not to prevent the buying of the goods, for in that case no revenue at all is received, but so as to allow the exchanges to take place as nearly as possible as before, only taking out a little from the gains of each particular exchange, and relying on the large number of exchanges to make up a good deal in the aggregate. The real interest of a revenue tariff is to have large impor-tations, for it has been found by experience, and might have been anticipated on principle, that a low rate of tax brings in more revenue than a high rate of tax, which last always decreases importations on which the tax is levied. The exact mean must of course be found out by trial.

Then, in the second place, it is the interest of a revenue tariff, that the people shall pay no more money in consequence of a tax being levied than just the tax itself; and, therefore, a proper reve-nue tariff will only put taxes on goods such as are wholly imported from abroad, and not also made or grown at home ; for, if tariff-taxes are laid on such imported goods as are similar to goods had in the country, then the effect of the imposts is to raise the price of both the imported and the simi-lar domestic goods, since they come into competi-tion with each other, and the imported goods of course are raised in price by the tax, so that, the people in this case are obliged to pay more in con-sequence of the tax than the tax realizes to the government, which is against the interest of the revenue in general, and a revenue tariff in particular. A few years ago, when the tariff-tax on salt was higher than it is at present, one-half of the salt used in this country was imported and one half domestic: the tariff-tax raised the price alike‑ of all that was consumed, and the people paid twice as much on account of the tax, as the gov‑ ernment got from the tax, which is a very bad form of taxation as such, and which accordingly a revenue tariff will avoid, and lay its taxes on arti- cles which are wholly imported from abroad so far as possible, and if thought impossible in certain cases, it is still the interest of a revenue tariff as such, that an excise (a home tax) be laid to the same amount on the corresponding domestic goods, so that the principle be maintained throughout that the government shall get all that the people are made to pay on account of any tax.

Also, in the third place, it is the interest of a purely revenue tariff that its taxes be laid on as few articles as will realize the needful revenue, and all other imported articles be exempted. People do not like to pay taxes; and, besides, the taxes paid lessen by just so much the motives to continue the exchanges, which exchanges in turn are the only reservoir whence any taxes can be drawn. Accordingly, the commercial prosperity of any people depends very much upon the kind and amount of their taxation, and remissions of taxes have been found to work like magic upon

the ability of the people to pay taxes, by relieving
them at several points and thus enabling them to
pay more and easier at the one point. The buoy-
ancy of trade is greatly promoted by relief from
vexatious interference and onerous payment at
many points, so that it becomes able and willing to
bear comparatively large drafts at the one point
selected by government. Whenever there are a
few articles of universal consumption, like tea and
coffee, which are wholly or mostly imported from
abroad, and a few other articles, like wine and
spirits, on the domestic production of which an
excise corresponding to the tariff-tax on the imported part can be collected, a large revenue can
be realized to the government through a tariff,
whose rates shall be comparatively low, whose
items shall be comparatively few, and whose burdens shall not be felt beyond the taxes actually
paid to government. No very great objections lie
against such a tariff as this, although we shall see
in our chapter on Taxation that there is a more
excellent way to get revenue even than this. It
illustrates the feeling among intelligent men that
all tariffs are destined to pass away, that the
Emperor of Brazil, when shown a few years ago
the new custom-house at St. Louis, and when told
that it would last 400 years, exclaimed, " What !
You do not mean to say that there will be any
custom-houses 400 years from now ! "

What is deceptively called a " protective " tariff
is directly the opposite of a revenue tariff in its

three fundamental principles as just sketched. No word could be worse chosen, if accuracy of description were desired, than the word "Protection" to describe what passes under that name. Some persons may indeed be temporarily "protected" against foreign competition in their business by high tariff-taxes, but they are so protected at the immediate expense of all their fellow-citizens, and ultimately at their own expense. The system is short-sighted, greedy, and hence self-destructive. *A protective tariff is a schedule of taxes laid on imported goods with a view to raise the price of certain home commodities, by cutting off foreign competition in them.* All the arguments of protectionists in favor of their system, and all their objections to free trade, imply when they do not affirm, that the purpose of "protection" is a rise of price of the "protected" commodities. We shall judge the protectionists by what they *say*, and also more especially by what they *do*, — when allowed to have their own way. We have had in this country since 1861 an avowedly protective tariff, to which we shall go for illustrations of what protection proposes and accomplishes.

In the first place, in accordance with its ground-idea, a protective tariff levies very high taxes, so as to exclude the taxed commodity altogether, or to raise its price by means of the tax to the point to which it wishes to bring up the price of the protected home commodity. As a rule, there is a market price for similar commodities of the same grade, and foreign and domestic commodities of one grade tend toward one price; and if the foreign commodity has been taxed on coming in, the tax of course must be added to its price, and the price of the domestic commodity corresponding tends to rise to the same point. It will not *always* rise to that point, because domestic competition may keep it down somewhat, and the foreigner may be willing temporarily to sacrifice a part of his profits for the sake of keeping the market; but the tendency, the theory, the promise, and the practical working, of a protective tariff is just to do that. High duties, therefore, have always been the cue of Protection. Between 1875 and 1880, the American people paid on woollen cloths imported an average of 59 per cent *ad valorem*, on other woollen fabrics 72 per cent, on carpets 55 per cent, and on bunting 95 per cent. On fine wools imported, the average tariff-tax was not less than 100 per cent; and foreign-built ships are absolutely prohibited from carrying the American colors, or having an American registry. All this is in the interest of protection. From 1816 to 1880, there was no competition whatever with American ship-building, because protection has chosen to exclude foreign ships altogether; and it is an interesting commentary on the principle of restriction, that ocean ship-building has practically ceased in the United States under the perfection of protection. We can no longer build ships on account of protection, and are forbidden by protection to buy them, and the American flag has mostly disappeared from the ocean.

I refer to these instances here in order to show the fondness of protection for high duties, and even for regulations in the nature of prohibition. The duties on coarse woollen blankets, in tho decade 1870–1880, were so high as practically to preclude their importation. This is consistent with the idea of protection, but it is not consist· ent with the idea of revenue, nor is it consistent with any liberal ideas on the subject of exchanges in general. Let us notice two or three effects of these high duties: — (1). The effect on revenue to lessen it. The best illustration of this principle was exhibited in the United States internal revenue tax on distilled spirits:

1868. Direct tax of $2 per gallon on distilled
    spirits; aggregate revenues . . $18,665,000
1870. Direct tax of 50 cents per gallon; ag-
    gregate revenues $55,606,000
1874. Direct tax of 70 cents per gallon; ag-
    gregate revenues $49,444,000

If the purpose be to get revenue from foreign goods, the goods must be allowed to come in; but if the purpose be to get protection so-called, it is better that the goods be kept out by the tax. Protection has been almost perfect in coarse woollen blankets, and the revenue has been virtually nothing. Protection has been perfect in ships for 65 years, and not a penny of revenue from them of course. Complete protection annihilates revenue; protection nearly complete almost annihilates revenue; is it not fair to conclude, that high duties are hostile to revenue? It is not denied that high duties may bring in considerable revenue, and at the same time afford considerable protection; but it *is* denied, that they can do this without making the people pay a great deal more than the treasury gets, which is surely not a good scheme for revenue. Low rates of duty are best for revenue, and high rates are best for protection, and, therefore, revenue and protection are incompatible with each other, and all attempts to combine them will be at the expense of one or the other.

(2). The effect on exchanges to discourage them. Tariff-taxes, like all others, come out of the gains of exchanges, and if these taxes be heavy, the motives to trade are lessened on both sides; the foreigner realizes less on what he sends over, and the native realizes less on what he sends back, in consequence of these protective taxes; if the tax shuts out, as it sometimes does, the foreign product, the foreigner loses that market entirely, and, what is usually lost sight of, the native loses, so far forth, his own market entirely; for, we cannot be too often reminded that trade is a mutual thing, if we will not buy we cannot sell of course, if a tariff keeps out foreign goods it thereby keeps in domestic goods that want to go out for a market, and the wound inflicted by protective taxes is thus a double wound. In order to

ɩnable certain protected interests to get an artificial price for their products, certain foreigners
lose their best market; and what is more, certain
citizens lose *their* best market against these foreign
goods shut out ; and what is more still, all native
consumers of that class of goods have to pay much
more than the goods are worth in a free market,
a part of the extra price indeed going to the government in the form of taxes, but generally a
larger part going to favored individuals in the
form of unearned bounties. Is not one industrious citizen as deserving as another? And what
right has government to take away his market
from one citizen, who only asks to be let alone to
make profitable exchanges, in order to make an
artificial market for another citizen, who clamors ˙
for government help to exalt himself and thereby
depress his fellow-citizens? An excellent authority [1] has calculated that on the average of
dutiable goods the price of the corresponding domestic goods is enhanced to the extent of at least
two-thirds of the duty. Thus, the foreigner is
harmed by protective taxes, (which is poor policy
in the end,) the citizen ready to exchange with
him is harmed also, (which is worse policy,) and
there has been besides a disturbance of prices by
which some citizens *get* more than they should
and other citizens are compelled to *pay* more
than they should, (which is the worst possible
policy.) It is not strange that Exchange depre-

[1] Hon. Robert J. Walker, ɩn 1847.

cates such an unjust, unnatural, and disturbing scheme.

(3). The effect on morals to loosen them. When citizens see that their government is a respecter of persons, that rich. and otherwise influential men can get laws passed for their individual behoof, and that the cry of thousands weighs little against the unjust claim of one, popular regard for government declines of course, respect for laws declines of course, the smuggler never yet failed to accompany high protective duties and never will, the selfish informer never fails to follow the smuggler, the legislator loses sight of the general good in the desire to please a few powerful constituents, bribes direct or indirect have had much to do with our protective tariffs, the public conscience is demoralized by the spectacle of interest and influence ruling in high places, large fortunes acquired through favoritism enthroned in law provoke envy and ill-will, the poor are angered at and ready to despoil the rich, the rich in turn contemn the unorganized though plundered poor, and society gets secretly disorganized and by the ears in consequence of a departure from the path of impartial justice. With one or two partial exceptions, a protective tariff has never been enacted in this country but in the teeth of an unyielding and bitter opposition; the instincts of the masses have been naturally enough against all such legislation; it was a piece of such legislation in 1828, that roused the ire of South Carolina, and led, through the action of Mr. Calhoun and others, to the doctrine of nullification, and became a mainspring to the series of misunderstandings and jealousies, that culminated in the late civil war; in short, protective tariffs bred mischiefs and war in Europe for 150 years, and have given birth in this country to more of demoralization and disintegration than any other one thing except slavery. If, then, high duties lessen revenue, wound exchanges, and loosen morals, is it not time for an intelligent people to abandon them?

Again, in the second place, in accordance with the aim of the system, protection chooses for the incidence of its taxes those foreign goods which would otherwise come most into competition with its favored domestic goods, and thus contradicts the most important principle of a revenue tariff. Tea and coffee, for example, are wholly imported from abroad, and tariff-taxes upon them, consequently, will raise the price of nothing else. They are among the best things to tax, because they are in universal consumption, and because the government will get all the people are made to pay under the tax. But protectionists as such do not like such taxes. They do not serve their ends. In 1872, under a deceptive cry of a " Free breakfast table," the tea and coffee taxes, easily realizing many millions of dollars to the treasury, were repealed under the lead of a protectionist congressman, for the sake of afterwards holding on to the protective taxes by the plea that any further reduction of revenue would be dangerous. The eye of the protectionist as such is never on his country's treasury, but always on the extra price of some domestic articles. Consumers of these articles bear the whole burdens of the extra price caused by the tariff-tax to both the imported and the home-made.

It is impossible to tell exactly how much of their forced contributions goes to the treasury, and how much to the protected individuals. Hon. H. C. Burchard of Illinois, à congressman unusually well informed and candid, not long ago calculated,[1] that of the contribution of each family in the United States on the average, under the iron, steel, cotton, and woollen duties as they were at that time, $5 went to the treasury, and $9 to manufacturers' dividends. I see no reason to question the substantial exactness of this. I know that in many single articles, as in salt formerly, and in blankets and bunting, the proportion was far worse than this. If we pass from particulars to generals, the figures become startling, and the wrong appears frightful. Take the two decades between 1860 and 1880, and putting the annual amounts of the domestic protected manufactures below the average as given by the three censuses, and reckoning also the rates of duty assessed on the corresponding foreign goods below the *actual* tariff-rates from year to year, and conceding that the domestic goods were

[1] Speech of May 25, 1876.

raised in price *only half so much* as the average
duty paid on the corresponding foreign goods for
the same time, and we have then these results in
figures, which, were they not demonstrably below
the truth, would be beyond belief; namely, calling the annual domestic product of protected
goods but $3,000,000,000, and the average duty
by which they were protected but 40 per cent,
and their own rise of price in consequence of the
duty but 20 per cent, then the American people
paid needlessly under the tariff $600,000,000 every
year, or $12,000,000,000 in the 20 years, not one
penny of which money went into the Treasury of
the United States. Indeed, the best protective
duty is that which pays least into the treasury,
and most into the pockets of individuals; and is
it any wonder that the so-called " protectionist
interest " was so strong in the two decades referred to, — so strong as against the masses of the
people and as against the thinking men of the
people, since it had the power, under the forms
of law, to distribute "where it would do the
most good " for its own ends, this enormous sum
of $12,000,000,000?

The effect of this distribution was seen in the
apparent complacency of Congress in this mon-
strously unjust system, and in the acquiescence
in it, if not advocacy of it, on the part of the vast
majority of the newspapers of the country. But,
in the early spring of 1880, white printing-paper
advanced 50 per cent in price; and then there

arose a universal outcry of the newspapers for the removal of the 20 per cent duty on paper, and also of the duties on paper-pulp, chemicals that enter into the manufacture of paper, type, and even the type-metals. It is one thing to have to see your neighbors pay high prices under protective duties, and quite another thing to have to pay them yourself, as this instance shows; and Congress, too, was startled for once out of its venal satisfaction in a false system, because these 7,000 newspapers stood very near to the sources of political life, while the cry of 70,000 ordinary and unorganized citizens would not have produced a ripple in that body. Newspapers can voice their own grievances, and compel attention to them, while the minds of the masses of the people are confused as between "revenue" and "protection," and, besides, they have no organs by which to make themselves felt in the National Legislature.

One of the worst things about protective duties is, that the forced contribution under them is usually drawn from the pockets of those who are least able to pay it, and passes over into the pockets of those who are best able to do without it, and who cannot show the least claim to it. The *average* duty on woollen cloths 1861–1881 was almost precisely the same as the duty on silks, namely 60 per cent; and, the coarser and cheaper the cloth, the heavier was the rate of duty, because there was a duty *per pound* combined with a duty *ad valorem*, and hence, the coarser the cloth the higher the duty paid, and the higher could the price be carried up of the coarse domestic cloth. The fundamental injustice of a protective tariff is made much greater by its throwing its *special* burdens just where they ought not to borne, namely, on the poorer classes. The duty on cheap bunting has been more than 35 per cent more than on silk; and the poorer patriot, who wanted to hoist the colors of his country on the Fourth of July, had to pay over 95 per cent on his material if imported, while his rich neighbor, who could afford a silk flag, paid but 60 per cent on *his* material.

Almost precisely one-half of the people of the United States get their living from agriculture, but, from the nature of the case, these cannot be benefited by protective duties, while the burdens of a protective tariff fall heavily on them, both directly and indirectly; directly, because many of the things they buy are thereby raised in price, and indirectly also, because the things they sell are thereby depressed in price. This last will be very evident, when we reflect, that the foreign market for American products is curtailed in just the proportion in which the American market for foreign products is curtailed by a restrictive tariff. If foreign products are kept out of this country by obstructive legislation, then we may be perfectly sure that our own products are for that reason kept out from other countries, or reduced in value there. Two nations are nothing more than two individuals expanded and multiplied, and the same principles which apply to individuals in trade apply to nations also; so that, if a nation refuses to take what would be naturally brought, it virtually compels, so far forth, other nations to refuse what would be naturally carried. So, since our products exported are largely agricultural products, cotton, grain, pork, bacon, lard, and so on, and the demand for these, and, therefore, the value of them, are assuredly lessened by our refusal to take products freely in pay for them, the losses of a protective tariff fall especially upon the farmers. By the census of 1870, only 3 per cent of all the persons engaged in industrial pursuits in this country were employed in the cotton, iron, steel, woollen, and worsted industries, which are all highly protected industries. It is the many who pay, it is the few who profit, under protective tariff-taxes.

It is pleasant to see, in accordance with the principle of the last paragraph, that lessening the tariff-taxes always increases the volume of exports *per capita*. For example, in 1849 British exports were but $10.93 *per capita*, an increase of but 33 per cent over 1839; while in 1859, the end of the first decade of comparative freedom of imports, the exports had risen to $22.11 *per capita*, an increase of 105 per cent in the ten years. In 1869, remissions of import-duties being of course fewer for that decade, exports had risen to $29.79 *per capita*, that is, an increase from 1859 of 35 per cent. Even in 1878, a year of bad crops in Europe, and of extraordinary crops in the United States, the exports of the latter were only $12 *per capita*. If a nation will not *buy* freely, it can by no possibility *sell* freely.[1]

Just so, if we compare the imports of those articles that are especially a gauge of the degree of the comforts of the common people, we find, for example, that British imports of *sugar* in 1852, just after the principal remissions of tariff-taxes, were only 28.15 pounds *per capita ;* while in 1877, twenty-five years after, they had mounted to 54.06 pounds *per capita*. Only two pounds of *tea* apiece for the British population in 1852, while in 1877 there were 4.52 pounds apiece. Just so also of the increase of the carrying trade under freedom: in 1849, the British merchant-marine consisted of 3,096,342 tons, but in 1878 it had reached 6,236,124 tons, an increase of 101 per cent.

Then again, in the third place, a protective tariff contradicts another principle of a revenue tariff, in that its tendency is to tax many things instead of few, and make the taxes themselves complicated instead of simple. Undoubtedly, the few persons who get themselves protected first, would like it all the better if nobody else would ask to get protected. But their very success tempts others. When the Legislature begins to grant favors of this sort, where shall it stop? It had better never

[1] See and compare an excellent little book by Hon. S. S. Cox, entitled "Free Land and Free Trade," pp. 34, 35, 55, 85, 114, and indeed *passim*.

begin! It will stop only when combinations of sufficient influence and power to impel it forward can no longer be organized. The natural tendency of protection is to try to protect many things, because others are sure to clamor, and because it will pretty soon require log-rolling and combination to maintain what has already been secured.

The woollen manufacturers of this country, who had long been protected, found in 1867, that they must help the wool-growers, who had not yet been protected, to get a heavy duty upon foreign wools, — the very thing the manufacturers did *not* want, — or else the wool-growers would turn against and help overthrow the duties on foreign woollens. The result of the compromise was the Wool and Woollens' tariff of 1867, of which the most favorable thing that can be said. is, that it is difficult to say whether the wool-growers or the wool-manufacturers have been the most harmed by it. The manufacturers were now obliged to pay over 100 per cent duty on fine wool, if they used the foreign, as many of them did, and were thereby placed at an immense disadvantage as compared with English and German manufacturers, who obtained their wools without any duty at all, and were consequently able to undersell our own manufacturers of fine cloths in our own market, even after paying the duty on cloths! This result re-acted upon the wool-growers, who found that hampering the manufacturers with high duties did not conduce to their own prosperity.

If there had been the same demand for wool as before, and they the only source of supply, they would have reaped a rich harvest; but there was *not* the same demand as before, because many branches of the manufacture require that different kinds of wools be mixed, and the makers having no longer a free market to pick from were curtailed in the manufacture, and the demand for even domestic wool fell off, prices declined, millions of fine-wool sheep in Ohio and elsewhere were slaughtered for their pelts and carcasses, and the decade 1870–80 was more discouraging both for the growers and the manufacturers than any other decade of our history. Many of the most intelligent woollen-manufacturers of the United States, who were formerly protectionists, were convinced by this remarkable experiment in tariff-tinkering, that free *materials* are of much more consequence to them as manufacturers than any rate of tariff-duty on foreign cloth can be.

This instance of combination illustrates the tendency of protection to many and complicated duties. When England began to abandon protection in 1842, the number of her tariff-taxes was 1150; and, on an actual count in 1868, the number of distinct rates assessed on different articles in the United States tariff was 2317; since protection was wholly abandoned in the former country, its tariff can be easily written on the palm of a man's hand; and even in the latter country, in which protection is more or less domi-

nant still, the number and grades of dutied articles
are much less than they were ten years ago. For
the year ending March 31, 1876, the entire customs'
revenue of Great Britain was derived, 38¾ per cent
from tobacco, 30¾ per cent from spirits, 18¼ per
cent from tea, 8¾ per cent from wine, and only 3½
per cent from a few other miscellaneous articles.
British customs' duties at present put into complete practice with the best results the three
principles of a revenue tariff already enunciated.

It is also the usage of protection to combine
specific and *ad valorem* duties upon the same
article, that is, a certain duty proportioned to the
quantity, and in addition to that a certain duty
proportioned to the value. For example, the duty
on one grade of wool was at one time 10 cents per
pound and also 11 per cent *ad valorem*. Under
these rates, if the value of the unwashed wool at
the port of exportation were (as it was) about 10
cents a pound, then the combined duty would be
about 111 per cent. One object in thus combining
both kinds of duty upon single articles is to conceal from the people as much as possible the actual
rate of duty, and this is at the same time the great
objection to the combination. No government
can afford to trifle with its people in the matter of
taxes. If any thing ought to be open, above-board,
clear, and thoroughly known beforehand, it is the
amount of contribution demanded by a government
from its citizens; but under these combined duties
it is impossible for any importer, still less for the

people, to know what will be demanded, because the *ad valorem* duty will depend on the price of the article at the place of exportation, which can never be exactly foreseen. The importer, or his agent, must take oath both to the quantity, (which is easy,) and also to the exact market price at the place and time of exportation, (which is sometimes difficult or impossible.) Phelps, Dodge & Co., an honorable firm in New York, were mulcted in $271,000, one-half of which went to an informer, because a few invoices, through no fault of the firm, appeared to have been undervalued. The firm, although they paid the money, asserted their innocence, and did not suffer one iota in public opinion; but the law suffered in public opinion, and some minor features of it were afterwards repealed, and it is to be one of the triumphs of the immediate future within intelligent nations, that there will be no combination of two kinds of duty on the same article, and also that specific duties will mostly or wholly take the place of duties per value.

An important report on tariff reform was made in 1876 to the Superior Council of Commerce in France, in which the gathered opinion of the Chambers of Commerce, the Chambers of Agriculture, of economists, functionaries, merchants, and manufacturers, throughout France, pronounces with great unanimity not only in favor of the renewal of the commercial treaties with other nations, that is, in favor of reciprocity in trade, but also in favor of converting the *ad valorem* into specific duties. " It is easy," this report points out, " to check fraudulent declarations of weight and measure, but it is extremely difficult when the value of a commodity is in question. Fair in appearance, these *ad valorem* duties are really as unequal as any others, and their collection gives rise to all sorts of difficulties between importers and the customs' officials, to fraud, and to vexation." The good results to France of the adoption of the principle of commercial treaties in 1860 are seen in the fact that in fourteen years the imports and exports of that country increased from 9,689,360,000 francs to 13,810,000,000 francs, in spite of war, revolutions, and dismemberment. The tariffs of Great Britain and Germany are already free, with trifling exceptions, from all *ad valorem* duties.

Free Trade is the opposite of Protection, and not of customs' duties properly levied for revenue. The phrase is not indeed well chosen, though it has been long consecrated by usage, on account of the possible ambiguity of the words. The phrase may mean the abolition of all tariffs, — the allowed introduction of all goods into any country without any tax at all, — but it is not in this sense that the words have become famous; it was not for this that Cobden and Bright and their compeers agitated England from centre to circumference, nor has it been in this sense that discussion and action on free trade have gone forward in this country. The animated controversies of a century have settled the technical meaning of free trade as the opposite to that of protection; in which sense Great Britain, certainly since 1860, has been a free trade country. Free traders as such are satisfied whenever the tariff of their country contains no tax except those laid with a single eye to simple and equitable taxation. There are those, however, and their number is increasing, who believe that even revenue tariffs constructed on the principles already indicated are not a proper instrument of taxation, and who think it more feasible to destroy protection by overthrowing tariffs altogether than by reducing them to the purely revenue form. They would lay the axe at the root of the tree. The International Free Trade Alliance in New York was founded [1] on this principle; and the great prime-minister of England, Mr. Gladstone, expressed himself a few years ago in Paris as inclining to the belief that a better method of raising a revenue may be devised than that by means of any form of a tariff.

Still, as no one of the leading nations has as yet abolished its tariff, and as all are likely to pass through the phase of a purely revenue tariff before they come to absolute free trade, and as the alternative of tariff or no tariff is rather a question of scientific taxation than of practical commerce, — a question that we shall discuss under its appropriate head in the final chapter, — it has seemed wiser to me for economists and philanthropists to

[1] These figures come from the official documents of the national government, and were stated, as in the text, by Senator Blaine.

assail and overthrow an actual grievance, an unjust discrimination as between classes of citizens, which common people can easily understand, than to undertake through more complicated processes of reasoning to convince them that any tariff is necessarily wrong. There ought to be no mis· understanding among those whose common end is the removal of "protection," whatever difference of opinion there may be about the most available means to compass that end. Commerce is such an unspeakable blessing to the nations, that any thing which essentially interferes with it should be stricken down by some means or all means; and while I shall use the words "Free Trade" in their conventional and controversial sense, my readers will find that the arguments already adduced and yet to be adduced will lose nothing of their significance and work no confusion in their minds, even if they should adopt the other view of the meaning of these words. I proceed to add a few succinct arguments in favor of Free Trade, and, in connection with these, the corre-. sponding objections to Protection.

1. *Free trade would bring the production of the world to its maximum.* There is in the world a certain amount of capital and a certain amount of industry These, if left to their own keen sense of interest, without any interference with their natural markets, will make the aggregate amount of production in the world as great as that amount of capital and industry can make it. By no pos·

sibility can protection, which is only restriction, bring *any new motives* to bear on producers universally. Even liberty brings no new motives to bear, but it gives perfect play to all the natural motives to production, among which the desire to better one's condition by exchanges is almost universal, and these motives are sufficient for all the interests of production. Even if they were not sufficient, as they are, legislation is incompetent to increase them on the whole ; and protection only pretends to increase the stimulus at a few points by reducing the stimulus at other points. If, then, a free commerce distribute this aggregate production over the earth in accordance with the simple law of supply and demand, we shall have not only the greatest production, but the most perfect distribution. But if government steps in by a restrictive tariff, withdraws capital and industry from their freely chosen posts of activity, prohibits exchanges that would otherwise be made, and commands commodities to be manufactured or grown in localities in which they would not naturally be manufactured or grown, then, obviously, the aggregate production of the world is made less, and its distribution becomes less perfect.

2. *Free trade is in accordance with the natural indications of Providence.* The countries of the earth differ widely in point of climate, soil, natural productions, established industries, and habits of the people ; and with these diversities of relative

advantage spring up the impulses and the gains of international traffic; usually considerable distance, and frequently other natural barriers also, have to be overcome in order to carry on this trade, and it will only be carried on when, notwithstanding all this, the trade is still profitable to both parties; so that, there is a plain indication of Providence that such countries should trade with each other, and thus each share in the peculiar good of each, and perhaps communicate through a mutual economic benefit some higher good each to each. Naturally, under freedom, the nearer nations will trade most with each other, for the same reason that the volume of each nation's domestic trade is larger than the volume of its foreign trade. For instance, we might expect that the United States, being nearer to and quite as diverse from Mexico and the South American States than and as England and France, would have a larger share of the trade on this continent; but the figures for 1874 show, that while this country sent to those neighbors but $28,000,000 of exports, France sent to them $62,000,000, and England $105,000,000. This could never have happened, if the United States had obeyed nature, and allowed a mutual free trade. Under the reciprocity treaty between the United States and the British North American provinces, the aggregate of exchanges went up in one year from $20,691,000 to $33,494,000, and in ten years to $84,000,000, or more than fourfold. When reciprocity was repealed in 1866, and the restrictive duties became operative again, the exchanges fell in one year from $84,000,000 to $57,000,000. Protection, being unnatural, not only destroys trade, but also makes the protected country weaker and weaker relatively to less protected or free-trade countries. In 1857, United-States ships carried five-sevenths, or more than 71 per cent, of all the imports and exports of the country; while in 1878, after a long period of unprecedented protection for goods and of absolute protection for ships, American bottoms carried less than two-sevenths, that is, less than 29 per cent, of the total foreign cargoes, and free-trade *foreigners* carried our old proportion of more than 71 per cent! Under protection, Belgium's sales of her products to other countries increased *in a whole decade* (1840–50) only 124,100,000 francs, while *in one year* (1871) under a comparative free trade they increased 198,600,000 francs. Protection accordingly thwarts nature, and nature is perfectly sure to take her revenge. Why should not the nations open their ports to foreign products, since that is nothing but opening the widest possible market for their own products? Why should not the time longed for by the poet Whittier be hastened on and welcomed? —

"When strand shall closer lean on strand."

Why should stupid and wasteful obstacles be thrown across the realization of the splendid apostrophe of Tennyson? —

"Fly, happy, happy sails, and bear the press;
Fly, happy with the mission of the cross;
Knit land to land, and blowing heavenward
With silks and fruits and spices, *clear of toll*,
Enrich the markets of the golden year."

3. *Free trade means abundance and cheapness,
while protection means scarcity and dearness.* The
common reason alleged for protective duties is, that
those goods would otherwise come in so cheap that
similar goods could not be manufactured in this
country at a profit. Suppose they could not, what
then? Is it *the manufacturing* that people want,
or is it *the goods?* Which is ultimate in the field
of exchange, the efforts or the satisfactions? But
what we are concerned with now is the admission
made by protection at the outset that things are
naturally too cheap, and that protective duties are
an instrument to make them dearer. The admission is honest, and the result actually follows. If
any one is doubtful on this point, let him try a little
experiment, — let him propose to almost any protectionist manufacturer to remove the duty that
protects *him*, and note the nature of his reply.
This manufacturer may have denied in argument
a hundred times, that protective duties raise the
prices of goods, but the style of his answer to
a proposal to take off that particular duty will
lay bare his deepest thoughts on that subject.
A hundred to one, he will say in substance,
"The removal of that duty will enable the for-
'eign manufacturer to undersell me." The duty

is in the interest of scarcity, and hence of dearness.

What might of course be anticipated from the nature of the case, the price-lists actually show. In 1872, the Michigan Central Railroad relaid its track in Detroit with steel rails costing ninety-seven dollars (gold) per ton, while at the same time the Canada Southern Railroad was laying down the same kind of rails within a distance of half a mile (across the Detroit River) at a cost of seventy dollars (gold) per ton. Protection in the United States made all the difference. An indefinite tax on freight and passengers must make up to the road the wretched tax of twenty-seven dollars per ton extorted in the interest of the makers of steel rails. I have myself seen price-lists, according to which the Onondaga Salt Co. of Syracuse, N.Y., offered to lay down salt, freight paid, at various points along the Grand Trunk Railroad in Canada at much less per barrel than any American citizen could buy the salt for in Syracuse itself! I am happy to be able to add that the salt duties have been since then very materially reduced.

Instances like these might be multiplied indefinitely, but I will only instance further, in illustration of the opposition of protection to plenty, that during the summer of 1876, the sugar-planters of Louisiana and Texas tried to defeat the then pending Commercial Treaty with the Sandwich Islands, because it admitted free of duty into our ports all unrefined sugars from those islands. The Treaty, however, was ratified, and practical free trade exists between this country and that; and it is an interesting illustration of the way in which knocking off fetters from foreign trade immediately revives some domestic trade, that within twenty-four hours of the passage of the bill giving final effect to this treaty, the sugar-refiners of San Francisco had taken steps to renew that decayed industry there. It is still more interesting to see how the whole volume of that trade between us and the Islands mounted up under the Treaty: for twelve years prior to and including 1876, our average imports from there were $1,200,000 a year, while in the calendar year 1877, the first full year under the treaty, they rose to $2,200,000; during the twelve years before 1876, our *exports* to the islands averaged $860,000, but in the very first year under the treaty they jumped from $800,000 to $1,800,000! That is to say, in the first year of reciprocity, imports show an increase of 83 per cent, and exports an increase of 125 per cent! Freedom means plenty.

4. *Free trade fully recognizes the rights of private property, while protection, by curtailing, virtually denies them.* The right of property, in the last analysis of it, is the right to sell something, that is to say, the right to buy something. Nothing is property that cannot be sold ; and any legislation that withdraws any service whatever from its best and freely-chosen market destroys a part of the

value of that service. It is a stab at the right of property. Protection says; — You shall not buy in that market, unless you pay a tax designed to *prevent* your buying in that market; which is tho same as to say, You shall not sell *your* product in the market where you can get the most for it; which in turn is nothing in the world but robbing you of a part of your private property ostensibly for the benefit of another's private property, that is, that somebody else may sell a domestic product for more than it would otherwise be worth. Thus this bad system is tainted on the one side by tho principle of slavery, and on the other by the principle of socialism. To take away a part of the proceeds of one's industry is not indeed so bad as to take away the whole, but the principle is the same, and it is the principle of slavery.

What is taken from its citizens by a just government in legitimate taxation is rightfully taken, and, on the part of good citizens, is voluntarily and cheerfully rendered; but what is taken by "protection" out of the pockets of one class of citizens ostensibly for the benefit of another class is wrongfully taken, — is in principle robbery on the part of the government and slavery on the part of those who submit to it without protest. On the other side, and what is even worse, protection recognizes the principle that government may properly take a part of the proceeds of ono man's industry to reward another man's industry with, which is the root-principle of socialism, and a menace to the rights of private property. If government may properly take some of the reward of my industry and offer it as extra reward of my neighbor's industry, it may properly take some of the rewards of the industry of both of us to feed and clothe the idle, and it may even distribute at will the property of the rich among the poor. There is no stopping the applications of the principle till the very extremes of socialism are reached, if the principle itself be once admitted. If protection be right, then Proudhon was also right; — "*Property is theft.*" So logically is the theft of property by protection connected with the doctrine that property is theft. Much of the late and present dissatisfaction in this country of laborers with capital comes by subtle inferences from this principle instilled into their minds by protectionists. The principle itself is solemnly and comprehensively denied. The fruits of every man's industry belong to *him*, save only that part which government may properly take for its own support.

Free trade recognizes this grand principle of liberty and property. John Bright wrote one of our citizens these truthful words: — "Protection has upon it a taint of the great wrong of slavery. It does not steal the laborer, but it steals his labor, it taxes it cruelly, it lessens its result and its profit, and turns it into channels less useful to the laborer. It says to your cultivator of the soil: You must not exchange your quarter of wheat or yo ir barrel of flour with an Englishman for the cloth or the hardware he would give you for it; only with an American who will give you so much less for it. It was so with us 30 years ago. Our weavers could not exchange with your farmers a piece of cloth for a barrel of flour, but only with an English farmer who offered him half a barrel. So the protection system has in it much of the evil of slavery, for the labor of the laborer is not free ; it is by force of law diminished in value. This can only exist in a free country from the ignorance of its people. Happily the fraud is too transparent to live long."

5. *Free trade allows a natural and stable cost of production, while protection enhances and hazards it.* We have already seen how numerous and delicate are the factors that go to make up the cost of production of commodities, and how important it is to the producer to be able to calculate and rely upon the cost of these factors. If the cost of his raw materials, for example, be artificially increased by tariff-taxes, it affects at once the cost of his product, it affects his market in accordance with this general principle that a higher price narrows a market and a lower price broadens it, it perhaps excludes him altogether from a market in which his competitors get their materials free of tax, and it introduces an element of uncertainty and instability into his business, all which is discouraging and hazardous.

An illustration may be found in the effect on

the boot and shoe business of New England of the imposition of duties on hides and leather, and especially on lastings or serges.. The export trade, which was quite considerable, was nearly annihilated in consequence of these duties; which, so far as the lastings were concerned, were the more remarkable, inasmuch as they were not thought of when the duties were put on, but, as they came under the technical tariff-description, duties had to be paid on them to the great disarrangement of that branch of the business that used them. A tax on a raw material has this peculiarity, that it has to be advanced at the outset, and becomes with the profits on it a rapidly accumulating element in the ultimate price of the product, inasmuch as this tax with profits has to be advanced over and over again as many times as the product changes hands between inception and ultimate sale. Tariff-taxes are quite apt to be laid on raw materials, and increase thereby the cost of production of all the commodities into which these materials enter. The duty on pig-iron, although it was reduced in 1872 from $9.00 to $7.00 per ton, was and is one of the worst duties in our tariff. (1.) It was needless. Pig-iron had been made in this country at a profit for more than 150 years before it bore any duty at all. It was first dutied in the tariff of 1816. (2.) It has been variable. The rate has been at 7 different figures between the years 1842 and 1880; and, as pig-iron is raw material to hundreds of commodities, it is plain that an unstable cost of production of all these has been one consequence of the duties; and, as instability of cost means miscalculations and bankruptcies, that even the production of pig-iron itself would have been more prosperous without any duty at all. (3.) It has raised the domestic price of pig-iron. It was falsely claimed that high duties imposed for a time would so stimulate the domestic production that the price here would be lower than that abroad. Years upon years of high duties gave us no lower prices of pig-iron than the price was in 1850, but on the contrary the average price for 14 years (1860–74) was $5.22 per ton higher than the average for 14 years under the tariff of 1846–60. A higher duty on pig-iron has never failed to give a higher average price to pig-iron in our markets, and a lower duty has never failed to be followed by a lower average price. The motives of the men who have succeeded in getting the duties put on, their piercing clamor when it has been proposed to take the duties off, and the actual price-lists of the markets, all tell the same story: nevertheless, the instability and uncertainties of prices under protection rarely, if ever, foster the protected industry so much in the long-run as an assured freedom would foster it in connection with the freedom of all other industries. The steadiness of prices under free trade as compared with their variability under protection is exceedingly well illustrated also in the prices of breadstuffs in Great Britain before and since the abolition of the corn-

laws. The corn-laws were protection applied
to British agriculturists in the shape of heavy
duties levied on the importation of foreign grain;
after a good season, grain was reasonably cheap,
the presumption being that the islands could feed
their own population in the good years; but after
a bad harvest or two, prices rose frightfully, poor
people starved, food *had* to be imported and pay
the duties, and domestic grain rose of course to
the price of the foreign with duties added. In
March, 1801, wheat in England was 156 shillings
·a quarter, barley 90s., and oats 47s. In August,
1812, wheat was 155s., while in July, 1814, it was
only 68s. Such alternations in the price of food
are fearful, and are the natural result of such protective legislation; while, since the trade in corn
has been free, the price never varies more than a
few pence to the bushel, because any deficiency in
the native harvest is instantly supplied from the
United States or from the Baltic provinces. Free
trade gives stability to all costs of production, and
to all prices, so far as it is possible in the nature
of things to have stability in values. The commerce of the world is like the tides of the ocean,
— apparently disturbing, yet really regulating, the
natural level.

6. *Free trade is the friend of the so-called laboring
classes, while protection is their enemy.* This might
be inferred with certainty from the nature of the
case, even if·experience had not confirmed it over
and over again. The value of things produced
depends in part upon the demand for them, and it

always must be for the advantage of all those who contribute towards the production of any thing, that the demand for that product be as strong as possible. The wages-class are as much interested in having a strong demand for the products they help to create as are the capitalist-class, since wages quite as much as profits come out of the proceeds of the *sale* of those products. Whatever, then, tends to increase the *demand* for material products in general, must tend to the benefit of the wages-class. But free trade must increase the demand for such products, inasmuch as it opens up for them a world-market in the place of a one-country market. Free trade allows foreigners to bring in their products freely to exchange against native products; foreign products cannot be bought beyond the point at which native products are sold; money may come in as a medium in both exchanges, as will be explained in the next chapter, but that does not alter the fact that at bottom it is an exchange of products other than money against products other than money; really the only reason why foreigners bring in their products is to get the native products in return; therefore, the demand for native products is necessarily increased by opening the ports freely to foreign products; and, therefore, the wages of those who labor on the native products now in enhanced demand must be enhanced also. I invite any protectionist, who feels disposed to try his hand at it, to break in two this simple chain of reasoning.

I admit, that branches of business artificially brought in and sustained by protective duties, in competition with countries in which nature rather than law favors the production, may collapse in the healthful shock of free exchange, because they are too sickly for any healthful shock of any kind. Why should they not collapse? There is no loss, on the whole, in their collapsing. They are unprofitable branches of business by confession, otherwise they would not demand to be supported out of the resources of the community, that is to say, by taxing their neighbors in order to continue to exist. The sooner all unprofitable branches of business cease to be prosecuted in any country, the better for that country and for the world. The prospect of ultimate profit under natural condi tions is sufficient inducement to try all needful experiments in new directions of production; and the proper test of the propriety of continuing any branch of industry beyond the period of experiment is the natural, God-appointed test of free exchanges. All branches of industry are equally natural, provided only they are profitable, provided only they are adapted to the circumstances and conditions under which they start. Agriculture is no more natural than manufactures, inasmuch as agriculture itself cannot go forward without implements, and without the means of clothing and housing the tillers of the soil. The point is, that men should follow natural conditions, and enter upon branches of business just so fast as they become profitable, and just so far as all the circumstances favor them. Such branches of business, and no others have any economic right to exist, instead of being harmed by free trade, are necessarily made more profitable by it, for such is the diversity in natural conditions and customs within the countries that each in many things has the advantage over all the rest, and the opportunity of each to sell to all the rest as well as at home the products in which it has an advantage makes a demand for such products which cannot be otherwise than favorable to the laboring classes.

As an illustration of the effect of free trade in increasing the demand for native products, I will give a few figures from the official Reports of Great Britain and France. In Great Britain, between 1854 and 1868, exports in general increased over 72 per cent *per capita;* exports ot cotton, nearly threefold; of woollen manufactures, fourfold; of linen, fourfold; of iron and steel, fivefold; of leather, sixfold; of haberdashery, nearly sevenfold; of woollen yarn, eightfold; and of machinery, tenfold. In the same interval, imports in general increased almost 66 per cent *per capita.* Under the commercial treaty with England, comparing 1860 with 1868, the volume of French commerce increased over 37 per cent; exports to England, over 155 per cent; of butter, more than twenty-fold; of eggs, nearly sixfold; of wines, fivefold; of silks, woollens, and cottons, nearly threefold. Whose labor produced these enormously increased exports? Whose wages

were ever reduced by an enlarged demand for
the products of labor? The truth is, that free
trade not only increases the wages of laborers
through an enlarged demand for their products,
but also brings comforts and conveniences home to
thousands, who, under a restrictive policy, would
have to go without them. French butter and
French eggs are now almost as cheap on the English side of the Channel as on the other.

As a matter of fact, too, a matter of daily
observation and testimony, the condition of the
laboring classes both in Great Britain and France
has greatly improved as the restrictive systems of
those countries have been gradually broken down.
John Bright says, that the wages of English laborers in all skilled employments have risen at least
25 per cent under and in consequence of free trade,
while hours of labor have been abridged and
staple articles of food reduced in price. In four
years from 1870 to 1874, paupers decreased in
England 23 per cent. Not to speak of Germany
and other large nations, the little State of Tuscany in Italy affords a most instructive example,
because exhibited on a small scale apart from
other influences, of the injurious effects of protection, and the marvellous power of recuperation
under freedom.[1] Never better than in Tuscany
was the wisdom learned out of bitter experience,
— the wisdom once compressed into the homely
sentence, "Just let the people look after their

[1] History of Free Trade in Tuscany, by James M. Stuart.
London, 1876.

own business ; they know it better than any minister of state."

Not only does free trade open up to the so-
called laboring classes better fields of labor in
order to supply broader markets, but also the
removal of protective duties lowers the price of
most of the commodities they are accustomed *to
buy*. The laborer gets more work and higher
wages under freedom; and, what is better, each
dollar he earns goes further in purchasing. The
sole purpose in laying the protective duty is to
raise the price of the domestic product; those
products are preferred for protection that are consumed by the masses of the people, such as
woollens, cottons, all forms of iron goods, lumber,
common window-glass, lead pencils, and cheap
carpets; and accordingly, when all such duties
are thrown off, the prices of the common necessa-
ries of life go down as a matter of course, and
of course as a matter of fact. If *not*, why do
protectionists object to the removal of the
duties ?

It is because protective duties are *designed* to
raise prices, and *do* raise prices, that the instincts
of the common people are opposed to such duties,
and that the interests of protectionists are opposed to their removal. As a good instance of
how prices go down, as protection goes off. let us
look at the quinine duties abolished by Congress in 1879. In April of that year, sulphate
of quinine was quoted in the Druggist's Circular
at $3.80 to $4 per ounce. Powers and Weight

man, manufacturing chemists of Philadelphia, had a virtual monopoly of the trade under the twenty per cent duty, and protested that its removal would drive them out of the business *without making quinine any cheaper.* The law abolishing the duty went into effect July 1, and quinine was quoted that day at $3.40 per ounce. In December it declined to $2.60, after which the Russian Government became a large purchaser, raising the price to about $3.25 in April, 1880, which is about such a reduction as the removal of the duty would lead us to expect. This fall of price took place, too, in the face of a disastrous war between the South-American States that produce cinchona bark, the raw · material of quinine. The chemists referred to did *not* go out of the business, — quite the reverse, — although somebody presented a memorial to Congress, in the spring of 1880, begging for, at least, a ten per cent duty on quinine.

7. *Free trade defends older and worthier interests than those that have become vested under protection.* A minority of the Ways and Means Committee of Congress reported adversely in May, 1880, to the lessening of tariff-taxes, ostensibly because certain interests, like the glass, iron, and woollen interests, have been more or less built up under these protective taxes since 1860. What if they have been thus built up? *At whose expense have they been built up?* Has not agriculture as much claim to the forbearance of Congress as glass-making, for example, has to its special favor?

Congress cannot favor one interest without laying
a tax-burden on other interests ; and the point is,
that these interests, and especially agriculture the
chief of them, are quite as old and quite as
worthy, and quite as *respectable* in asking to be
let alone, as any special interest is that begs the
privilege of taxing its neighbors for its own up-
building. If such special interest, having once
got such taxes put on others for its own benefit,
becomes thereby a "vested" interest, if such
taxes become " sacred " by mere usage, then they
never can be rightfully thrown off! That argument, if admitted, will last too long! The validity of the argument is utterly denied. An original wrong never becomes an ultimate right by
lapse of time: no interest can become vested by
preying on other interests, and especially on interests older, worthier, and more self-respecting.
Dr. Eliot in his History of the United States,[1]
while discussing the first national tariff, confesses
this conflict and wrong: "The interests of the
Northern industry, its shipping, its commerce, and
its manufactures, called for a very different policy
on the part of the government, *from that demanded
by the Southern agriculture.*" That original wrong,
afterwards repeated and aggravated, rankled in
the breasts of the wronged till it developed the
Calhoun theory of the Union, and issued in the
Civil War. The only proper way to deal with

[1] Page 283. Compare with this the strange remark, — too
empty and foolish for such a thoughtful writer, — concluding the
first paragraph of page 280.

taxes that were put on the many for the benefit of the few is to cut short their career of mischief by immediate abolition.

As free trade can only appeal to the sense of justice, and the broad and generous impulses of the masses of men; and as no man can have any *motive* aside from these impulses, and aside from his own liability to pay an unjust tax, to advocate free trade; and as no man is specially authorized to voice the wants and the rights of the poor: while, on the contrary, protection from its very nature makes a strong appeal to the selfish greed of a comparatively small number of men, at whose instance protective duties are *always* put on, if at all, and who can easily combine, and *do* combine, to carry out their ends; it is not strange, looking at human nature as it is, that " Protection " is able to hold its own for a time, against the general interests, even in an enlightened country, and sometimes also to get back its own for a time even after the true system has been once entered upon. Protectionists are possessed of every art of the lobby ; they seem always to have plenty of money, and to know how to use it for their own ends; being obliged to " make the worse appear the better reason," they become adepts in sophistry, which often seems to deceive themselves ; and they sometimes have the boldness to appeal to popular demonstrations, as when " a grand picnic to enforce the theories of protection " was held in Ohio, June 5, 1880! All this is indeed strong language; but Political

Economy, as the Science of Sales, has no patience, and ought to have no patience, with a
narrow scheme whose end is to *lessen* sales and
make their terms more *onerous*. It is not a mere
difference of opinion, it is the existence of Political Economy as a body of scientific principles,
that is involved in this matter. If protection be
sound, there is and can be no science of Political
Economy: happily there *is* such a science.

But all this also furnishes an adequate explanation of the apparent re-actions from free trade
from time to time, like that in France after the
German War, and like that in Germany some
years later. These re-actions, however, were
moderate, and will doubtless prove temporary.
English re-actions, though often confidently predicted, have never come in sufficient force to make
any stir in the House of Commons. English re-actions *go hard* against such facts as these, of which
British official statistics are full; namely, the exports of British products advanced from £63,596,-
000 in 1849, to £256,257,000 in 1872, an increase
of 303 per cent; and, what is still more illustrative
of the *mutual* benefits of freedom, the tonnage of
vessels entered and closed in British ports increased between 1840 and 1878, — *foreign* tonnage
452 per cent, and *British* tonnage 443 per cent.[1]

7. *Free trade has the sanction of all ages of the
world, while protection is at once a novelty and a
decrepitude.* Antiquity, though perfectly familiar
with customs' duties, knew nothing whatever of

[1] Financial Reform Almanack for 1880, p. 151.

the doctrine of protection. Neither did the
Middle Ages. England, in the course of the
seventeenth century, developed the system, which,
in the course of the nineteenth, she loathingly
rejected. The new centuries are certainly bringing in many new and good things; there is constant progress in science and in the arts of life;
even in the realm of exchange, new things of
great importance, like the check and the clearing-
house, have come in and been acknowledged to be
good; the charge of novelty is not necessarily
conclusive against any thing — many new things
are good, and many old things are bad; but, then,
on the other hand, trade is very old, all nations
have engaged in it from the beginning, some grew
very rich by means of it,[1] and all experienced
the reciprocal benefits of it; money, as a medium
of exchange, was invented before Abraham's day,
and there were in his day certainly, and probably
long before, as there have been in every generation
since, merchants as a class; the minds of men
were employed about trade, they must have perceived the grounds of its utility, and though they
did not develop the science of it, though they
made many mistakes about it, yet it seems strange,
if there be any truth in the matter of protection,
since that concerns the fundamentals of trade,
that no one of the ancients should have had even
a glimmer of that truth.

Aristotle threw out a good deal of light in

[1] See the 27th chapter of the Prophet Ezekiel.

various directions upon the subject of Political Economy, but it never occurred to that gifted thinker that it would be a good thing to try to stop by statute a mutually profitable trade between nations! There was plenty of hostility between nations in ancient and mediæval times, and often great restrictions on intercourse between them, but I find no hint coming down from those times of the central point of modern protection, namely, that it may be ultimately *profitable* to curtail by legislation a presently profitable international trade. Under all the circumstances, it is against protection, that it never was thought of until the middle of the seventeenth century. It is against protection, that it had its origin in the bitter rivalry and hostility of England and Holland. It is against protection, that, having been thoroughly tested by Great Britain for almost two centuries, it is now acknowledged through every organ of public opinion there, that the system was *always* maintained at a loss. It is against protection, that other nations, having copied the system from England and tried it long, are only just behind England in abandoning it in scorn.

It is against protection, that its influence is waning in every enlightened country in the world. It is against protection, that the United States, in which it has been dominant for two decades, have yet recently made a free-trade treaty with the Sandwich Islands, and are likely soon to make another with Canada. It is against protection.

that the Mercantile System so-called — the doctrine of the Balance of Trade — in *connection* with
which restrictive tariffs had their birth, has long
ago been discarded as false by all thinkers, statesmen, and nations.   In one word, it is against protection, that it came in so late and is going out so
early.   On the other hand, it is altogether in favor
of free trade, that it has always been in the world
and always will be, and that it has fought and is
fighting in a dozen different nations a good fight
with its great enemy, and has already substantially
won the battle.

9. *Free trade is in harmony with the spirit of
progress, while protection is directly opposed to it.*
It will be admitted by all, that the past progress
of the world has been in the direction of freedom.
The great struggles have been around three points
as centres; first, freedom of person; second, freedom of opinion ; and third, freedom of exchange.
As the result of the struggle around the first
point, personal slavery has now mainly disappeared from the earth; as the result of the
struggle around the second point, the freedom of
opinion and its expression, and especially of religious opinion, has gained great triumphs in all
lands, although much yet remains to be done
before its complete triumph is assured; while, as
the result of the struggle around the third point,
one barrier after another has given way, one
monopoly after another has been conquered, until
now it is pretty generally agreed that freedom of

exchange is just as sacred as freedom of person
and of opinion, and the struggle, which is in
entire harmony with the others, will certainly
never cease until the liberty of contract and delivery, subject only to conditions of morals and
health and revenue, shall be international and
universal. The spirit of free trade is the spirit
of peace and good-will. It is the spirit of self-
interest certainly, but then it is an enlightened
self-interest that sees that another's loss cannot
permanently be one's own gain. It is the spirit of
give and take. It is the spirit of live and let live.
It is a lower and yet beneficent application of the
apostolic words,[1] — "Look not every man on his
own things, but every man also on the things of
others." It is in harmony with the tendencies
and ongoing of things in this world. It has in it
all the elements of stability and permanency. It
is itself a sign of progress, and it paves the way to
progress in other directions.

I have recently met with a passage in one of
our daily newspapers,[2] which is so just in sentiment and so clear in expression, that I will quote
it entire: —"It is a matter of notoriety, demon-
strable from contemporaneous English history and
social statistics, that the public morals of that
country have improved along with its prosperity
ever since the principle of free, unshackled trade
was adopted. It was the first of the long series
of reforms that have characterized English legisla-

[1] Phil. ii. 4.   [2] Chicago Tribune.

tion during the past quarter of a century. It was followed by an improvement in all kinds of taxation, until the revenue is raised upon the smallest number of articles of luxury and to the relief of the largest number of people. It opened the way for the growth of the liberal sentiment which has encouraged social, political and religious freedom. The extension of educational facilities, the dis- establishment of the Irish Church, the liberalization of suffrage, the establishment of free schools, are all reforms that never would have been realized if the power of reform had not first asserted itself in the derogation of the injustice of high tariff. Incident to these and other measures for the amelioration of the condition of the English people have been the growth of intelligence and education, the increased power of enlightened public opinion, the improvement and purification of the civil service and the decrease of crime, until to-day the English Government is cited as a model in its assurance of individual rights and personal liberty, as the English people are noted for the high degree of prosperity. All this has not only been accomplished under freedom of trade, but free trade was the starting-point from which these conditions took their impetus."

On the other hand, protection cannot bear a searching inquiry into the motives of the men who practically get the protective duties put on. They are thinking only of an artificial price for their particular product, and not at all of the

other far-reaching consequences of their action.
That some of their fellow-citizens are cruelly
taxed as consumers in consequence of their action,
that others of their fellow-citizens lose in part or
in whole the market for *their* products in consequence of their action, and that foreigners lose
also in part or in whole *their* market in consequence of their action, weighs but little in the
mind of the practical protectionist. I have it
on the very highest authority, — the authority of
experienced men who have served at different
times on the Ways and Means 'Committee at
Washington, — that the individuals and delega
tions who come before that Committee in behalf
of new or higher protective duties, come in the
barest selfishness, without a thought or care of
anybody's interests but their own. Can a system
like this, so shortsighted and greedy, so obstructive to natural and wholesome tendencies, building
so little on permanent elements in man and nature,
claim to be a part of the progress of the world?
Can restriction hold its own in a fair comparison
with freedom?

It is not needful, in a book like the present, to
go further into detail with the arguments for a
free commerce, or to refute in detail the arguments
for protection. Enough has been said to indicate
the profound conviction of the writer, and, I venture to 1 pe also, enough to determine the delib-
erate judgment of the reader, that international
commerce is good; that God intended it as a part

of the education and well-being of mankind; that
restrictions on it, except in the three cases already
so often mentioned, are economically and morally
evil; that a tariff, if it be had at all, should be
had as an instrument of simple taxation only; and
that a protective tariff is, and from its nature must
be, a cause of loss to other nations indeed, but of
greater loss to the nation imposing it.

The history of the Colonies, which now form
some of the States of this Union, and the history
of the Union itself, confirms in a striking manner
the justness of these general conclusions. That
history makes ridiculous the plea that artificial
stimulus is needful in order to bring in new industries into any country. Most of the great industries of this country sprang up, not only without
any artificial stimulus, but also in spite of the
hostility and vigilance of the mother-country.
As early as 1638, the manufacture of linen, cotton,
and woollen cloths was commenced at Rowley in
the State of Massachusetts.

The mother country envied the Colonies the
profits of the manufacture of woollens, and as
early as 1698 laid a prohibition upon the exportation of colonial woollens, even from one Colony
to another. Parliament crowned its many acts of
interference with colonial woollens by prohibiting
in 1732 (the birth-year of Washington) the exportation of hats. Ship-building, commenced in
1631, was firmly established as an industry by the
first generation of civilized men inhabiting New-

England shores. Brick-making, glass-works, and the manufacture of salt, were all begun in Massachusetts before 1640. Tannery and shoe-making began about that time, and within 20 years boots and shoes became articles of export; while in 1643 the younger Winthrop established iron-works at Braintree and Lynn, in the same State, which, after some losses, were successfully prosecuted.[1] In 1721 New England alone had six furnaces and nineteen forges, and there were many others in Pennsylvania and Virginia. Parliament enacted in 1750 that no more mills should be erected in America for slitting or rolling iron, or forges for hammering it, or furnaces for making steel; and in certain cases, agents of the crown were authorized to tear down such establishments as "nuisances."

How far all the arts of navigation had been carried in the Colonies before the Revolution, any one may read in Burke's famous speech on Conciliation with America. How far the products of the loom, the forge, and the anvil, were already being exported, in spite of British legislation, to other countries, any one may see in Lord North's last proposals and concessions to ward off the Revolution. The history of this country from the first day to this day is a continuous refutation of the pleas and arguments for restraining its foreign trade.

[1] See 9th Annual Report Mass. Bureau of Statistics and Labor, 1878.

We may group as follows the fundamental points of the present chapter : —

1. *Commerce is an exchange of goods for the mutual* BENEFIT *of the respective owners.*

2. *A free commerce does not oblige parties to exchange, but merely* PERMITS *them to do so.*

3. *The Constitution of the United States* GOES VERY FAR *towards securing to all its citizens the benefits of a free commerce.*

4. *A tariff is a scheme of* TAXES *levied by a government on imported goods.*

5. *Revenue and protective tariffs are the* OPPOSITES *of each other in all essential points.*

6. *Protective tariffs are designed to* PREVENT *revenue, and to gather spoil from the many into the pockets of the few.*

7. AGRICULTURE *and the unorganized masses of the people are the chief prey of Protection.*

8. *Opening ports to foreign products is opening* MARKETS *for domestic products.*

9. FREE TRADE *maximizes products, harmonizes with Providence, means abundance, recognizes rights, makes stable the cost of production, is the friend of the laboring classes, defends from attack the worthiest interests, has the sanction of all ages of the world, and is one with the spirit of progress.*

10. *History affirms that all industries are equally* NATURAL; *and hence no one has the right to subsist at the expense of the others.*

11. *Political Economy as the Science of Sales* MUST *denounce protection, which deranges and curtails them.*

CHAPTER IV.

MONEY.

MONEY is always a pleasant topic to discourse about. Through the influence of association, the very word has come to have an agreeable sound; and the thing itself, especially in the form of gold or silver coin, is an object of beauty, as well as of ·great utility. Even a Bank of England note, which rarely gets much soiled by usage, inasmuch as, once returned to the bank, it is never re-issued, and its average life is computed to be not more than three days, is not a disagreeable thing to look at; neither are our present national bank-bills and greenbacks offensive to the eye, until, by much usage, they become dirty and mutilated, and even then they are still convenient things to have. Money, too, almost always has upon it in some form the symbol of its nationality, it bears the image and superscription of Cæsar, and so becomes associated with patriotic love of country.

Another thing that gives interest to the subject of money, is the fact that it is a human invention, and therefore completely intelligible, inasmuch as

men can always understand what men have devised. Undoubtedly, the conditions of exchange
were so pre-ordained as to make money of some
sort an almost indispensable instrument of society,
and to make the invention of it a comparatively
easy task to the human mind, still, we can go back
in history to a time when there seems to have
been no money, and we can trace in tolerably clear
outline the gradual introduction of various forms
of money, until Pheidon, King of Argos, first
coined silver money in Greece in the first half of
the eighth century before Christ. The Homeric
poems, probably about a century older than the
time of Pheidon, make no mention of money,
though gold is several times alluded to as an article of value, and most of the words expressive
of value refer to cattle or horses or products
of agriculture, various things being mentioned in
these poems as worth so many oxen. It is plain
also from the Latin word for money, *pecunia*,
which is derived from *pecus*, a sheep, that cattle
were the earliest form of money among the Romans, as they still are money among some of the
tribes of Africa.

The word money is derived from an epithet of
uncertain meaning attached to the name of the ·
Goddess Juno. On the Capitoline Hill in Rome
was a temple dedicated to Juno Moneta, and the
Roman mint was a building annexed to this temple, and the epithet of the goddess passed over
first to the mint and then to that which was

coined there. The Romans first coined silver in
the year 269 B.C., but they had coined money of
bronze (copper and tin) for some centuries previously, and Pliny states that this bronze money
was stamped at first with the image of cattle
(*pecus*), whence its name (*pecunia*). This is an
interesting statement, because it implies that the
first pieces of coined money were regarded as the
equivalents in value of the cattle whose image
they bore. It implies that cattle were an early, if
not the very earliest standard of value ; and that
when the convenience of the metals as such a
standard first suggested itself, these were coined
or cut into such size as made the pieces represen
tative of the value of the animal whose outline
was stamped on them. Gradually was lost in the
minds of men this connection between the two,
and the bits of metal came to stand independently
in their own right as valuable things.

The earliest recorded mention of the precious
metals, in Gen. xiii. 2, confirms the precedence of
cattle as a standard of value, and, in the order
of the words, perhaps foreshadows the connection
just alluded to, and certainly implies, what is
proved by other evidence, that silver came earlier
than gold to be a standard of value ; — " And
Abram was very rich *in cattle, and in silver, and in
gold.*" The earliest recorded mention of a purchase and sale, found in Gen. xxiii., and belonging
to a time about 2000 years before Christ, throws
much clear light upon the conditions of trade in

that early time, and gives us a glimpse of the kind
of money then in use. The wife of Abraham
being dead, he bought from · Ephron a field in
Machpelah as a burying-place for her, and he
" weighed to Ephron the silver he had named in
the audience of the sons of Heth, four hundred
shekels of silver, current money with the merchant." The pieces of silver were weighed, not
counted, just as the Bank of England still weighs,
not counts, coins received. Yet the money was
" current," that is, cut for purposes of circulation
to certain ostensible weights, as the shekel, (originally a weight), yet requiring a balance to make
the exact value sure. The monuments of Egypt
and of Assyria give us pictures of such a weighing,
used in those countries from a very remote time.
The Scripture passage shows that there were in
Abraham's time " merchants " as a class. It
shows also, that, in the absence of written documents, living witnesses authenticated the facts of
trade. It was " in the audience of the sons of
Heth, before all that went in at the gate of his
city, that the field and the cave were made sure
unto Abraham for a possession."

Now, in the light of what has already been said,
it is easy to see what is the essential nature of
money. *It is a go-between. It is a standard of
comparison in values.* All values of every kind
rest back for their basis on a COMPARISON; and
some things are compared directly with each other,
and exchanged directly against each other without

any reference to any third thing as a standard of comparison; while most things are first compared with the standard, even when they are not actually exchanged against the standard, and their relations in value to other things are ascertained by means of the standard. Money itself is a valuable thing, else it could not serve as a standard in values. Something that has length (an inch) must be used as a standard of length, something that has capacity (a pint) must be used as a standard of capacity, and something that has value (a dollar) must be used as a standard of value. The value of money comes and goes under precisely the same conditions as the value of any thing else, it stands in its own right just as any other valuable thing does, and the only peculiarity of it is, that *its* value is made a means, — a standard, — of comparing together the values of all other things.

Let me simply illustrate these points; — If I have a penknife for which I have no immediate use, and my friend has a patent inkstand for which he has no immediate use, and each of us happens to desire this possession of the other, we may exchange penknife for inkstand without ever thinking of any third thing, as a dollar, with which to compare the two things. This is a case of value. The penknife is worth the inkstand, and the inkstand is worth the penknife. This is a case of what is called Barter, or direct exchange. Money plays no part whatever in such

an exchange. But such exchanges are relatively
uncommon. Almost all things are sold either
actually for money, which thus becomes an intermediate and equivalent merchandise, or at a
value *estimated* in money, which thus furnishes
the aid of its *denominations* for a transaction
which may be settled up otherwise than by the
use of money itself.

Thus ; — The stationer, thinking it likely that
I, or somebody else, will want an inkstand, and
my friend, or somebody else, will want a penknife,
buys these commodities in the market in order to
sell them again at a profit; I pay him a silver
dollar for the stand, and my friend pays him a
silver dollar for the knife ; our wants are both
supplied, as before, but this time through the
agency of money, which acts in this case as a
convenient commodity, an equivalent merchandise, a thing with which the other thing is compared and is pronounced equivalent; but if my
friend and I have reciprocal dealings with the
stationer, he furnishing us things from time to
time, and we furnishing him things other than
money from time to time, there is no need that
money pass from us to him in pay for the inkstand and penknife, at least at present, but there
is need that we know what value on account of
these two things will be reckoned against us in
the final settlement, and this can only be through
the use, not of money itself, but of the *denomina-*
tions of money. He charges us each one *dollar*

and we are bound to furnish him at some time either with an actual dollar in return or with a dollar's *worth* of something.

This example illustrates the important fact, that money as a denomination is used in thousands of cases, as in estimates, bargainings, cases of mutual indebtedness in the clearing-house and elsewhere, in which money as a commodity is not used at all, or if at all, only to pay off small balances. Whether the thing-dollar or only the denomination-dollar be used, the nature of money as involving *a comparison*, as involving *a standard*, is equally illustrated. Strictly speaking, money as such has but one function, namely, *to serve as a standard of comparison throughout the whole realm of values, to serve as a means of reducing to one common measure all values whatsoever.* Much confusion has arisen, and still exists, even among eminent writers, from not distinguishing clearly between what belongs to money as a certain valuable thing having qualities in common with all other valuable things, and what belongs to it *as money*. All money has *value* of course, else it could have no function in the realm of values, but besides value, which it has in common with ten thousand things, it has something additional and peculiar, something imparted to it by the opinion, custom, or law, of the community, and that something is just this, that it shall serve as a means of commensurating all other values with each other. It is commonly said, that money is both *a medium of exchange* and *a measure of value;* and Professor Jevons[1] has even tried to make out that there are two functions more, namely, *a standard of value,* and *a store of value.* I myself formerly endeavored to distinguish carefully the medium‑quality from the measure‑quality, as if these two were *co-ordinate;* but I am now, after much reflection, inclined to maintain that money as such has but one characteristic difference from other forms of value, namely, this *standard*-quality, to which all other values are constantly referred.

When money passes from hand to hand as a medium in exchanges, that is to say, when men sell services of all kinds for actual money received, what is it that makes the money so universally acceptable? Of course, the main reason is its *value,* that is to say, it can be used at once or at will to purchase other things with. The service has just bought the money, and now the money will buy any other service offered for sale. But other things besides money, as wheat, cloth, butter, have value as constantly in time, though not perhaps as steadily in amount, as money has; but these things, whatever they are, are not so acceptable in exchanges as money is; why not? Simply because money through the action of society in law or custom has an additional attribute, which these other forms of value lack, namely, the attribute of being a *standard.* This additional attribute

---

[1] Money and the Mechanism of Exchange, p. 13.

is not what imparts its *value* to money, since an ounce of uncoined gold is *worth* within a very small fraction as much as an ounce of gold money, but it makes the money a far more convenient instru-ment to purchase with, inasmuch as money, having now the attribute of making all other values easily commensurable with itself, becomes at once some thing which everybody is willing to receive, be-cause everybody knows in general what its power will be to purchase all other things. In other words, money becomes a medium of exchange just because it has become a measure of values; and there are not in reality two functions of money, still less four, but only *one*.

When the United States at one of its mints coins a piece of gold weighing $25\frac{4}{5}$ grains troy, of which 23.22 grains are pure gold, and calls that coin a " dollar," and makes the " dollar " the unit of accounts, and makes the coin a legal tender for debts to the amount of a " dollar," it transforms a bit of bullion into a piece of money. What has really been done? The mint has *not* imparted its *value* to the gold piece, because the bullion was worth substantially as much as the coin now is, and the United States does the coining absolutely for nothing, but it *has* imparted a most important attribute to the gold piece, by virtue of which its value becomes a legal measure of the value of every salable thing in the country, and by virtue of which, *being such a measure*, it becomes accept-able to the extent of its value in every pecuniary transaction in the land. This view seems to me to simplify the subject of Money very much, and I am confident that it will be found to be scientifically correct, and we shall have many means of testing its accuracy as we proceed.

I cannot at all see my way clear to agree with Mr. Macleod, who is able however to fortify his opinion by the great name of Bastiat, and who is himself an economist of the first rank, when he affirms[1] that money is a simple representative of Debt. " The quantity of money in any country represents the amount of Debt which there would be if there was no money ; and consequently, where there is no debt there can be no money." The unfortunate use by some countries of a paper-money, which is indeed a form of debt, gives some plausibility to the notion that money is a representative of debt; and perhaps the fact, that money is frequently used to pay debts previously contracted, and that debts are usually contracted in the terms of money, gives some additional plausibility to this view ; but as Mr. Macleod himself goes on to say, that " no substance possesses so many advantages as a metal for money," and that " all civilized nations therefore have agreed to adopt a metal as money, and of metals, gold, silver and copper have been chiefly used," I do not see how he can consistently hold that a gold dollar, or a gold sovereign, whose value is in no sense due to the process of coining, whose value is

[1] Elements of Banking. London, 1576.

as substantive and independent as any value in the world can be, becomes through coinage and circulation a representative of debt. Instead of saying, as he does, " where there is no debt there can be no money," I should confidently say, where all transactions are settled in solid money there can be no debt.

Gold and silver money are an independent and equivalent merchandise, made indeed by coinage a measure of the value of all other merchandise, but not losing through coinage their own quality as merchandise, only taking on by means of coinage an additional quality fitting them to be a standard of value ; paper-money is strictly nothing but *a promise to pay* the merchandise (gold or silver) which the proper authority has coined as the standard money of the land, and which alone furnishes the denominations in which even the paper-money and all other credit-obligations are reckoned ; so that money is always either an equivalent merchandise, or a promise to pay it. Paper-money certainly represents a debt, but gold and silver money represent nothing but themselves, only the national stamp on them makes them and their denominations a convenient n eas- ure of all other values.

What is a dollar? Practically since the year 1834 a dollar has been a metal compound, consisting of nine parts pure gold and one part a hardening alloy, and weighing 25⅘ grains troy. There is no mys- tery about it. That is a dollar. It is a substantive thing, visible, tangible, ponderable, and valuable. But when the law makes just that thing *a dollar*, it establishes the *value* of that as the unit of all other values, and of course at the same time constitutes the denomination-dollar as a kind of language through which values may express themselves in estimates, bargainings, and so on. It is competent for Congress to say that the dollar hereafter shall consist of 2) grains of gold nine-tenths fine; but the effect of that would be to reduce the unit of value 23 per cent, or in other words, to raise the value of all things measured by the new dollar 23 per cent.

Congress indeed tried from the beginning, and again in 1878, to make another *kind* of dollar out of silver; but these attempts ceased in 1853, and it is yet too soon to judge how the renewed attempt of 1878 will issue; but it is strictly true to say, that between 1834 and 1880, with exceptions too trifling to disturb the point now in hand, the *standard*-dollar of the United States was the gold dollar just described. To try to make a double standard at all, is doubtless very unwise ; and it is exceedingly unwise for any government, unless in view of imperative public reasons, to change the standard to which the people have been accustomed, for the same reason that it is unwise, except as before, to change the standard of weights and measures. After each change in one or the other, every thing has to be adjusted to a new unit

It is indeed very desirable that there should be an international and universal system of coinage, that is to say, that the money of one country, having been so minted as to bear simple ratios to the coins of other commercial countries, may circulate freely throughout the world. The French franc-system has already gained great prevalence in Europe and parts of Asia, and if our gold dollar were lowered 3.5 per cent, and the English sovereign also lowered 0.83 per cent, very simple relations would obtain between francs, dollars and sovereigns; — 25 francs would just equal 5 dollars, and each would just equal 1 sovereign; or, 1 dollar would equal 5 francs, and each equal 4 shillings. The unification of French, English, and American money in this or any other way would doubtless be followed by the action of all other commercial countries bringing *their* money into harmony with these unified coins; and to bring about such a grand result as this would justify any country in changing its unit of value. This is done simply by changing the *weight* of pure gold or silver in the unit coin. As the value of coined money depends on the weight of pure metal in it, the relations in value of different coins depend on their respective weights; for example, there are 113.001 grains troy of pure gold in an English sovereign, and 23.22 grains in an American dollar, accordingly, one sovereign is worth $4.8665, and by recent law of Congress the two are made equivalent. Thus we see what a dollar is, what a sovereign is, what is any other unit of value: it is a certain weight of a precious metal authenticated by the government through the process of coinage as of such and such weight and fineness.

What is a dollar-bill? It is nothing in the world but a *promise to pay* the dollar just described. It may be issued by a bank, or it may be issued by a government, it is a promise still — nothing but a promise. Here comes in Mr. Macleod's idea that money represents a debt. Paper money *does* represent a debt. A dollar-bill is a *sign* that the issuer owes the bearer one dollar. If the issuer redeem his bill with a gold dollar, as he is bound in terms and in honor to do, the debt is paid, the transaction is completed; while the holder of the gold dollar holds no debt against anybody, nobody is obliged to take his dollar, the government that coined it has nothing to do with it any more, it is a piece of ultimate property, it is the unit of value, not a sign but the thing signified, not a debt but a quittance. A dollar-bill is a piece of credit-paper that goes by faith: a coin-dollar is a piece of metal, authenticated indeed as to weight and fineness by the stamp of government, and thus made a convenient standard of value, but otherwise requiring no faith in anybody, — it goes by sight. Paper-money is promise, coin-money is payment. This distinction is of great importance, and, if clearly seen and firmly held to, will guide my readers safely through all the mazes of what is called the "currency discussion."

Bank-bills will be thoroughly discussed in the coming chapter on Credit, and I will here only call attention to the incongruity of ever making a mere promise to pay a legal tender for debts. Parliament indeed makes the bills of the Bank of England legal tender for debts within the realm, *but only so long as the bank redeems them in coin on demand*, which condition removes of course the chief objection to such legislation; and Congress in 1862 made the Treasury notes, commonly called greenbacks, legal tender for all debts within the United States except interest on the public debt and the taxes levied by the tariff. These notes are still legal tender, though their value has varied in this interval as compared with gold from 35 cents to just one hundred cents to the dollar. A promise should always rest on the free faith of the receiver in the good faith of the issuer; and, therefore, to *compel* people to accept a *promise* is a moral and monstrous incongruity. To continue to give in this manner a forced circulation to mere promises to pay which were so long unfulfilled and depreciated has at once weakened the discredit, disarranged the industries, and lowered the morals of the people of the United States.

Common language recognizes alike as money these national coins of gold and silver and these paper promises to pay them, — both those issued by banks and those issued by government for the purpose of furnishing a circulating medium ; and science, while insisting on the fundamental distinction already made, has no motive to restrict the current meaning of the word money. Money, then, may be defined to be *that value which law, or usage equivalent to law, requires creditors to accept in payment of debts.* The question What is money? and the question What is the best money? are quite distinct questions, and while we shall try to answer both questions fully in their place, we will for the present, for the sake of simplicity and the clearer understanding of some points, dismiss all thoughts of paper-money, and consider that money consists only of gold and silver coins. In doing this, we will not forget that a great many other things besides gold and silver have been used as money at one time or another. We have already seen that the sole characteristic of money as such is that it serves as a standard value with which to compare all other values, and as such a standard — value being what it is — it possesses of course a kind of *generalized* purchasing-power, which fits it to pass from hand to hand as a medium in ordinary exchanges. A good many different things have served these purposes in different ages and countries, and we will notice a few of them, more as a matter of curiosity than as necessary in order to understand the nature and functions of money as such.

Before Pheidon coined silver in Greece, copper skewers were used in that country as money, of which six were equal to a drachm, which was both a coin and a weight, the coin worth about 17 cents of our money — nearly the same as a Roman *dena-rius* — and the weight about 66 grains avoirdu-pois; — the word drachm being derived from δράγμα, *a handful*, and the sixth part of it, called an *obol* from the Greek word meaning *a spit*, was also both a coin and a weight, which makes it evident that these skewers were used in connec-tion with roasting meat, and that one of them was both a unit of value and of weight. Cattle have been employed as money among pastoral people in almost all periods of the world, and are still em-ployed for this purpose in Africa. Cowry shells are used in the East Indies and also in Africa in place of small coins, and have sometimes been imported into England from India to be exported in trade with the coast of Africa : these count in Bengal at about 3200 to a rupee (46 cents).

The New England Indians used as money belts of beads, the white ones made out of the ends of periwinkle shells and the black ones from the black parts of clam shells, of which 360 made a belt or string of *wampum*, as they called it, the black beads being counted worth twice as much as the white ones ; and the English colonists accepted the wampum in their exchanges with the Indians, regarding a string of white as equivalent to 5 shillings and a string of black to 10 shillings, and afterwards made it a legal tender for small sums among themselves, and even counterfeited it.

The Carthaginians had a kind of leather money, which may have originally enclosed bits of the precious metals, but which came to circulate as bits of leather only; and several times in Europe, in the middle ages and even since, kings have resorted to the issue of leather money, of which there are specimens in the British Museum.

According to the travellers Polo, China had in the 13th century a money made from the middle bark of the mulberry-tree, cut into round pieces and stamped with the image of the sovereign, which money it was death to counterfeit or to refuse to take in any part of the empire. Cakes of tea have passed as money in India, and elsewhere; and it is said, that at the great annual fair at Novgorod in Russia, the price of tea has first to be determined before the prices of other commodities can be settled upon, since that is a kind of standard of values in that great mart. Bullets once passed in Massachusetts at a farthing apiece, and were legal tender for debts of less than one shilling. Salt has been current money in Abyssinia; codfish in Iceland and Newfoundland; tobacco in Virginia; beaver-skins in New Netherlands; pieces of silk in China; nails in Scotland, according to Adam Smith, which is a forcible reminder of the old Greek skewers; iron was money in Sparta; leaden money was known to the ancients, and is still current in the Burman empire; the earliest coins proper were undoubtedly of bronze, a mixture of copper and tin, and Sicilian, Roman, and old British coins of tin alone are known to have been struck; and Herodotus makes the statement, that the Lydians of Asia Minor were the first to make a coinage of a mixture of gold and silver, called *electrum*, very ancient specimens of which are still existing.[1]

Indeed, such is the necessity of some standard of value in order that exchanges may reach any considerable development, that we shall not be surprised to learn that many other things besides these mentioned have served in primitive states of society as such a standard. Experience, however, as civilization has advanced, has already driven the nations for the most part to drop these tentative and factitious standards in favor of the precious metals as the best material for money. Gold and silver coins are now acceptable in almost all parts of the known world; and in many parts of the world nothing else is acceptable as money; so that, experience has demonstrated in their almost universal adoption the superiority of these metals over all other forms of money; and we shall be able to give, further on, some excellent reasons why gold and silver furnish the best money.

Assuming now, for the present, that coins of these metals are the only money, this is the place to see exactly what the uses of money are. These uses are two; and they both spring out of the one characteristic of money as the chosen standard

[1] See comments on this passage in Macleod's Economics, vol I. 367

with which all current values are compared. Gov‧ ernments usually appoint the standard, that is, determine by law the weight and fineness of that coin whose denomination furnishes the unit of reckoning; but even if governments failed to do this, the people would not fail to establish and maintain a standard for themselves. Such a standard being chosen in a gold coin called a dollar, and these dollars being minted freely for the convenience of the people, my readers will see clearly how they come to have their first use as money by becoming *a medium in exchanges*. A true medium always stands between two other things and serves to relate them to each other. Such a medium is money.

Having been appointed as a standard for values, a person having any thing to sell immediately compares his product with the standard, determines in his own mind how many multiples or sub-multiples of the standard his product will bring, that is to say, how many dollars or cents it is in his judgment worth, and offers his product for sale to anybody who will give him his price. *Price is the value of any thing expressed in money.* It is not certain that anybody will be found who will give him that exact sum ; because, as we have seen, it takes two to make a bargain ; but the seller is willing to sell his product for as much of the standard as he can get, because, being the *standard*, he knows that other people are also comparing their products with that, and that, if he possesses the standard, they will be

willing to sell their products for his money on precisely the same principles as he is now willing to
sell his product for their money. It is in this way
that money becomes a medium of exchange. It is
a standard first, and a medium afterwards; not a
medium first, and a standard afterwards. Or, as I
would rather put it, it becomes a medium in virtue
of being first a standard. The use of the thing
waits on the nature of the thing: the function of
the thing follows the constitution of the thing.

Now, the effect on exchanges of having a medium of exchange is simply marvellous. It multiplies exchanges indefinitely on every hand, because no man is obliged to wait before he sells his
product till he can find somebody who both wants
this product and has to sell the precise product which
the first man wants, he sells at once for money to
any man who but wants his product, assured that
with this medium in his pocket he can buy the
products which he wants at his own convenience.
While seeming at first sight to complicate, it
really simplifies trade. It introduces a valuable
thing, — valuable in its own right, — but which
everybody wants, not for its own sake, but because
it will purchase from everybody what each person
wants more than he wants the money. It is
gladly received, but as gladly parted with. Everybody wants to take it in, and everybody wants to
pay it out. It is good to sell for, simply because
it is good to buy with.

It affords no ultimate satisfaction to human wants,

except to the miser, who, as his name indicates, is a *miserable* being, but it is a medium through which those wants are really satisfied. It brings buyers and sellers together commercially, no matter how far separated they may be locally. If there be a market for any product anywhere on the face of the earth, there will be some middleman who will buy that product for money, and, transporting it, it may be to the antipodes, will sell it again either for more money, or for some product that he wants himself for an ultimate satisfaction, or for some product, which, being transported back, will sell again for more money than that originally given. In trade, there is, or ought to be, no dividing lines, no repelling barriers, no hostile nationalities, no local prejudices, no such differing media of exchanges, as shall prevent a legitimate product produced anywhere from finding open its appropriate market anywhere else. Money should be, and largely is, a universal medium the world over. Wherever it is, it draws products towards itself in the way of exchange, and in turn, products draw it out again in the way of further exchange. It is, in some respects, like the gravitation of the earth in relation to that of the moon: — it draws and is drawn in turn.

Especially does such a medium, being divisible into small parts without loss, draw out from society a multitude of small services, which otherwise would certainly not be rendered at all. Were it not for the attractive power of the pennies, for example, newspapers and flowers and apples and many other such things would not be sold as they are upon railroad trains. A medium of exchange in which everybody has confidence, minted in such sums as meet the public convenience, facilitates greatly exchanges which would perhaps take place any way, and calls out multitudes of exchanges which otherwise would not take place at all. David Hume describes money as the grease which makes the wheel of exchange turn easier; which is right so far as it goes; but money does more than make a pre-existing wheel revolve easy; it enlarges the circumference of the wheel itself, multiplies the spokes, broadens the rim, and strengthens the hub.

It must be borne in mind, however, great as is the power and the benefit of money as a medium, that it is still only a *medium*, — a means to an end, — and that what may be called the *real* exchanges of society are in services which minister to an ultimate satisfaction. What people really and ultimately want is not money, but food, clothing, homes, farms, factories, utensils, furniture, books, education for their children, various means of display, and innumerable other means of personal gratification. The possession of these is mediated by money, but the aggregate value of these in any country by far surpasses the aggregate value of all the money there.

According to the Census of 1870, the real and **personal** property in the United States amounted to $30,000,000,000 in that year, while the aggregate of money in that year was certainly less than $800,000,000. This would indicate a ratio of property to money of 40 to 1. Unfortunately, much of that money was paper-money depreciated; unfortunately, also, the inflation of prices that always accompanies a depreciated money made the aggregate of national values in that year larger than it would otherwise have been given. We must remember that money is a *medium*, and, though vastly important as such, is little in amount relatively to the value of that which it helps to circulate. The right quantity of money in any country is a matter that will take care of itself without any need of anxiety on the part of anybody. There is a natural demand for money for these purposes of exchange, and gold and silver enough to answer these purposes are perfectly sure to come into and stay in any country without any decree or legislation. The supply is sure to wait on the demand. Let the mint of the country coin for all parties bringing bullion, and there will be just money enough and no more. If perchance too much be coined, the excess will flow off to other countries in trade, and if perchance too little, bullion will be sure to be knocking before long at the doors of the mint. This is one of the things that take care of themselves perfectly. No government needs to lay awake of nights over the matter of sufficiency of money, provided only they allow no other than gold and silver money within their jurisdiction.

We have now seen that money is a tool of exchange, and as this particular tool is made of gold and silver, of course it will cost something to maintain and repair it. Gold and silver coins will wear out. But they do not wear out so fast as many people seem to think. Careful calculations in the Report of the Director of the Mint in 1862 indicate that such coins in active circulation lose on the average $\frac{1}{2400}$ of their weight each year. Considering how perfectly they do their work, considering how beautiful they are as works of art, considering that it would take 2400 years to wear them all out, and considering the difficulty not to say impossibility of finding any adequate substitutes, we may reasonably conclude that gold and silver coins are a cheap and durable instrument. Their first cost is considerable: so is the cost of any first-class machine. It costs something additional to keep them up to full weight and beauty : so also it does to keep in good repair and efficiency the machinery in a mill. No argument is good for the displacement of gold and silver coins by what is deemed a less costly money, which will not equally apply for the displacement of the good machinery of a factory by cheaper and less efficient substitutes.

This first function of money, namely, to serve as a *medium* in exchanges of all kinds, is a delicate and most responsible function, demanding for the instrument that performs it the complete confidence of everybody year in and year out; and the function cannot be satisfactorily performed except by a tool that costs something. To mediate *values* well requires something highly and steadily *valuable*. With reference to a given volume of business, it is cheaper for a country to keep a smaller stock of coins in a more rapid circulation than a larger stock moving more sluggishly, for the same reason that it is cheaper with reference to a given amount of work to keep any tool employed constantly than occasionally, namely, the interest on the outlay is thus soonest secured.

For example, $1,000,000 changing hands five times a day will do the work in exchange of $5,000,000 changing hands but once a day. But the interest on the two sums for the day is in the ratio of 5 to 1. It is true that the rapidly circulated coins are abraded faster than the sluggish ones, but this will not begin to balance the loss of interest. The quantity of coin needed to make the exchanges will adjust itself to the habits of the people and to the conditions of business in any country; and it is well for individuals and corporations to remember, that, the more rapidly they circulate the coin that comes into their possession consistently with the uses to which they have determined to put it, the better for everybody with whom they deal, and the cheaper for the country furnishing the coin. He doubly pays who quickly pays. Quick payments all around imply relatively small stocks of coin and healthful conditions of business.

The second function of money, — both functions resulting alike from the nature of money as an appointed standard of value, — is to serve as a *measure of value* in cases in which no money as a medium is required to pass. Considering that value is always determined by an exchange, the *standard* of value must necessarily be a medium, that is, something actually exchangeable against other things; and it is equally necessary that the *name* or *denomination* of this standard should come to be used in the minds of men as a general measure of values in future contracts, credits of all kinds, calculations and bargainings.

To illustrate by matters mainly parallel; — Many years ago, Edward Troughton[1] of London, a mathematical-instrument maker, took great pains to obtain and authenticate a standard inch, which has ever since been called " Troughton's inch; " and such was the great reputation of the man and his work, that that inch was greatly sought after by English speaking peoples as a means to correct and verify their measures of length. It became a standard inch. As such, it must offer itself as a tangible and measurable thing to all who wished to ascertain its exact length and use that length thereafter as a standard. This having been fre-

---

[1] Graduates of Williams College who had the privilege of attending the lectures of the late Professor Hopkins on Phys.cs, will recognize my indebtedness to him for this illustration.

quently done, and a copy of that inch being generally diffused for purposes of comparison, the
denomination-inch derived from that came to be
usable in the minds of men as an ideal measure of
length. It is still so used. Men talk about
inches, and calculate by inches, in thousands of
cases in which no actual inch is used as a measure.
Still, in every case of doubt, dispute, or difficulty,
recourse is had to the actual inch. The ideal inch
is kept steady in the minds of men by frequent
reference to the outward and actual standard.

Just so with dollars and cents. As a standard
of value, the dollar must be an actual medium
passing from hand to hand in exchanges, but in
so passing its denomination impresses itself on
the minds of men as an ideal measure of values,
which they can use, and which they constantly do
use, without handling the dollar itself. But, as
before, there needs to be a check on the conception and use of ideal dollars, by a constant recurrence to palpable, actual thing-dollars. The
denomination only comes into existence in connection with the use of the thing, cannot possibly
exist independently of it, and needs constantly to
be reduced to it (as it were by actual contact) in
order to be useful as a measure.

The French writer Montesquieu asserted that
there was in use among the inhabitants of the coast
of Africa in the last century what he called "an
ideal money," "a sign of value without money,"
the unit of which was called the *macoute*, which

was subdivided also into ideal tenths called pieces. This statement was startling, as implying a denomination without the thing denominated, as implying a standard of value which had no basis in a valuable thing. It was discovered, however, afterwards, that this money of account had its origin, just as we should suppose it must have had, in an actual *macoute*, namely, a piece of stuff, a fabric, which they had used first as a standard of value, and afterwards its name as a money of account. It may be taken as settled, that, in order to have and maintain the name-dollar, we must first have and maintain the thing-dollar. · Moreover, it is important to observe, that, when the thing-dollar is changed, there is no corresponding change in the *name* by which we denote it. We call it a dollar still.

In 1834, our gold dollar was reduced 4.45 per cent in weight, and 1.81 per cent in fineness, but it was still called a dollar just the same. Only, as the new dollar was now the standard, and was considerably less valuable than the old one, the minds of the people became gradually accustomed to associate the word *dollar* with a lessened purchasing power; the *measure* in men's minds slowly followed the fortunes of the now lighter coin, and became lessened, although the same name attached to the coin; so far forth as the change in the coin was concerned, all prices were a little higher than before, and the denomination-dollar meant a little less — measured a little less —

in men's minds than before. This is one of the most delicate points in Political Economy, namely, that a word spelled and sounded as before comes silently to mean more or less, according as the *value* of that whose name the word is becomes more or less. The *value* changes first, the *measure* changes next, and the *denomination* does not change at all.

It is a very important inference from this, that the only way to keep the *measure* of values steady is to keep that *thing* steady, whose denomination furnishes the measure. There has been no change in our gold dollar since 1834; if there had been no other legal-tender dollar in this interval of now about forty years, we should have had as steady a measure of value in this country as it is possible in the nature of things to have; and there is no measure used among men any thing like so important to be maintained as uniform as possible year in and year out as the measure of value; since contracts are made in it, annuities are measured by it, debts are incurred in the light of it, bequests are made in the terms of it, expectations are built on it, and all business breathes through it. Any change in it, making it measure more or less, involves an inevitable loss to many persons, involves a shock to business confidence and a shattering of many hopes. The measure *inch* is important to human welfare, and so is the measure *pint* and the measure *pound*, yet all these combined are less vital to the interests of men than the measure *dollar.* To maintain this measure uniform should be one of the first aims of Society; since money is, as Mr. Carey has well called it, the instrument of association, and its denominations accordingly should mean the same from January to December, from one decade to another.

Unfortunately, legislation, which has been so often in manifold ways a foe to exchanges, has proved their greatest foe precisely at this point. For example, in 1862, the Congress of the United States enacted a law, that its own paper promises to pay gold dollars should pass in lieu of the dollars themselves, and should be a *legal-tender* for all debts public and private, except tariff-duties and public debt interest. This law, substituting the shadow for the substance, the sign for the thing signified, the promise to pay a dollar for the dollar itself, changed for many purposes of domestic trade and calculation the old measure of value. The real dollars of course abandoned in scorn the circulation in which they were legally regarded as of no more consequence than the unfulfilled promises to pay them. With a new *medium*, there came in of course a new *measure*, if that can properly be called a measure, which varies from day to day and from month to month. The gold dollar, nevertheless, continued to be the standard, the unit, with which the variations of the greenbacks were compared from day to day. For more than sixteen years the value of the greenback dollar as thus compared with the gold dollar varied with almost every business day and often also on the same day. What would be said of a measure of length or capacity, — a yardstick or a quart cup, — which varied like that?

The variations from day to day, however, were little in comparison with the changes from year to year. The first greenbacks were issued in the spring of 1862, and before that year was out they were worth (October) only 72 cents in gold. In the course of the next year, their value zigzagged between the two extremes of 80 and 58 cents in gold. During 1864, they were worth in January 65, in July 35, and in December 43 cents in gold. During the succeeding years, their value slowly rose on the whole, — falling and rising, — till it reached 89 cents in 1875, 94 cents in January, 1877, 98 cents in January, 1878, and 100 cents in the last days of that year. The bill "to provide for the resumption of specie payments" was signed by President Grant Jan. 14, 1875, and was to become, and did become, operative Jan. 1, 1879.[1]

Now, several things are to be observed in the light of the facts just narrated: (1) That this paper medium, having driven gold and silver out of the common circulation in accordance with a universal law soon to be explained, and notwithstanding it was constantly compared for certain purposes with the gold dollar still used for tariff-

[1] I have used for these figures the excellent table in Bowen's Political Economy, and Mr. Editor Richardson's little pamphlet, "Paper Money."

dues and public-debt interest, and notwithstanding it varied in actual value (assuming gold to be the standard) from 35 cents to 100 in every dollar, *was* CALLED *a dollar all the time*, and consequently, the dollar-measure, so far as there was one in ordinary business, varied with the varying purchasing-power of the dollar-bill. What a *measure* that was for a commercial people for sixteen years! An india-rubber yardstick for measuring cloth is a suitable symbol for it. Rational calculations in business became impossible. (2) That, as a result of this uncertain money and variable measure of values, a gigantic commercial crisis dragged its slow length along for five years between 1873 and 1879; failures were innumerable, losses uncountable, and business despondency well-nigh universal. There can be no question, though from the nature of the case it cannot be demonstrated, that the losses. of property resulting directly and indirectly from the adoption of this false system of a paper legal-tender were a hundred-fold greater than all the expense would have been in securing and maintaining an honest dollar during all those years. The country was exporting in all those years raw gold and silver enough to keep up to the brim a reservoir of gold and silver coin. (3) That the making a paper-money *legal-tender* has little or no effect either way upon their value in the market. While they were full legal-tender for debts (except in two cases) these greenbacks depreciated 65 per cent. Some notes of the government "not bearing interest, but payable on demand," issued in 1861, remained at par, because they were *redeemable*, though not originally a legal tender. Both were alike promises-to-pay; but the redeemable non-legal-tenders kept up, while the irredeemable legal-tenders went down. Some convenience, indeed, is added to a paper money by making it a legal-tender for debts, but the very making it legal-tender implies some doubt on the part of the government of the validity of its own promises. If the government is going to *fulfil* them according to their tenor, what need to *compel* people to take them? So that this artificial quality added to a paper-promise does not seem to add to its *value*. (4) That the disuse of the gold dollar in ordinary payments in consequence of the use of the cheaper paper dollar probably made the gold itself cheaper than it otherwise would have been, inasmuch as there was a less *demand* for gold, and a lessened demand for any thing (other things being equal) always lessens the *value* of that thing. If this were so, then the daily comparison of the greenback with the gold dollar did not indicate fully what the depreciation of the paper would have been had the gold still circulated, — in other words, gold itself was cheaper than was natural, and so the premium on gold as compared with paper money was less than the average inflation of other prices. That this *was* so, seems to be proved by the regular exportation of the annual product of the mines during those sixteen years, and also of a considerable portion of the stock of coin had in hand in 1862. Still, while it is not claimed that gold under *any* circumstances is an absolute standard of value, which is a contradiction in terms and an impossibility in fact, but only that it is the best attainable standard, and better when the sole legal-tender and a part at least of the current money, the gold dollar, though practically demonetized and discarded, was the only accessible standard of comparison during this interval of the destruction of natural values, and doubtless gave us results when compared with the paper at least approximately accurate.

Perhaps it ought also to be noticed in this connection, that, since gold was in demand as a medium during those sixteen years for two limited purposes only, namely, by merchants in order to pay their tariff-dues, and by the National government, and also at least by one State government, — that of Massachusetts, — in order to pay the interest on their bonds, and became in consequence more than ordinarily a mere commodity; the variations in the daily quotations may sometimes have been owing to the greater or less difficulty than usual in getting gold for that day. In such cases " *corners* " are easily made.

We arc now in position to entertain the proposition *that gold and silver constitute the best money.*

1. The first and main reason for the truth of this proposition is, that these metals have been found by experience to be less subject to fluctuations in their value than any other articles known

Since money is the standard of value, it follows that that which is to serve as money must be both *valuable* and as little as possible subject to *variations* in value. Gold and silver meet this essential test better than any thing else. Many other things have been tried, as we have seen, but these have all with one exception, namely, paper-promises, been long ago discarded by all the more civilized nations in favor of gold and silver. Sagacity, which early lighted on these metals as money, has been confirmed by experience, which has steadily and increasingly held on to them as money; and it has been the perception on the part of the most enlightened minds, that these metals maintain their *value* steadier than any thing else, that has kept them, and is likely to keep them, the money of the world.

It is true, that silver has experienced during and since 1876 a remarkable decline in value, and that it has been subject heretofore to some considerable variations, particularly after the discovery and conquest of the silver mines of the new world by the Spaniards, and that the perception of this, together with the undoubted difficulty of maintaining a double standard consisting of gold and silver both, has led some of the leading nations, as England, Germany, and the United States, to make gold alone the standard, and use silver only for subsidiary coins; still, after all, it remains true that silver, next to gold, constitutes the best money, and that gold and silver together in right adjustments constitute an almost ideal and perfect money. In respect to the present decline of silver, it must be said, that the average price in gold for the 30 years prior to 1876 was nearly 60 pence an ounce in the London market; that in the year named it experienced a sudden fall, and went down for a few days to the neighborhood of 46½ pence; that it has since been slowly rallying, and now stands at about 52 pence; that the only explanation of this great decline is the present and prospective fertility of the silver mines in the western parts of the United States, and the fact that Germany, having adopted the sole standard of gold, seemed to menace the silver market with the sale of her old silver; and that no reasons are known why the value of silver as measured in gold may not be hereafter as *steady* as it has been heretofore, though there seem to be some reasons in the superior productiveness of silver mines and in the abandonment of the double standard by some of the nations why silver may rule at a lower *value* in gold than heretofore.

Indeed, silver has already pretty steadily, though on the whole very slowly, declined in its power to purchase gold from the earliest notices of their comparative value till the present time. Livy mentions that their relative value was 1 to 10 about 189 B.C.; Suetonius says that Julius Cæsar on one occasion exchanged the two at 1 to 9; under the early Roman emperors it was 1 to 12, and from Constantine to Justinian about 1 to 14   In Greece, it was much the same, since Herodotus mentions it as 1 to 13, in his day, which was the fifth century before Christ, though Plato, a little later, calls it 1 to 12. In England, before the discovery of America, it was about 1 to 10; after that discovery and its consequences, silver declined till in 1717 the last legal rating of the two put them at 1 to 15⅕; and in 1816, the double standard was abandoned, silver was practically demonetized by debasing the coins in weight, and since then has only been legal-tender to the amount of 40 shillings.

In the United States, when the mint was first established in 1792, the legal rate of exchange for the two metals was fixed at 1 to 15, which proved an under-valuation of gold, and tended to drive the gold coins abroad; in 1834, this difficulty was sought to be remedied by a new legal valuation which made the rate 1 to 16, and this went too far the other way, and led to the exportation of silver coins; and in 1853, the double standard was abandoned by the United States also. Still, silver held its own in the market, and even for a while gained upon gold, standing in 1859 at 1 to 15⅓, since which time silver has grown cheaper, standing much of the time since 1876 at about 1 to 18. Notwithstanding these variations as towards each other, and consequently as towards all other salable things, gold and silver have been in the past the steadiest in their value of any articles known among men, and are likely to continue so in the time to come, and we are able to give some good reasons for this.

(1.) The demand for these metals is very steady. They are wanted for two general purposes, first, for use as money, and second, for use in the arts. Probably not far from one half of the aggregate of these metals in the world is in the form of money, and the other half in the form of plate, utensils, art-works, and ornaments. It makes no difference, so far as value is concerned, for what purpose any object is desired; and the demand for these metals for use in the arts and for purposes of ostentation contributes to the steadiness of their value just as much as the demand for them as money; and the result of this demand has this additional advantage, that there is always at hand in the form of plate a reservoir from which a chance chasm in the coin may be replenished, or an extra demand for it met. As a parallel case, barley is steadier in its value than it otherwise would be because it is in demand for food and also for malting purposes. It is the combined demand for all uses that helps to give any thing its value; and accordingly, it is fortunate for the interests of gold and silver as money, that there is a constant and well-nigh universal demand for them in the useful arts and for purposes of luxury. Since the value does not depend on one use but on many uses, an ounce of bullion of standard fineness destined for the smelting-pot of the artisan is worth within a trifle as much as an ounce of coined money.

The Bank of England is obliged by law to buy all bullion and foreign coins of standard fineness offered to it at £3 17s. 9d. per ounce, which, when coined, only make £3 17s. 10½d.— a difference of three halfpence. If, in the progress of civilization, less gold and silver should be desired for purposes of ostentation, more doubtless will be wanted in the useful arts, and much (perhaps more than at present) in the form of money, so that there is a prospect of a steady demand for them in the future, as there has been in the past, and this steady demand is one condition of a steady value, and a steady value is the grand condition of a good money.

(2.) The cost of production of these metals is very uniform. Correspondent to a steady demand there is a steady supply under circumstances giving a pretty uniform cost of production the world over. Nature herself has indicated, in a manner not to be mistaken, her intention that these metals should be the money of the nations. She has scattered them almost all over the earth, not much on the surface where they can be gathered without difficulty, but in the rocks which require to be crushed before they will yield their treasures. There were surface washings in California from the rocks already disintegrated by nature, but these were soon exhausted; special inventions have facilitated mining as well as other branches of industry; some mines are richer by nature or better located than others; yet, on the whole, the obstacles are pretty much the same everywhere — the cost of production is remarkably uniform. If the ores become richer, they are apt to be deeper down in the bowels of the earth. Water becomes an enemy, as well as gravitation. Sentinels of some sort guard faithfully their Golden Fleece.

Sometimes it becomes more profitable to work over again the slag of former ages through improved modern methods than to make fresh incursions into the rock, as a French company is now working in the once-used material of the silver mines of Laurium in Greece — those mines to which Xenophon gave his attention in the earliest known treatise on Political Economy. There is an illusion in the minds of some men, as if it were possible for many to get rich suddenly by mining, through overlooking the fact that the value of gold and silver depends on desires and efforts just like every other value. If men should find a mountain of gold, they would also find that its value would decline in some proportion to the now greater ease of obtaining it. As it is, the cost of production is large and steady, and this is the second condition of a steady value.

(3.) The great quantity of these metals is favorable to their steady value. The accumulations of ages are so vast, that they receive the annual tribute from the mines, much as the ocean receives the waters of the rivers, without sensible increase of its volume, and part with the annual loss by abrasion and shipwreck, as the sea yields

its waters to evaporation, without sensible diminution of volume. The yearly supply and the yearly
waste are small in comparison with the whole mass;
and therefore the relation of the whole mass to
the uses of the world, as well as the purchasing-
power of any given portion, remain comparatively
steady. Quantity is not an element in *value*
strictly so called, but, in connection with durability, it *is* an element in *steadiness* of value.
Slight changes scarcely affect a great mass of any
thing so imperishable as gold and silver. The
mountain streams are indeed washing down the
sides of Greylock, in plain sight from my window
at this moment, but Greylock looms as high and
stands as firm as when the eye of the first white
man rested on it. It is probable that production
at the mines might cease altogether for a little
interval without very sensibly enhancing throughout the commercial world the value of gold; as it
is certain, from experience, that a production
largely augmented only gradually diminishes its
value.

The mass of the precious metals has been aptly
compared to the heavy balance-wheel in mechan-
ics, which preserves an equable and working condition of the machinery under any sudden increase
of the power, and even when the power is for a
moment withdrawn. So far as the annual production from the mines exceeds the yearly waste,
a natural and beautiful provision is made for an
increased demand for use in currency and in the

arts, without much disturbing the previous relation of supply and demand. Perishable things,
like apples, lose their value rapidly under an
abundant supply, because they must be used soon
or never: durable things, like silver and gold,
especially when they exist in great mass and
under a steady demand, hold their value steadily
amid temporary changes, and thus furnish another
condition of a good money.

(4.) The fluency of these metals is favorable to
a steady value. They have great value in small
compass. They can be carried easily from place
to place without any loss. They are in strong
demand almost everywhere in the world. Whenever, from any cause, they become relatively in
excess in any country, and thus lose a portion of
their previous purchasing-power, there is an immediate motive to export them to other countries
where their power in exchange is greater, and
thus the equilibrium tends to restore itself. There
is both a private and a public gain in thus carrying them away, because they will buy more abroad
than at home, and because their export helps
maintain at home and abroad their own steady
value, which is a great *public* gain. Formerly, the
nations were so foolish as to prohibit the export of
gold and silver. Cicero tells us, that this was
done at Rome: — " The Senate solemnly decreed
both many times previously, and again when I was
consul, that gold and silver ought not to be
exported." Adam Smith tells us, that there are

acts of the old Scotch Parliament which prohibit under heavy penalties "the carrying gold and silver forth of the kingdom."

England, France, Spain, and probably every other country in Europe, did the same thing; Spain especially, which became proprietor in the sixteenth century of the mines of the new world, suffered immense losses through her prohibitions, since the precious metals, which came in in mass in treasure ships from the West, were smuggled out in detail in galleys and fishing craft. At length, England, under the powerful influence of the East India Company, which found it profitable to export silver to the East, repealed her prohibitions in 1663, and gave that Company and private traders liberty to export freely. At present, no civilized nation attempts to prevent the export or import of gold and silver; and the remnants of prejudice in this country against exporting gold are fast dying out. The gold is not given away; it is sold, and sold for more than it will bring at home; otherwise it would not be carried abroad. There is the same immediate gain in this as in other exchanges, with the great incidental advantage in addition, that such action tends to keep the value of the metals pretty uniform everywhere. Under freedom, they go and come at will. In 1850–1860, both years inclusive, the United States exported $502,789,759, coin and bullion, and during the same period imported $81,270,571, coin and bullion. These metals may be called the blood of international commerce, and there are natural arteries and veins for them to flow through ; they will go, as the blood does in the body, where they are most wanted, and will return as freely when they are wanted most at home.

It may be laid down as an axiom, that no country will export, for the sake of getting other things, those things which are more needful for its own welfare ; and there need be no fear that any nation which cultivates its own advantages under freedom will ever lack a sufficiency of gold and silver for all purposes of money. The greater the enterprise and skill, the keener the development of all peculiar and presently available resources, the more honorable and free the commercial system, the surer is any nation, whether it be a gold-bearing country or not, of securing the gold and silver which it needs. This is so, because *there* will be a good market to buy in, and they who *have* gold will resort thither to buy. Great Britain is not a gold-producing country, but London nevertheless is the bullion market of the world. The precious metals flow into and away from that market, just as the tide flows up the Thames and ebbs away again, because the business of the world centres in London, and wherever *business* is there must be *money*. Now, the fluency of gold and silver, by which they pass so easily in commerce to those places where their present value in exchange is greatest, and return as easily when the conditions are reversed, tends powerfully to keep their value

steady throughout the commercial world, and consequently to make them the best standard of
value, that is, the best money. ,   •

(5.) The durability of the precious metals is
favorable to the steady value of the money made
from them in this respect also, that the coins on
occasion may pass very rapidly round i: the circulation without much loss from abrasion, and thus
temporarily do the work in exchange, which would
otherwise require an enlargement of the mass of
money. An increased rapidity of circulation,
which coin is capable of without impairing it,
meets the temporary *extra* demands for money
without increasing the *stock* of coin, and thus
tends admirably to keep the value steady within
certain limits. If the *mass* had to be increased in
brisk times, then its *value* would decline in slack
times. When enterprises are multiplying and
exchanges are being permanently increased in
number and variety, then there must be a larger
amount of money, and this larger amount will be
secured in the ways already indicated, with perhaps slight disturbances of value; but the temporary ebbs and flows of business need have no
effect at all on the mass of metallic money, but
only on its movement, and its value consequently
is not disturbed at all. This delicate function of
faster and slower movement cannot be so well
performed by paper-money, partly because that is
rapidly worn out and requires new issues, but
mainly because there is no such confidence in mere

promises as is always and everywhere accorded to gold and silver coins. Great pains have sometimes been taken in this country to get paper-money out into circulation, and off to a distance from the place of issue, so ·that it cannot easily get back : it does not go of itself, as go and come the coins. This fifth point, though subordinate to the others, is worthy of enumeration along with them, and is another ground of the steady value of gold and silver money.

2. The second general reason why gold and silver constitute the best money is the important fact, *that governments have little to say or do about the value, quantity, or mode of circulation, of such money.* In all essential respects such money is wholly self-regulating, while its only competitor in civilized countries, namely, paper-money, is always the creature of some government, which determines the conditions of its issue, and attempts, at least, to secure the reality of its redemption. We have already seen that coins do not owe their value to the stamp of the government, since the metal in them is worth within a trifle as much before coinage as after. Coinage publicly attests the quantity and quality of the metal in the coin, and that is all. Of the value of their coins governments say nothing. They can say nothing. That depends on men's judgments, and not on edicts at all. No law of the United States can add a fraction of a cent to the value of a gold dollar. The law says, that a gold dollar shall

consist of 25⅘ grains troy of gold nine-tenths fine, the mint stamps it as of that weight and fineness, and it thereafter takes its own chance as to value. Government has done with it. It is now in the hands of the people.

If the government, however, thinks it best to maintain a double standard, that is, a silver dollar legal-tender to all amounts alongside a gold dollar equally legal-tender, then it must take upon itself to decide the relative value of the two metals each in each. Thus England said in 1717, that 1 ounce gold in her coinage should equal 15⅕ ounces silver in the same ; the United States said in 1792, that 1 ounce gold in their coinage should equal 15 ounces silver, and again in 1834, that 1 ounce gold should equal 16 ounces silver ; but no one of these edicts happened to hit the market-rate of the two each in each at the time, and the market-rate thereafter in each case did not pay any attention to the law, but adjusted itself independently under the law of supply and demand, shrewd debtors paid their debts in whichever metal happened at the time to be relatively cheaper, exporters sent abroad in balances the metal legally undervalued at home, and practical difficulties arising from these sources led both these countries, the former in 1816, and the latter in 1853, to discard the double standard. Silver coins in England are only legal-tender to the sum of 40 shillings.

In 1878, after 25 years' experience of the single standard, the United States returned to the old method through a law requiring the minting in large quantities of a silver dollar of the old weight and fineness, that is, 412½ grains, $\frac{9}{10}$ fine. This dollar contains precisely the same amount of fine silver that the American dollar has always held; namely, 371¼ grains. If any reader quick at figures will divide this sum by 23.22, the number of grains of fine gold in a gold dollar, he will find the ratio to be substantially 16 to 1, just as it was established in 1834. The law of 1878 made this silver dollar legal-tender for all debts, public and private; but the fall in the value of silver, under natural law, overrode the statute, kept the silver dollar below par in gold, and kept it also out of general circulation. When silver bullion is worth about 52 pence in London, our silver dollar is worth about 88 cents in gold. We have also *subsidiary* silver coins, which are only legal-tender to the amount or $5; and these, since 1875, are minted on the metric system; so that two half-dollars, or four quarters, or ten dimes, weigh each just 25 *grams*, or 385.8 *grains*, $\frac{9}{10}$ fine; and consequently a nominal dollar's worth of small silver is really *worth* 6½ per cent less than a silver *dollar*-piece. Our five-cent nickel piece is both subsidiary and doubly metric: it weighs 5 *grams*, and five of them laid along in order are a *decimeter* long, and they are legal-tender for only $1. The three-cent nickel piece, like the five-cent, is 75 parts copper and 25 parts nickel, and debts of sixty cents can be legally paid in them. The one-cent piece is 95 parts copper and 5 parts tin zinc, and debts of four cents can be paid in them. Governments, accordingly, while they make a public profit out of the issue of *subsidiary* coins, — their value as money being much above their value as bullion, — and while, if there be a double standard, they must determine the *legal* relation of the two metals to each other, can *not* settle the *actual* relative value of the two, which follow their own laws, and pursue their own course, with very little reference to mints.

While the United States went back, in 1878, to the double standard they had once abolished, several of the principal nations have taken the opposite tack. The French, for example, had the single (silver) standard till 1803, when the double standard was introduced in the *legal* ratio of 15.50 : 1; but the value of silver in gold was *really* less than this down to 1850, averaging 15.65 : 1; between 1850 and 1866, silver rose to 15.19 : 1; but it sank again gradually, till in 1878 it stood at 17.92 : 1, though the coinage of silver had practically ceased in 1876, since which the French have had the single (gold) standard. Germany passed from silver to gold by the laws of 1871 and 1873, the latter of which ordered that silver should not exceed ten marks per head of population. At the close of 1879 there were in circulation 1,550,000,000 marks gold, and 856,-

000,000 marks silver, that is,· 37 per cent silver, showing that the law of 1873 had not been fully carried out. The Scandinavian kingdoms in 1873, ·and Holland in 1875, adopted the single standard of gold. The latter, indeed, established a ratio of 15.625 : 1, but the coinage of silver was sus-· pended, and the coinage of gold made free.[1] All these facts illustrate the main point we have now in hand.

Governments, too, wisely leave to the people the whole question of the quantity and mode of circulation of their principal and wholly legal-tender coins. The Bank of England is obliged by law to buy and pay for in coin all gold bullion offered it for sale, paying for it three half-pennies less by the ounce than the bullion will make of stamped coin. This is the same thing as coining for all comers all the gold they bring at a seignior-age of .032 per cent, practically equivalent to free coinage. By the law of 1874, the United States charge nothing for coining gold; the French government charge .216 per cent seigniorage on gold coins; so that, practically, it is left to the people to say how much money they will have coined, and, having received it from the mint, they are at liberty to do just what they please with it, — they may hoard it, they may melt it up, they may circulate it at home, they may export it abroad, at will. Now, it is a great gain to have

---

[1] Most of the facts in this paragraph are drawn from Meyer's Konversations-lexikon (first supplementary volume, 1880).

a money with which the government has nothing
to do except to mint it, — a money that asks no
favors, needs no puffing, never deceives anybody,
knows how to take care of itself, is always respectable and universally respected.

3. The third general reason why gold and silver constitute the best money is found in their
physical peculiarities, by which they are *uniform
in quality, conveniently portable, divisible without
loss, easily impressible, and always beautiful.* Pure
gold and silver, no matter where they are mined,
are exactly of the same quality all over the earth.
Gold is gold, and silver is silver. · The gold mined
to-day in California differs in no essential respects
from the gold used by Solomon in the construction
of the Temple, and the silver out of the Nevada
mines is the same thing as the silver paid by Abraham for the cave of Machpelah.   Nature with her
wise finger has thus stamped them for the universal money; and a universal coinage, that is, coins
of the same degree of fineness, and brought into
easy numerical relations with each other in respect
to weight, and, though coined in the four quarters
of the globe, yet current everywhere by virtue of
universal confidence in them, for which the first
grand provision is this uniformity of quality, is
one of the dreams and hopes of economists, that
is yet to be realized in the future.

Gold and silver are sufficiently portable for all
the purposes of modern money.   Their weight is
little relatively to their value.   A thousand dollars

in gold are not indeed carried so easily as a bill of exchange or a bank-note; and expedients are easily adopted, and have been in use since the days of the Romans, by which the transfer in place of large masses of coin is for the most part obviated; these expedients will all be explained in the following chapter on Credit; our proposition does not deprecate at all the use of these expedients of commerce, which are mere credit and not money proper; but for money proper, for that which gives birth to and maintains the *denominations* of value, for that which passes from hand to hand in ordinary exchanges, we do maintain that gold and silver coins are conveniently portable. I have myself carried across the ocean, incased in a glove-finger and borne in a vest-pocket, a troy pound of English sovereigns worth about $230, scarcely conscious of their weight, although easily re-assured of their presence by a touch of the hand. The experience of those countries, like France and Germany, in which the money has been mostly metallic, has not pronounced it onerous on account of its weight; and, at any rate, it is better to accept all the other immense advantages of gold and silver money, together with a little inconvenience as to weight, if one chooses to insist on that, than to adopt substitutes every way inferior as money, except that they are lighter in our purses. They are unfortunately " lighter " in other respects also.

Moreover, gold and silver differ from jewels,

and most other precious things, in that masses of them are divisible, without any loss of value, into pieces of any required size. The aggregate of pieces is worth as much as the mass, and the mass as much as the pieces. This is a great advantage in money, because for the convenience of business, a considerable variety of coins is required, and the proper proportion of each kind is a matter of trial, and if any kind be minted in excess of the demand nothing more is required than to remint in other denominations, and the whole value is thus saved to the currency in the most convenient form.

Then, gold and silver are easily impressible by any stamp which. the government chooses to put upon them. Indeed in their natural state they are too soft to maintain long the impress of the die. Accordingly, for coinage purposes they are alloyed with another metal, chiefly copper, since by a chemical law, whenever two metals are mixed together, the compound is harder than either of them in a pure state. Most of the nations now use in their gold and silver coins one-tenth alloy, but England still adheres to her ancient rule of one-twelfth only. So compounded, coins receive readily and retain for a long time with sharp distinctness the legend and other devices chosen for them to bear. In monarchical countries, the head of the reigning sovereign is usually stamped upon the coins; and there was a curious debate in the first Congress of the United States, whether the heads of the successive Presidents should not similarly be impressed upon the coins minted during their respective administrations; but this proposal was negatived, as was also a motion to substitute the head of Columbus, and an emblematic figure representing Liberty was then hit upon and has been since continued.

Quite recently, some of our coins have been made to bear the appropriate legend "In God we trust." The national coat of arms is frequently impressed upon coins in the various countries, by which means patriotic associations are connected with the current money. Although the alloy hardens the coins, yet after long usage they will lose a part of their weight by abrasion, and governments usually indicate a short weight, after coming to which the coins are no longer legal-tender. An English sovereign weighs 5 pennyweights $3\frac{171}{623}$ grains, containing $113\frac{1}{623}$ grains of fine gold, and when it falls below 5 pennyweights $2\frac{3}{4}$ grains, it loses its legal-tender character. There is an English half sovereign in gold; five- two- and one-shilling pieces in silver; and pence, halfpence, and farthings in bronze. The bronze coins are only worth about one-fourth of their nominal value; and pence and halfpence are only legal-tender to the amount of one shilling, and farthings to the amount of sixpence. One English shilling equals $24\frac{1}{2}$ of our cents, gold.

Lastly, gold and silver, when coined into money, are objects of great beauty. This is no slight recommendation of these metals for the money of the world. They are clean. They are beautiful. Their perfectly circular form, thé device covering the whole piece, the milled and fluted edges, the patriotic emblem whatever it be, the religious or other legend, and their bright color, are all elements in their beauty. The educating power over the young of a good coinage well kept up, æsthetically, historically, and commercially, is a matter of consequence to any country. A whole people handling constantly such money cannot fail to receive a wholesome development thereby. The new German coinage, in contrast with the old money of the German States, furnishes an illustration of all this. The new German coins from highest to lowest are very beautiful, and have already tended, and will tend more and more to a true German nationality.

The new German unit is the *mark*, equivalent to 23.821 óf our cents, gold. The principal coin is the 20-mark piece, containing 7.1684 grams of fine gold. The English sovereign contains 7.3224 grams fine, the French 25-franc piece contains 7.2581 grams fine, and our five-dollar gold piece contains 7.5230 grams fine. It is one of the great problems of the future to remove in some way these slight differences, and thus practically to unify the money of the world. The mark-system is decimal, being subdivided into groschen and pfennigs. It is quite like our dollars, dimes and cents, although each of these denominations is rather more than four times larger than the corresponding German ones. For the present, until the old silver is gotten rid of, the Prussian thaler is still current, passing as equivalent to three marks. The new mark-system is a skilful modification of the old Prussian money, while at the same time it is completely decimal, as the old system was not. This partial national continuity is the only thing that goes to reconcile one to the often regretted fact that the new German mark was not made equivalent either to the English shilling or to the French franc.

The French franc and its multiples, notwithstanding the ugly fraction in their metric weights, have already gained great triumphs as towards a universal money. France and her colonies, Belgium, Switzerland, Spain, Italy, Greece, Roumania, and Austro-Hungary in part, have now a common money based on the French franc. Austria began in 1870 to coin gold pieces of eight and four florins, the same in weight and fineness as the French 20 and 10 franc pieces; and decreed in 1873, that foreign gold pieces of the French system be accepted in Austro-Hungary in the ratio of 2½ francs to the florin. The five-franc gold piece, which is the unit of the system so far as the gold coinage is concerned, weighs 1612.9 milligrams; the multiples of this unit are decimal, or at least divisible by 5; and while the coins in these countries bear the emblems preferred by each they are legal tender in all.

Our gold dollar weighs 1671.8 milligrams, and
if it were in future coining to be reduced so
as to be equal to five francs, American gold
would thereafter circulate freely wherever the
French napoleon (20 francs) now circulates, and
this would tend powerfully to make the *dollar*
as a denomination the future universal unit, as it
is already the unit in many countries, and as the
French have no simple name for their five-franc
piece. This would require our dollar to be reduced in weight 3.5 *per centum*. Then, if the
English sovereign were lowered 0.88 per cent in
weight of fine gold, the following very simple
ratios would obtain, namely, 25 francs = $5 = £1.
Even this would leave the German mark out of
harmony with the rest, but as the Germans have
already adopted bodily the metric system from the
French, it is not too much to hope that they will be
willing to listen by and by to some modifications
of their system in order to bring it in some way
into harmony with that of other nations. I con-
fess, that to my mind the fairest prospect to an international and universal coinage lies through the
adoption on the part of Great Britain and the
United States of the French five-franc unit, to be
called a *dollar* in all languages, and to be the exact
equivalent of 4 English shillings, and of 2 Aus-
trian florins.

Before passing to discuss paper-money briefly, I
must explain what is coming to be called " Gresham's Law of Currency," from Sir Thomas Gresh-

am, a financier of the time of Queen Elizabeth. Aristophanes, the Greek comic poet, had noticed even in his early day that good coins of full weight were apt to be crowded out of the circulation by the lighter and poorer pieces, and, mistaking the cause of this, satirized his countrymen unmercifully for preferring bad coins to good, and demagogues, like Cleon, for rulers, to honorable citizens. The following are the verses : —

" Oftentimes have we reflected on a similar abuse,
In the choice of men for office, and of coins for common use;
For your old and standard pieces, valued and approved and
 tried,
Here among the Grecian nations, and in all the world be-
 side,
Recognized in every realm for trusty stamp and pure assay,
Are rejected and abandoned for the trash of yesterday;
For a vile, adulterate issue, drossy, counterfeit and base,
Which the traffic of the city passes current in their place I
And the men that stood for office, noted for acknowledged
 worth,
And for manly deeds of honor, and for honorable birth;
Trained in exercise and art, in sacred dances and in song,
All are ousted and supplanted by a base, ignoble throng;
Paltry stamp and vulgar mettle raise them to command and
 place,
Brazen counterfeit pretenders, scoundrels of a scoundrel race ;
Whom the state in former ages scarce would have allowed
 to stand
At the sacrifice of outcasts, as the scapegoats of the land."

Gresham was the first to explain fully what Aristophanes had noticed and falsely referred to the bad taste of his generation. It is true always and everywhere that *an inferior money, so long as it circulates at all, drives a superior money out of the circulation ;* and this is rather creditable to human nature than otherwise, when the true ground of it is perceived. In most spheres, what is excellent tends to displace what is inferior, but in the sphere of money the exact reverse takes place, and bad money drives out the good, for the simple reason that money is an instrument of exchange, and nobody wants it except to buy with, and so long as the government and the community treat light coin and full coin as of equal value in current exchanges, receiving them indifferently in payment of debts and of taxes, it is clear that few persons will give in payment of debts and of taxes what is really and elsewhere worth more so long as what is really and elsewhere worth less will go just as far. The inferior pieces will abide in a market where they will fetch just as much as the superior pieces, while the superior pieces will take on a form or migrate to a place in which some advantage can be gained from their superiority. Thrown into a crucible, or exported in commerce, this superiority immediately manifests itself; and therefore into the crucible or into the channels of foreign trade it might be predicted that such money would be thrown, and all experience testifies with one voice that into exports, melting-pots, or private hoards, such money always goes.

This principle is now called Gresham's Law, and

it applies equally to purely metallic currencies and to currencies mixed of coin and paper. The city of Amsterdam founded its famous bank in 1609, because the clipped and worn foreign coins circulating in that then great mart of trade drove out the good money which the mint of the city constantly poured in. There was no paper-money in Amsterdam before or afterwards; the bank became a bank of deposit merely; it took in all the old coins at their intrinsic value, and had them re-minted at full weight; gave depositors a credit on its books for all they brought; adjusted accounts between merchants and others by mere transfers on its books; and thus took away all uncertainty from bills of exchange drawn on parties in Amsterdam, which had been before at some ten per cent discount, bringing them up at once to par, and thus making it for the interest and convenience of every business man in Amsterdam to have these simple dealings with the Bank, which in turn enjoyed unlimited credit in the commercial world for nearly 200 years.

The great English re-coinage of 1696 was compelled by similar causes; the previous working of Gresham's Law as between the old silver and the new — the worn stamped money and the fresh milled money — caused great confusion in business, great bitterness in society, and great hopes among the Jacobites that they would be able by means of the prevailing discontent to overthrow the yet scarcely established revolutionary government of William and Mary.[1] Thus we see that there may be *depreciation* even among coins. Depreciation implies of course a *standard*; and whatever any coins are worth *less* than the standard coins of that kind is their depreciation. But Gresham's Law has its most marked operation in mixed currencies, and the word " depreciation " is commonly used of paper-money to express its lack of equality in value with gold coin. This brings us to the subject of paper-money.

I lay down this proposition : — *A paper-money is only tolerable when it is instantly convertible into gold or silver.* This proposition rests back for its proof upon the nature of paper-money. *Paper-money is a promise to pay a certain quantity of gold or silver.* For example, in this country a five-dollar bill is a promise to pay five times $25\frac{4}{5}$ grains of standard gold. No other meaning than this is possible, since the bill does not read, This is five dollars, but, The United States will pay to bearer five dollars; and when we go to the statutes to find out what a dollar is, we ascertain that the United States have said that a dollar is $25\frac{4}{5}$ grains of standard gold. It is, indeed, true that in 1878 Congress enacted that $412\frac{1}{2}$ grains of silver coined nine-tenths fine should *also* be a dollar : but at present these coins are not meant in the minds of men when they give and take promises to pay *dollars*; they are stowed away by the million in the sub-treasuries of the United States, and silver certificates, so-called, are issued to all de-

[1] Macaulay's History of England, chap. 21.

positors of them ; so late as the autumn of 1880, they had come very little into general circulation : and consequently the name *dollar* still attaches itself to the 25$\frac{4}{5}$ grains of gold, and not at all to the 412$\frac{1}{2}$ grains of silver, although both are alike legal-tender for all debts public and private. If, however, what are technically called "the exchanges" (and these will be fully explained in the next chapter) should turn strongly against this country, and silver continue in the markets of the world to be cheaper than gold in the ratio 1 : 16, and gold accordingly be drawn off in considerable foreign payments, in this case the silver dollar is likely enough to become the *current* dollar, and thus also the *standard* dollar; and as a result of this the *denomination-dollar* would shift at once to the silver, and thereafter represent the *value* of that, and not the higher value of the gold. Then, in accordance with Gresham's law, the silver would expel the gold altogether from the circulation, and the country would have in effect the single (silver) standard, and also a cheap dollar in which all promises to pay would be met.

In all cases, therefore, the nature of paper money is perfectly clear: it is a mere promise to pay so much gold or silver. In all the leading nations of the world, it is a promise to pay gold. Now, if the promise be kept, if the gold be forthcoming on presentation for payment, then paper-money is tolerable, its value is equal to that of the gold promised, because it brings out the gold promised; but if the promise be not kept, if the gold be refused, then the paper-money is dishonored, it becomes intolerable, it *depreciates* as compared with the gold promised but not paid; and if it have a forced circulation, that is, if government compels creditors to receive it in payment of debts, a fearful injustice is done, creditors are cheated, the measure of value becomes variable as the wind, and irreparable mischiefs to business and credit follow as a matter of course.

Paper-money is issued either by governments directly, or by corporations instituted by governments. The nature of paper-money is essentially the same in whichever way it is issued; in the one case, it is the promise to pay of the government itself, good if kept and bad if broken, and in the other case, it is the promise to pay of organized bodies deriving their authority to act from the government, and the government itself usually feels responsible more or less for the way in which they act. Those banks which issue paper-money are usually so connected with the government in one way or another, that their circulating notes have a kind of government indorsement or guaranty. We will consider as specimens of such banks, the Bank of England, and the present national banks of the United States, looking at them now solely as corporations issuing paper-money. In the next chapter, we shall look at banks generally as institutions of Credit.

The Bank of England is the child of the English Revolution of 1688. It was incorporated by Parliament in 1694, in the midst of the struggle under Gresham's Law between the old coinage and the new, on condition that its stockholders should loan to government, then pressed for funds, the sum of £1,200,000, on which they were promised 8 per cent as interest, and £4,000 for management, per annum. On the strength of this capital stock, which was all invested in the government debt, the bank was allowed by law to issue an exactly equal amount of circulating notes, which at first however could only pass from hand to hand by successive indorsements. On several subsequent occasions, its capital stock was increased, that is, the stock-holders of the bank advanced more money to government, and each time the bank was allowed to issue an equal amount of notes additional; and it was provided that if the Directors issued notes exceeding the amount of their capital they should be liable in their private capacity. Afterwards they were released from this limitation, and were allowed to issue as many notes as they pleased, provided always they redeemed them in specie on demand.

In about two years from its establishment, the bank fell into difficulties from having received the old coin and being obliged to pay out the new; its enemies made a run upon it, and it was obliged to suspend payments; and in February, 1697, the notes were 24 per cent below par. Just then, came the first parliamentary act increasing the capital stock, one-fifth of which increase was receivable in bank-notes, which brought them up to par. In 1709, the capital was again increased, and the interest on the whole debt reduced from 8 per cent to 6. In 1711, the limitation on the amount of issues was removed; and in 1716, the bank was exempted from the operation of all usury laws: why the bank only, and not other people as well, the Act of parliament does not state.

In 1720, and again in 1745, when the Young Pretender made the last rally of the Jacobites, there were severe runs upon the bank; on both occasions, in order to gain time, notes were paid in shillings and sixpences, and best friends were said to be accommodated first, who returned the bags of morey as fast as they received them. In 1759, £15 and £10 notes were first issued, no previous note having been for less than £20. In 1782, the debt of the government to the bank stood at £11,642,000, most of which bore but 3 per cent interest. During the following great war with the French, the constant demands of the government for money could not be met, and the bank continue to give its usual accommodations to merchants, and consequently private credit wavered and there was a run upon the bank for cash, under which the bank suspended payments in February, 1797, and did not resume them till May, 1821.

During this long suspension, government and the business men of London did their best to hold up the credit of the dishonored notes, *but they were not made a legal-tender for debts.* Government received them at par for taxes, and provided that business payments in notes should be held as payments in cash, if offered and accepted as such; debtors, having tendered bank-notes, which the creditor refused, had certain privileges before the law, which other debtors had not; and the notes, accordingly, had a certain legal recognition, *but not a forced circulation.* At this time also, the bank was first authorized to issue £5, £2, and £1 notes; and all its notes, being cautiously issued for some time, were kept quite or nearly to par in gold, which proves that under favorable circumstances an inconvertible paper can be kept at par by sufficiently limiting its quantity; while the same example proves a little further on what a bad money inconvertible paper is, inasmuch as, all restrictions being now removed and small notes authorized, the bank gradually expanded its circulation, and so stimulated speculation, until in August, 1813, its notes were at 30 per cent discount in gold. In the following years, the inevitable crisis occurred, a very large number of country bankers failed, the volume of paper-money decreased about one-half, and the notes of the Bank of England rose nearly to par in October, 1816. They declined again, however, after a partial attempt at resumption, and then gradually rose till the complete resumption began in 1821. In 1829, all notes whatsoever for less than £5 were forbidden to be circulated in England.

In 1833 when the bank charter was renewed for the ninth time, the bills of the Bank of England were declared to be a legal-tender for debts, *so long as the bank paid them on demand in legal coin, but no longer.* In 1844, Sir Robert Peel caused to pass Parliament an Act under which the Bank of England is still administered, and under which the bank is divided into two distinct departments, the Issue department and the Banking department. The Issue department is the only one we have any thing to do with now, and its operations are entirely simple, almost self-acting.

Under the law, the Directors of the bank have transferred to the Issue department £15,000,000 of securities, most of which is the debt of the government to the bank, and also gold coin and gold and silver bullion in varying amounts according to their discretion but averaging about £15,000,000. The Issue department is authorized to give over to the Banking department notes to the exact amount of the securities, coin and bullion thus deposited. The Banking department can get notes only from the Issue department, and the Issue department can issue notes only to the Banking department, and only to the amount of the coin and bullion actually on hand in the Issue department *plus* the value of the securities already described. Consequently, the total power of the Bank of England to issue notes is limited to the sum of these two simple elements. Of course, the Banking department holds coin and bullion also for its banking purposes, and can get more notes at any time by transferring parts of these to the Issue department; but the law prescribes that silver bullion shall only be held by the Issue department to the extent of one-fourth of the gold coin and bullion held by it at any one time. This whole legislation has made the notes of the Bank of England a very safe medium of exchange. Since May, 1821, no note has been presented for payment, which has not been immediately cashed.

Still, the system is not perfect. In October, 1847, during a severe commercial crisis, government authorized the bank to violate its charter, and to issue notes at its discretion. This extraordinary authority quieted the panic in ten minutes. and no more notes were actually issued than the previous legal limits allowed. Again in November, 1857, in the next great crisis, the Banking department fell into difficulties, and could not have continued to discount another day, when government suspended the law a second time, and bade the bank issue notes at discretion, but not to discount for less than 10 per cent. This permission worked as before, the panic vanished, and the legal limits did not need to be exceeded. Again in 1866, there was a very severe crisis, and on the 10th of May there was a general run on all the London banks, and it is said that one bank alone paid out £2,000,000 in six hours, and after banking hours that day it became known that the house of Overend, Gurney & Co. had suspended with liabilities of over £10,000,000 — the largest failure that had ever taken place in London — and that evening the government sent word to the bank to issue notes in discounting at its own discretion at not less than 10 per cent. The bank advanced in this way £12,255,000 in five days, one million pounds of which was to our country-man, George Peabody, which saved him from otherwise inevitable failure, and his gigantic fortune to the benevolent and patriotic purposes to which it was afterwards put.

It may well be questioned whether a fundamental restriction, which has to be removed on every occasion of extraordinary pressure, ought not the rather to be abolished; and, if so, whether the division of the bank into two departments is of any further practical use, and whether the directors may not now be safely trusted to govern the issue of their notes as they govern the amount and rate of their discounts at their own discretior It may also be gravely questioned whether England is any better off, or ever has been, for the issue of Bank of England notes to circulate as money. As a *banking* institution its merits and benefits are freely conceded, but it may reasonably be doubted whether as an institution for circulating paper-money it has ever added any thing to the prosperity of England.

The amount of Bank of England notes in circulation is about £30,000,000, one-half on the basis of securities, and one-half on the basis of coin and bullion. About £15,000,000 of other bank-notes are in circulation in England, making £45,000,000 in all; while at the same time, there are about £115,000,000 of gold and silver coin in circulation there. The ratio of coin to paper is nearly $2\frac{1}{2}$ to 1. Very nearly the same ratio prevails in France. If there were no paper-money at all in either country, the system of checks, which is thoroughly established in England but less so in France, would obviate for the most part all burdensome transfers of coin.

The present national banks of this country are a second illustration of institutions chartered by government issuing a paper-money. These banks are organized under a law of Congress approved in February, 1863. They invest their capital stock in the bonds of the United States, which are deposited with an officer in Washington called the Comptroller of the Currency, who holds them as security that the banks redeem their notes and otherwise obey the provisions of the organic banking-law, but pays the interest on them to the banks so long as these conditions are fulfilled. Ninety per cent of the amount of such bonds thus deposited with the Comptroller is then furnished to the bank in circulating notes engraved and registered by the United States, unless the capital of the bank be over $500,000 and under $1,000,000, in which case only 80 per cent is furnished in notes; and if the capital be between $1,000,000 and $3,000,000, only 75 per cent of it is returned in notes; and if the capital be over $3,000,000, only 60 per cent; but by the law of 1870, no *new* bank can be organized to issue more than $500,000 of notes, no matter what the capital stock may be. All the banks are required to keep 5 per cent of their circulation in lawful money with the Comptroller at Washington for the purpose of redeeming their notes on presentation there; and in seventeen of the principal cities of the Union, the banks are required to keep 25 per cent of their average deposits in lawful money as a reserve, and in all other places 15 per cent, with which to meet their various obligations over their own counters.

By the law of 1875, all restrictions on the aggregate circulation of the national banks are removed, but provision is made to retire 80 per cent of the amo nt of notes issued thereafter to new banks, or old banks increasing their circulation, in the other paper-money of the country, namely, in the greenbacks so-called, until these be reduced to $300,000,000. When this law was passed, January 14, 1875, there were in circulation of national bank-notes $351,861,450, and of greenbacks $382,-000,000; under the operation of this law, and of other causes, the bank-notes outstanding, and the greenbacks too lessened in volume, — the average sum of the two having been about $700,000,000 for several years.

The banks can curtail their circulation at will, and recall their bonds from Washington; — and they can recover and increase their circulation at will by pledging more bonds again. Under this system, it is scarcely possible that any note-holder can suffer any loss, though depositors may, for the United States undertakes to redeem all notes, at first from the 5 per cent reserve in their hands, and then, if necessary, by selling the bonds in their keeping. A few banks have failed, a few more have wound up their affairs as national banks, and about 2,100 are now in operation all over the country. Prior to the resumption of specie payments in 1879, these bank-notes were redeemable in "lawful money," that is, in irredeemable greenbacks; but since then, the greenbacks themselves having become redeemable in gold or silver, all the paper-money of the country may be said to be redeemable. It would certainly be simpler if there were but one kind of it, and it probably would be better if there were none of it. The various expedients of pure credit to be described in the next chapter would seem to obviate any need of any form of paper-*money*. But, whatever may be thought about that, the *amount* of paper-money in our system is excessive relatively to the amount of coin in the hands of the people. The amount of paper-money per head of population is just about double that in England, say $14 to $7. So far as our system of national banks creates *money*, I have never seen any thing that leads me to think that it has added, or is likely to add, any thing to the property or happiness of the people of the

United States. In many other respects the system is admirable, and its author was the late Secretary of the Treasury, and Chief Justice of the United States, Salmon P. Chase, who borrowed the outlines and some of the details of the scheme, however, from the State bank system of New York.

I will illustrate the other kind of paper-money, that, namely, issued directly by governments, by giving some account of the present greenback money of the United States. This will serve as a sample. Many governments, particularly revolutionary governments, have issued directly an irredeemable paper-money; and the *assignats* of revolutionary France, and the *continental money* of these American states one hundred years ago, will occur to many minds as examples. Those were never redeemed at all; and, I believe, there has never been in the world an example of the complete liquidation of such money by any nation. The first batch of this money, consisting of $150,-000,000, was issued almost immediately under a law of Congress approved Feb. 25, 1862. These notes of the United States, made nominally payable to bearer but at no specified place or date, and not on interest, were made legal-tender for all debts public and private, except customs-duties and interest on the coin-bonds of the United States. It was also expressly stipulated in the law that these notes might be funded in sums of fifty dollars, or multiples thereof, in the six per cent bonds of the United States.

In less than a month after the passage of the first legal-tender act another act was passed at the request of Secretary Chase, approved March 17, 1862, declaring $60,000,000 more of demand notes previously authorized but not made legal-tender to be legal-tender in like manner, and for the same purposes, and to the same extent, as the first notes. July 11, 1862, the President approved another law authorizing the issue of $150,000,000 more of just such legal-tender notes, fundable as before in six per cent bonds, and $35,000,000 of these notes might be of denominations less than $5, but not fractional parts of $1. January 17, 1863, the President approved of a joint resolution of both houses of Congress authorizing $100,000,000 more of legal-tenders to pay soldiers and sailors, but in doing so, he uttered a solemn protest against the policy of thus inflating the currency by forced means, which, he said, " has already become so redundant as to increase prices beyond real values, thereby augmenting the cost of living to the injury of labor, and the cost of supplies to the injury of the whole country."

March 3, 1863, a very comprehensive act was approved, authorizing loans to the extent of $900,-000,000, authorizing also $50,000,000 of fractional currency redeemable in sums not less than $3 in legal-tenders and receivable for all dues to the United States less than $5, except duties on imports, and taking away also after July 1, 1863, *the right to fund legal-tenders into six per cent bonds at par*, although on the back of some of these legal-tenders was printed this statement : " This note is a legal-tender for all debts, public and private, except duties on imports and interest on the public debt, *and is exchangeable for U. S. six per cent bonds, redeemable at the pleasure of the United States after five years.*"

It was a great breach of the public faith to take away in this indirect manner, or in any manner, from the people the right to fund notes into bonds, after it had been twice guaranteed in the laws authorizing the issue of the notes, and after the people had been *compelled* to take the notes, and this accounts in part for the great subsequent depreciation of the notes, the excess of which could not, as was originally intended, be drawn easily into the funded debt.   By the act of June 30, 1864, it was provided that " *the total amount of United States notes issued, or to be issued, shall not exceed* $400,000,000, *and such additional sum not exceeding* $50,000,000, *as may be temporarily required for the redemption of temporary loans.*"   On the 31st October, 1865, there were outstanding $454,218,038.20 of United States notes and fractional currency.[1]

While the greenbacks were still depreciating on the whole, creditors were constantly cheated by being *compelled to receive* less value than they had contracted for ; and, after they had begun to appreciate on the whole, debtors were *compelled to pay* more value than they contracted for.   Failures

See Hon. E. G. Spaulding's " Financial History of the War."

have been a consequence. Discontent has been ·a consequence. Fallacious theories of money have been a consequence. A wounded public credit has been a consequence. At times, rash speculation has been a consequence. At other times, long-continued depression has been a consequence. Great injustice as between classes of men has been a consequence. A universal financial uncertainty has been one of the worst consequences. Acknowledged difficulties in the way of a return to a better system have been another consequence. Paper-money in its best estate, that is, when certainly convertible into gold on demand, is a questionable good; but paper-money like the greenbacks, inconvertible, variable in value, redundant in volume, and having a forced circulation, is an unmitigated evil, whose power for mischief is indefinite and interminable.

How shall we get back to specie payments? *By restoring the fundable feature of the laws of 1862 removed in 1863, and by appointing a day in advance after which the legal-tender clause shall be inoperative and void.* If the people of the United States knew certainly that after the 1st day of January, 1879, a day already legally appointed for resuming specie payments, no paper whatever would be legal-tender for debts; and if they were allowed from now on to fund greenbacks freely into the 4 per centum long bonds already authorized, whose interest is too low to prove overattractive to the circulating medium, and thus too

rapidly deplete it; I believe that no other legislation is needed, unless it might be to require the
national banks to retain as reserve the gold interest on their bonds, to bring the country back,
doubtless not without something of shock and
disaster, to the good ground occupied between
1836 and 1862, the ground, namely, of a purely
metallic money, or bank paper instantly convertible into that. Between those dates, the national
government neither received for its dues nor paid
out for its debts any thing but gold and silver
coin. It should resume that position. And it
would be much better in my judgment, if the feature
of *circulation* were eliminated from the national
bank system, and those institutions were restricted
to a purely *banking* business, that is to say, to
dealings in credits of all sorts except credit-money.
If that be too great a good to be hoped for, the
patriotic citizen may at least indulge the hope
that those banks may be so managed and con-
trolled as never to issue any thing but a strictly
convertible money.

As money is always a thing of value, and as it
is the inmost nature of a thing as *valuable* that its
owner is at liberty to part with it on his own
terms, whoever owns money has an indubitable
right to loan it to others at any rate of interest
they may be willing to pay him. What are called
Usury Laws, therefore, that is, laws of the State
or the Nation forbidding persons to take more
than a prescribed rate of interest on money loaned,

are wholly out of character, and are now disappearing. Massachusetts, Connecticut, and Rhode Island have abolished their usury laws; and, as the national banking law enacts that the banks may legally take the interest allowed in their respective States, all limitations are removed in these three States. No evil of any kind has followed their abolition. Even in the States in which usury laws are still nominally kept up, they are notoriously disregarded. It is a queer distinction, when governments allow their citizens to make all other bargains and exchanges freely at their own discretion, and then forbid them to loan money at the market rates.

Governments are careful not to bind themselves in this manner, and of course they ought not to attempt to bind their citizens, because it is useless to attempt it, because there is no reason why they should succeed in it, and because, even if they could succeed in it, it would be worse for all parties concerned. Our government paid twelve per cent on a public loan in 1860, and could get but little at that, because its credit was then weak; which shows the absurdity of its forbidding a citizen to pay over seven, no matter how weak his credit or great his necessity. Such laws are injurious to the public conscience so far as they are disobeyed, injurious to persons of weak credit so far as they are obeyed, and injurious to the rights of capital whether obeyed or disobeyed. Let them be abolished.

In conclusion, we will give a summary of the principal points in this chapter.

1. *From the very nature of value, which always implies comparisons, a* STANDARD *of comparison becomes natural and useful: such a standard is money.*

2. *From being a standard of comparison in values, money comes naturally to be a* MEDIUM *in exchanges, passing from hand to hand to facilitate the ultimate exchanges of society.*

3. *From being a standard of comparison in values, the denominations of money come to be a* MEASURE *of all values whatever.*

4. *The only way to keep the* DENOMINATIONS *steady in meaning, is to keep the medium steady in purchasing-power.*

5. GOLD *has been found by experience to be the steadiest in purchasing-power of valuable things: therefore, it is the best money.*

6. *Subsidiary coins may be made of* SILVER; *but Gresham's Law forbids a double standard.*

7. *Paper-money is only* PROMISES; *promises are liable to be broken; and therefore promises do not make a good money.*

8. *Credits are good; but that does not prove that* CREDIT-MONEY *is good.* ·

9. *Credit-money is only tolerable when instantly* CONVERTIBLE.

10. *Money depreciated from the highest standard raises* PRICES, *but not of all things equally in amount or uniformly in time: it works, therefore, great injustice.*

11. *Any money inferior to the best works a national* LOSS *of necessity.*

12. *An universal coinage would be a vast international* GAIN.

13. *The interest of money should be* FREE *to all contracting parties.*

CHAPTER V.

CREDIT.

POLITICAL ECONOMY is the science of sales, or exchanges. It must, therefore, present clearly the principles applicable to all *kinds* of exchanges. We have already learned that there are only three kinds of things that are ever commercially exchanged among men, i.e., commodities, services, and claims. There are, consequently, only six cases of value possible, since something belonging to each of these classes may be exchanged against something belonging to its own class and also against something belonging to each of the other classes, making six possible cases of exchange. Commodities with the mode of their production and the law of their exchange we have already sufficiently considered ; there is nothing further to be added in detail in respect to personal services viewed economically; but the subject of Claims now demands and will certainly reward a complete explanation. It is to be noticed, that these three classes of things have a relation to the three grand divisions of time; commodities are property in the

production of the Past, services are property in
the production of the Present, and claims are
property in the production of the Future. What
these claims are in their nature, how they arise in
practice, their different kinds, the part they play
in the commerce of the world, and the modes in
which they are extinguished, are the general topics
to which the attention of my readers will now be
directed.

I have entitled this chapter " Credit," because
on the whole, that is the best word under which to
discuss the whole subject in hand. I have found
that the derivation of words usually casts much
clear light on the nature of that which is designat-
ed by them; and of two words having apparently the same meaning, that one is to be preferred
whose origin most illumines its meaning. The
word credit is derived from the Latin word CRE-
DO, *I believe*, and the corresponding term debt from
DEBEO, *I owe.* The term credit, accordingly, carries the mind at once to future time, and carries it
also to the personal action of a human will. As
there can be no credit without debt, and no debt
without credit, two persons, as in every other case
of value, must be involved in every case of credit;
and what connects the two persons together is the
belief of one of the parties in a virtual *promise*
made by the other.

Some exchanges are finished up at once, the
things exchanged and the ownership in them are
passed over then and there, and there is an end;

but the peculiarity of credit exchanges is, that the transaction is not then and there ultimately closed, but one (or both) of the parties exchanging relies on the good faith of somebody to fulfil in the. future a promise expressly or impliedly made in the exchange. A credit, then, may be defined as *a right to demand something of somebody;* and a debt may be defined as *a duty to pay something to somebody.* There are not *two* things in the relation between a creditor and a debtor but only *one* thing — not a right *and* a duty that can be separated, but a right *founded* on the duty and a duty *growing out* of the right. The single bond connecting the two persons is called in the Roman Law, which is clear and full on the subject of credit, an Obligation. It may also be termed a Contract. It may also be termed indifferently a Credit, a Debt, a Claim.

It makes a great difference to individual persons whether they owe others or are owed by others, but what Political Economy has to do with is what *lies between* debtors and creditors, and not with debtors or creditors personally. This intermediate thing, or right, is *property.* It may be, and is constantly, bought and sold. The right to demand from the debtor at some future time an equivalent for what the creditor renders now, is the service which the creditor receives from the debtor at the time of the exchange. It is a clear case of value. Each renders to the other satisfactory equivalents. The right to demand a future equivalent is the present equivalent for the sake of which something else is rendered. All our definitions apply here perfectly. Considered as a mere case of value, the transaction may be said to be ended; but, considered as to the nature of the exchange which requires another exchange to complete it, the transaction is not yet ended, and we must follow it in its principles to the end.

The amount of transactions in credits is immense in every commercial country, and is becoming constantly greater. Not only are the exchanges very common in which the right to demand future payment is *one* of the services rendered, but the exclusive traffic in credits — exchanges of one form of credit for another — has already reached gigantic proportions in all parts of the world. The exchanges in currency values at 'the New York Clearing-House alone for the years between 1867 and 1876 have averaged $28,152,-711,026.68 a year; and during the same nine years the exchanges in gold values at the London Clearing-House alone also averaged $24,058,845,555.55 a year, calling $5 the equivalent of a pound sterling. With trifling exceptions representing balances paid in cash, these immense sums represent pure credits exchanged against each other on the principle of SET-OFF, which, with the whole operation of clearing-houses, will be explained pretty soon. These figures at only two commercial points are given, as samples merely, of the prodigious amount of transactions in credits throughout the world.

It is time now to explain exactly the nature of credit, and to remove a very common misapprehension that exists in relation to it. A friend of mine, a practical printer, was in my study a few days ago, and speaking of collecting his dues, he said ; — " When I have done a piece of work for a man, *he has got my money*, and I never hesitate to ask him for it." The sentiment of this remark is excellent, but its terms imply considerable misapprehension of the nature of credit. Has the debtor any *money* belonging to the creditor ? Not a penny. Would the creditor be justified in taking out of his debtor's purse, if he should happen to find it, the amount of his debt ? That would be downright stealing, just as much as if there were no debt between them. A debt is never the *money* owed to the creditor, but is always instead the personal *duty* of the debtor to pay the money ; that is to say, no particular money in the possession of the debtor, not even that which the creditor may have just loaned to him, belongs to the creditor so that he can seize upon it at any time — he has parted with his property absolutely to the debtor and has taken in lieu of it *a right to demand* something back, but not that particular money, or any other particular money. The debtor has the absolute property of what he has received, he can use it as he likes, and the creditor must wait until the debtor of his own free will, or compelled by the courts, responds to his personal duty to repay.

Thus the depositors in a bank part with their

property absolutely to the bank — the bank becomes absolute *owner* of it — and take in return a
right to demand a corresponding sum of the bank
at some future time. The Roman law recognizes
all this, and calls a debt a *mutuum*, because the
property passes over from creditor to debtor, while
it calls a thing merely lent, when the very thing
lent is to be returned, a *commodatum*.[1] The English
language has but the one word *loan* for two very
distinct operations, namely, for the loan of a book,
for example, which is to be returned, and which
may be reclaimed if the owner chance to find it,
the Latin *commodatum*, and the loan of money, or
other measurable thing, which is to be returned in
kind merely, which may not be reclaimed except
with the borrower's consent, the ownership of
which passes to him completely, the Latin *mutuum*.
The same ambiguity of course inheres in the Eng-
glish word *borrow*. There are two kinds of borrowing. Commercial borrowing, with which we have
now especially to do, passes the property over completely into the hands of the borrower, and gives
to the lender the *right to demand something of somebody*. This right is credit.

The duty of the debtor to pay exists entirely
independently of the question of fact whether he
has any thing in his possession to pay with, or not.
A debt is a claim on a *person*, not on a *thing*. As we
have already seen in the first chapter, value is always
determined by the mutual action of two persons,

---

[1] See Macleod's "Elements of Banking," p. 72 *et seq.* 1870.

and never resides in things separately from persons, so debt, which is one form of value, hinges
on the free action of persons, and Political Economy consequently has much more to do with *per-*
sons and much less to do with *things* than has
been commonly supposed.

Thus the Roman law, recognizing indeed the
legal obligation in a *commodatum*, in which there
is no exchange at all, called that right a *jus in re*,
a right to that very thing, but it called the right
to which a *mutuum* gave birth, which was a real
exchange, a *jus in personam*, that is, a right against
the person. It was also called a *jus ad rem*, which
is a personal right, and not a right *in re*. So when
goods are sold on credit, the property in the goods
goes completely to the buyer, and the seller takes
instead the right or property to demand their price
at some future time at the hands of the buyer.
It is a right against the person of the buyer, and
not against any specific goods or money whatever.
But this right he can sell, if he chooses, because
it is property.

This peculiarity of credit explains what many
have found it difficult to understand, namely, that
credit in all its forms is *an addition* to the mass of
other exchangeable property; thus, as above, there
are the goods, which are property, and there is
besides a present right to a future payment for
them, which is property also. This second property is a claim on the buyer of the goods for some
form of property to be rendered by him in the

future. In other words, a man can sell what he has not now in possession, provided there be a reasonable prospect that he will have it in possession at the time when he agrees to render it. The *belief* of the buyer that the seller will have it in possession and will render it to him is the foundation of all such *credit* transactions. The gain of such transactions is, that a *new value* has been created, a new purchasing-power, something in the realm of exchange additional to what existed before. Not only does the Past contribute to exchange in *commodities*, and the Present in *services*, but the Future also in *promises*, which create rights, which create values. Exchange is not shut up to the past and to the present: the future is also open to it to a certain degree. That degree is marked by the limits of rational probability. Credit is the right to demand something in future, and the value of the credit is the prospective value of that something, and if that something fails to come, the value of course is gone.

There is an actual addition to the world of values through credit, but not an unlimited addition. The degree to which credit can be carried depends of course on public confidence; the safe limits of credit can be learned only by a sagacious experience; the inherent dangers of credit arise from the uncertainties of the future; but the property in credit and the propriety of credit and the potency of credit are certain. At least 90 parts out of every 100 of the payments and receipts in mod-

ern commerce are in some form of credit rather
than in any form of money; in this country for
the past twenty years almost all commercial transactions have been mediated either by pure credit
or by credit-money; in Scotland, owing to their
peculiar banking system and "Cash Credits" to
be explained pretty soon, coin plays an almost
inappreciable part in business transactions; while
even in England, where bank-notes for less than
£5 are prohibited, it is estimated that not far
from 95 per cent of commercial business is mediated by pure credit.

A credit-right is commonly recorded on paper.
The paper is the evidence of the right, and not
the right itself. These paper documents are
termed Instruments of Credit, and may be divided
into two classes : first, Promises to pay, and second,
Orders to pay. We will now look at these varied
forms of Credit, and at their practical advantages
and disadvantages.

1. Book Accounts. This is the simplest form
of a promise to pay. A charge in a trader's books
is both a current and a legal evidence that the
person charged has received a certain service, and
has virtually promised to render the sum charged
as a return service. The promise is not indeed
express, but it is implied. If the person charged
·fails to fulfil this promise, fails to meet the creditor's right to demand from him, the law, in the
absence of any proof to make the charge suspi-
cious, collects it, if possible, and forcibly com

pletes the exchange. The convenience of this form of credit is so great that it is not likely ever to be disused; and as between people who deal much with each other is very useful, inasmuch as their respective book accounts are set off against en h other in settlement, and only balances are required to be cancelled in money. This form of credit, however, unless the parties are constantly becoming mutually indebted, is subject to some disadvantages to them both. (1.) The trader loses in this way for a time the use of a part of his capital. (2.) He cannot ordinarily make this form of debt to him, as he can other forms, a means of gaining credit from others. (3.) The number and amount of book debts as against any person are less likely than other forms of debt to become publicly known, and consequently the trader is liable to trust persons beyond the point of their solvency and his safety.

On the other hand, (1) the debtor is likely for obvious reasons to be charged a higher sum for each service than the cash customer would pay; and (2) debts contracted in this way are apt to accumulate more rapidly. than the debtor is well aware of; and (3) there is usually less satisfaction in completing by payment exchanges in a mass than similar exchanges one by one. It is for the benefit of both creditor and debtor, that book credits should be short in time, and settlements frequent, since thus only the creditor realizes the full gains of the exchange, and the debtor keeps fair his mercantile name. Doubtless, for many persons in many situations the best maxim is " Pay as you go ; " and even for those who find book credits an unquestioned advantage, the max im is excellent " Go and pay."

2. Promissory Notes. These are express prom ises to pay a certain sum of money to a certain person under certain conditions of time and inter-est, authenticated by the signature of the *maker* of the note, and usually delivered over to the *payee*. Such notes are issued by individuals, corporations, and governments. The interest on them is re-garded as an equivalent for the delay in payment ; and such credit given by one person to another is frequently made a means of obtaining other credit from another party still, as when such a note is discounted by a banker on the joint credit of the maker and payee through the payee's indorsement. The following is the usual form of a promissory note : —

$500.   LYME, N.H., Nov. 25, 1876.

One year after date I promise to pay D. C. Churchill, or order, five hundred dollars with interest at seven per cent, for value received.

DAVID TURNER.

The promissory notes of governments are usually called in this country *bonds*. They pledge the public faith by the signature of authorized officials to return the principal to the lender of the money with interest in the mean time at a specified rate

Sometimes the. time of repayment is distinctly specified, as was the case with all the bonds of the United States issued before 1865 ; at other times, the bonds are made payable *within* a date specified, as the so-called consols of 1865, 1867, and 1868, which are made payable not more than forty years from date ; while consols proper, like most of the British debt, and like the U. S. bonds authorized in 1870, are payable *after* a specified time at the option of government. The United States have recently negotiated bonds bearing 4½ per cent interest payable after fifteen years, and 4 per cents payable after thirty years.

These consols are so named from the " Consolidated " debt of Great Britain, which adopted for the convenience of the government this feature of non-obligation to pay the debt on a day certain. The United States have paid of late years various rates of interest on their bonds, of which the highest was 7.30 per cent in currency, and the lowest 4 per cent in gold. It is thought that even the 3½ per cents might be now negotiated at par, since the 4 per cents have been worth, at times, as much as 7 per cent premium in gold. States, cities, railroads, and other corporations issue similar bonds. Railroad bonds are frequently secured by mortgages on the road itself and its rolling stock and other property, and thus become a very safe form of investment.

3. Bank Bills. These are indeed also promissory notes of a corporation, but they have this pecu-

liarity that they are not on interest, and the bank offers as a sort of compensation for this to redeem the notes into coin on the demand of any holder It is this proffered redemption into coin that en-ables the notes of a bank to circulate as money, while the notes of other corporations equally solid do not circulate as money. The privilege of banks to circulate their notes as money, always gained under governmental regulations, and sometimes under special governmental security, does not essentially alter the nature of their notes; they are a form of credit; they are promises to pay on demand; and although they are commonly issued against another form of credit, namely, against the interest-bearing notes of individuals who resort to the bank for discounts, this does not make their nature differ-ent from the individual notes against which they exchange. It is an instance of exchanging one form of credit for a second which has a greater currency or validity than the first, and for this superiority of the bank credit the individual credit pays an interest, in other words, is discounted.

Bank bills which are actually and always con-vertible into coin on demand are a very conven-ient form of credit, and find no difficulty in being accepted as a substitute to a certain extent of coin money. But such notes are apt to become incon-vertible in times of commercial pressure. All the banks in the United States suspended specie pay-ments Dec. 31, 1861, and only resumed them Jan. 1, 1879. The present national bank bills are redeemed in greenbacks, and the government redeems the greenbacks in gold or silver at certain stated places. The greenbacks themselves were promissory notes issued by the national government directly, were not on interest, and were made legal-tender for debts as a sort of compensation for their inconvertibility and non-interest-bearing character. It may well be doubted, however, whether the making these notes a legal-tender for debts has ever added any thing to the value which they would have possessed as mere promissory notes of the government, or whether, if the legal-tender quality of them were now withdrawn, they would not continue to be as valuable as before. When specie payments were resumed by the government and by the banks, the national bank bills became very acceptable to the people, partly on account of the attitude of the national government towards them, which not only holds as trustee securities for their redemption, but stands towards them also as principal pledging the public faith.[1]

4. Bank Deposits. *A bank is an institution for the creation and extinction of credits.* As a merchant is a buyer and seller of commodities, so a *banker is a buyer and seller of credits*, buying some credits with other credits, and some credits also with money, and money also with credits. A banker needs some money in order to carry on his business, but the amount of his money is a mere trifle compared with the amount of the credits in which he

[1] Amasa Walker's Science of Wealth, page 233.

deals. The word *bank* meant originally a mass, an accumulation, as we still say, a *sand-bank*, and the *banks* of a river. The word was first applied to commercial transactions in Venice as early as 1171, when the Republic was at war, and wished to raise a loan. The Great Council ordered that every citizen should contribute one per cent of his property, receiving five per cent interest on this, and that commissioners should manage the payment of interest to the contributors, and the transfers of their stock. The loan itself was called in Italian *monte*, but as the Germans at that time held a considerable part of Italy, the German word *banck*, which means the same as *monte*, came to be applied to it. Thus the word *bank* in its commercial sense meant first a public loan — the aggregate of the contributions of the citizens of Venice — and also naturally the place where the commissioners paid the interest and transferred the stock.

The origin of the Bank of England was very similar to this, since the original stockholders were only contributors to a public loan, and the larger part of the capital of the Bank is invested in the public debt of England to this day. Gradually the idea of a public debt became mostly dissociated from the meaning of the word *bank*, while the other fundamental meanings still inhere in it. A bank is a place to which the money of other people is brought, as well as the banker's own ; and hence we speak of banks of *deposit :* it is a place in which one form of credit is exchanged for

another form; and hence we speak of banks of
discount : it is frequently a place where promissory
notes, designed to circulate as money, are issued;
and hence we speak of banks of *circulation.* These
three are the main functions of banks; and of
these the two former are, while the third is not, essential to banking. The central idea in banking is
for the banker to receive his customer's money and
credits becoming due, and to render in return for
these a *credit,* that is, a right to demand from him
an equal sum at a future time. The evidence of
this right is entered on the banker's books, and
thus becomes what is now called a DEPOSIT.

It is needful for my readers to understand distinctly what deposits are, especially as they are
very different in their nature from the *Depositum*
of the Roman Law, and different from what the
English word seems to mean. *Depositum* meant
any thing passed over to another person for safe
keeping, the ownership of which was not passed
over, and which formed no element of an *exchange.* ·
If an exchange took place, it was a *mutuum;* if
no exchange took place, the thing handed over to
another was a *depositum,* which very thing was
to be returned. Similarly, the English word *deposit* would seem to mean the thing deposited,
but in banking it does not. The ownership of the
money and of the credits deposited passes over
completely from the customer to the banker.
The latter has the right to do just what he pleases
with them; only his entry of the transaction in

his books is a virtual promise to pay that amount on demand to the customer, and he must be ready to respond to his customer's call, whenever the latter demands, not his own money, but so much of his banker's money. The deposit, therefore, is not the thing deposited, but *a credit purchased by the things deposited.* It is in this way that a banker buys money with credit. The customer has now the right to call on the banker by check or otherwise for such sums (not to exceed the deposit in the aggregate) and at such times as may suit his own convenience. He has such confidence in the banker, and finds it so useful to have dealings with him, that he prefers a credit on him to the possession of the money itself. The banker relieves him from the care of his money and bills receivable, and at the same time is ready to furnish him money or credit to meet his bills payable. This motive on the part of bank customers is so practically operative, that the average deposits in the banks of the city of New York during the nine weeks of August and September, 1876, was $228,-735,877.

The motive on the part of the banker to receive his customers' funds on these terms is the fact that he can safely use a large portion of these funds in other operations in credit profitable to himself, and at the same time be sure of being able to meet his customers' calls for money. He finds by experience that many of his customers wish always to have a balance in his hands; that

while some of them are constantly drawing on him
for cash, others of them are as constantly depositing with him in cash, and that consequently he can
use with safety a part of the money he has purchased with his credit to purchase other credits
with.

Deposit-banking may be illustrated by the practice of insurance: it is abstractly possible that
all the lives insured by a Life Insurance Company
may terminate on a single day, in which case no
life insurance company in the world could meet its
obligations; and it is also abstractly possible that
all the houses insured in a Fire Insurance Company might be burned in a single night, which
would cause the collapse of the soundest company
in the world; and so it is abstractly possible that
a banker might be called upon to pay all his
deposit-liabilities at once, which would break him
of course; but in all these cases of abstract possibility, there is on the other hand a *certainty* that
that supposition will never become a fact. Precisely to what extent a banker may multiply his
liabilities to pay on demand over the amount of
cash kept on hand for that purpose must be ascertained by experience in each locality with reference
to the general modes of doing business there. If
the banker has at any time misjudged, he must
sell some of the securities he has bought, or borrow money on them.

Taking up a chance report of the condition of
the Adams National Bank, at North Adams, in the

State of Massachusetts, at the close of business, Oct. 2, 1876, and I find that "individual deposits subject to check" were $344,482.16, while of "checks and other cash items," "bills of other banks," "silver coin," "legal-tender notes," in short, all the means available on that day to pay checks with, aggregated but $38,299.62. That was a little more than 11 per cent of the immediate liabilities, and yet, I presume, it was amply sufficient. Each depositor felt safe, and *was* safe; the bank was making a profitable use of the difference between these two sums; and the gain for the whole community from such operations in credit is, that a *new capital* has been thereby created, a new purchasing-power, something in the world of value additional to what existed before. It is of the very nature of credit that a new value is created by it. If credit be kept within due limits, if its obligations be assumed with a constant regard to the *uncertainties* as well as to the *certainties* of the future, it is a great blessing. But like all other great blessings, it is liable to be greatly abused. Deposit-banking, however, which is one of the best forms of credit, is being extended more and more every year, especially in all English-speaking communities.

5. Bank Discounts. It is because, in accordance with the primary meaning of the word *bank*, bankers gather up by means of deposits into their own hands values that belonged to their customers, as well as values that belong to themselves, that

they are able so largely to *buy*, that is, to *discount*, credit-paper offered to them by these same and other customers. The bank statement, from which I have quoted above, shows of "loans and dis- counts" $595,309.58. That was the amount of the promissory notes or bills of exchange bought by that bank at that time for the sake of the dis- count upon them. *Discount is the difference be- tween the face and the price of a debt.* I use the phrase "price of a debt" advisedly in order to make plain the fact that whoever gets a note or bill discounted at a bank *sells* it to the banker. It is not a *favor* done me by my banker when he dis- counts my note, it is a *trade* we make. The banker is not primarily a money-lender, he is a buyer and seller of credits.

When I take my note indorsed or fortified by another name to the bank, I do not go as a men- dicant asking a favor, I go as a merchant offering to sell something. If the banker does not care to buy my wares, I need not take it hard of him. Neither has he occasion to consult any thing but his own business interest in the premises. Pity has nothing to do with it, his personal respect for me has nothing to do with it, it is a simple question whether my paper is a good thing for him to buy then and there. If he concludes neg- atively, I have no more ground of offence, than if he should decline to buy my horse or house. My motive in selling the paper is to get either ready money or else the right to draw checks on him at my convenience; and his motive in buying it is to get the difference between the face of the note and the price at which I am willing to sell it. If this view of the matter, which is the true view, always prevailed on both sides of bank counters, it would be better than it is for all parties concerned.

It is more in accordance with genuine *banking* for the banker to pass over the price of the discounted note to his own books in the form of a credit due to the customer, than to pay the money over at once. Those who do the latter are called in England bill-discounters rather than bankers, and though most of our bankers do both, there is a strong tendency towards the separation of the two in this country also. The dependence of banking on ordinary business is something as follows;— manufacturers and wholesale merchants usually sell goods *on time*, as it is called, say three or six months. A debt is thus created. The manufacturer or wholesaler is creditor and the jobber or retailer is debtor. But debts, as we now well know, are property; and the creditor in this case wants to avail himself of his property at once for further production; and so he either takes a note from his debtor or draws a bill upon him, and this piece of property is ready for sale. The banker buys it, that is to say, the creditor passes over to him the right to demand payment of this debt at the end of three or six months, and receives from the banker either money or so much of the banker's credit, that is, a deposit in the banker's books in the creditor's favor. For this furnishing the creditor with money or with a more available credit in lieu of his mercantile paper, the banker charges a percentage. This is discount, and is the chief source of profit in ordinary banking. When the mercantile paper matures, the banker gets from the debtor its full face. Such bankable paper is the following : —

$1000.   WILLIAMSTOWN, MASS., Oct. 30, 1880.

Three months after date I promise to pay to the order of John Wadhams, one thousand dollars, payable at the Adams National Bank, value received.

JAMES L. SMEDLEY

John Wadhams' name on the back of this paper, and the requisite government stamp, make it, if the parties are "good," an acceptable note for dis- count. Two names are usually, not always, requi- site, since a note may be drawn payable to one's own order, but paper is discounted on the strength of all the names upon it. The form of the paper to be discounted makes little difference with the banker; a note is as good as a bill and a bill as good as a note ; his concern is with the genuineness of the signatures and with the financial solidity of the men who make them ; if he cannot discount all the paper offered, he gives the preference, of course, to regular customers and large depositors ; and most bankers prefer that a real business transac- tion should be at the bottom of the paper they

discount, rather than a mere accommodation between the parties signing, but the security of the
bankers is after all in the soundness of the men
whose names are on the paper rather than in the
nature of the commercial relations between them.

Bankers are substantially dealers in credit
rather than in money. Still, so far forth as they
buy discountable notes and pay for them in money,
they become money-lenders; and they become
such also by loaning out *on call* to those who have
collateral securities to pledge, such reserve sums
as they do not wish to invest in negotiable paper
on account of the *time* involved before such paper
matures. The following is the form of such a
pledge : —

$5000.   TROY, N. Y., December 3, 1876.

   *On demand we promise to pay to the Bank of Troy, or order,
five thousand dollars, for value received, with interest at the rate
of six per cent per annum, having deposited with said bank, as
collateral security, with authority to sell the same, at the Brokers'
Board, or at public or private sale, or otherwise at said bank's
option, on the non-performance of this promise, and without
notice, —*

   12 *shares N. Y. Central & H. R.*
   40 *do. Michigan Southern.*

                      FRANKLIN R. BLISS & Co.

The *rate of discount* charged by bankers, or by
bill-discounters, is a matter of the utmost impor·
tance both to business in general and to credit in
particular. Discount is the difference between
the face and the price of a debt, and if this differ

ence be very large, it is a discouragement to business, fewer notes are offered for discount, deposits consequently decline in amount, and the banks become less able to discount for the very reason that they have discounted less. Whenever there is a stable measure of value, a general commercial confidence, and a vigorous production of all sorts, in any community, there will be naturally a low rate of discount, and banks will share in the general prosperity, not through a high price for *every* piece of credit, but through a low price for *many* pieces of credit, and through the ability to use profitably the large deposits that are natural in such circumstances. When, however, there is commercial pressure, and a consequent strong demand for money or credit, a rise in the rate of discount is both proper and useful. Banks have a right to get all that they can for their services in an open market, and it is best for the public that they use this right, for then the services are sure to be rendered to those who most need them. The only practical way to find out who want money or credit the most is to find out who will pay the most for its use. A rising rate of discount in time of money pressure is somewhat like the brakes upon the railroad train. It manages the momentum. It graduates the supply to the demand. It tends to leave something to those most desperately in need.

It is a dictate alike of common sense and of copious experience that, in times of commercial panic, strong banks, instead of refusing to discount altogether, as has often been done, *ought to dis-count very freely indeed;* but, at the same time, they ought to raise the rate of discount very con-siderably, so as to shut off those who can forego the use of the money or credit, and leave the more to those who want it the more. The British govern ment has three times allowed the Bank of Eng-land to violate its charter of 1844, and to issue more bills in the way of buying therewith commer-cial paper than the charter permits, but it has coupled its permission with the condition that the Bank should not discount any paper *at less than ten per cent.* The permission on the one hand was wise and timely, for in each instance it dissipated a great panic in the course of a few hours, and it is plain to reason that free discounting on the part of those able to offer it in times of pressure tends powerfully to bring back confidence again; and so, on the other hand, was the requirement wise of a sharp rise in the rate of discount, so as to dis-criminate in favor of those whose needs were the greatest.

The Bank of England, as the principal bank in Great Britain, and as closely connected with the government, acts, and is designed to act, as a bank of support to the private and public credit in that country. Accordingly, while it does a regular business as a bank of deposits and discounts, it means to keep its rate of discount slightly above the rate demanded by private bankers and bill discounters in London, so as not to come into competition with them much in their ordinary business, and so as to act as a bank of support to them and all others in case of commercial pressure. All banks have just about so much credit to sell, and no more; most banks sell in ordinary times about all the credit they have; if the Bank of England did this, it would be useless in time of panic as a great national bank of support; accordingly, in ordinary times, it keeps its rate of discount above the market-rate, and is thus prepared to do good service in selling its reserve credit when the credit of the bankers below is exhausted. When *their* discount-rate rises, its rate rises a little more; and when they are at the end of their rope, there is usually an abundance of slack rope still in the great institution above.

As gold can be drawn out of the Bank of England by the checks of depositors as well as by the presentation of notes for redemption, the rate of discount becomes a matter of prime importance in the practical management of the bank. Whoever gets a note or bill discounted there, has the right to draw out the proceeds at will by check either in bank-notes, or coin, at his option. The whole line of deposits is a line of liabilities to pay out gold, if the depositors demand it. Accordingly, as these deposits come largely through discounts, whenever there is a strong tendency to draw out gold so as to weaken the reserves of the bank, the directors have an effectual remedy in raising the rate of discount. Of course, a rise in the rate of discount does not affect liabilities *already* incurred; but it tends to lessen the liabilities of the immediate future; because, the higher the price the bank charges for its credit, the fewer, so far forth, will be its customers, and the smaller its line of deposits. Debts are property; and those who have debts to sell do not like a high rate of discount, which is only another phrase to describe a low price for their property; and, therefore, higher rates of discount drive off from the bank some of the sellers of bills of exchange and promissory notes, and thus tend to stop a continuous drain of gold from its vaults. The Bank of England is managed throughout by so simple a matter as the turning back and forth of this magic screw of discount. If the rate is put too high, the bank loses business, and consequently profits; if the rates are kept too low, the reserves are endangered from a drain of gold, which depositors may put to a profitable use either at home or abroad.

And this leads me to say here, what we shall understand better when we have studied the course and par of international exchanges, that whenever the foreign exchanges turn for any considerable time against London, it is a sign for the directors of the Bank of England to raise their rate of discount; for, otherwise, the sums needed to pay off the balances of foreign trade would naturally be drawn from the reserves of the bank.

Also, whenever the rates of discount are decid-

edly higher in the neighboring countries than they
are in London, it is usual for the directors of the
Bank of England to raise their own rates; for,
otherwise, gold would certainly be drawn from
their vaults, and sent to Paris, Antwerp, Ham
burg, or Frankfort, as the case may be, in order to
buy therewith good paper in those markets where
the rates of discount are higher. Gold goes in
one night from London to the continent. To buy
notes of hand or bills of exchange at high rates
of discount with gold, is the same thing as loan
ing out gold at a high rate of interest; and my
readers perceive, accordingly, that it is not safe
for London to maintain for any great length of
time decidedly lower rates of discount than prevail on the continent.

This one fact illustrates on the one hand how
the world is more and more becoming *one* in its
commercial interests and methods, and on the
other hand how potent an instrument over both
domestic and foreign exchanges is a rising or falling rate of bank discount. London is the best
place to observe the potency of this instrument,
because London is the commercial centre of the
world; but the Bank of France, and all the other
great European banks have learned from the Bank
of England how to use the rate of discount. Indeed, in regulating wisely the rate of discount
from time to time in accordance with the state
of domestic and foreign exchanges consists the *art
of banking;* and, in the light of this, appears more

clearly than ever the anomaly and the mischief of usury laws.

In February, 1880, the amount of discounted paper in our *national* banks alone was $969,000,-000, an increase in ten months of nearly one-fifth.

We come next to speak of *Orders* to pay, which proceed from creditors, as *Promises* to pay do from debtors.

6. Checks. A check is a written order on a banker, or other person, directing him to pay to the person named in the check, or to *his* order, a certain sum of money. Of course, the drawer of the check is creditor with reference to the banker on whom it is drawn, but is at the same time debtor with reference to the person in whose favor it is drawn. Commonly, a check is drawn against a *deposit*, which, as we have seen, is a *debt* of the banker to the depositor. The depositor realizes this debt through a check, or series of checks. When the person drawing the check and the person receiving it keep deposits with the same banker, there is no need of any money passing at all in the premises, the sum being merely transferred in the banker's books from the credit of the drawer to that of the receiver.

The introduction of banks has largely changed the old methods of doing business. Men have found that it is safer and more convenient to deposit their money and bills becoming due with a banker, and to make their payments by checks upon him, than to keep their own money and to make their payments directly. The banker is will ing to do this business for nothing, and sometimes to allow the depositors a low rate of interest on balances left in his hands, in consideration of the privilege he enjoys of loaning out such proportion of the sums as he deems safe to other parties at a higher rate of interest. The custom of depositing one's funds with a banker, and the consequent use of checks, is widening constantly in commercial countries, especially in English-speaking countries, among all classes of people. It is difficult to say whether the advantages of the system are greater to the banker or to the depositor; both alike profit by it, as well as the community at large; and nothing illustrates better the nature and benefits of credit.

There has lately been instituted in England what is called the Check Bank, which is designed to bring the benefits of the check-system more easily to all classes of the people, even down to their small, every-day payments.[1] It is a Stock Company, which has entered into relations with nearly all the banks and bankers of the United Kingdom, and with very many colonial and foreign banks, by which check books are furnished for sale by the Check Bank through these associated banks which also agree to cash the checks, every check in which books indicates by printed and indelible perforated notices upon the forms what the utmost sum is against which that check can be drawn, and the aggregate of these sums is the price of the book less 1⅕ penny for each check in it, of which the penny is for the government stamp, and the one-fifth of a penny for the profits of the Check Bank. It is a great security against fraud when every check bears on its face the utmost amount for which it can be drawn. If the checks are actually drawn for less sums, the bank will give additional checks to the amount of the balance ; or the persons to whom they are paid out may give back the change, if drawn for the full sum, and the debt thus paid be less than that.

All money received for check books is left in the hands of the bankers through whom they are issued, or transferred to other bankers if needed by them to meet the checks presented. The checks are payable by any of the associated banks · or bankers. An interest is paid to the Check Bank on the balance of deposits held by these banks, and this, together with one-fifth of a penny for each check, is the only source of profit to the Check Bank. The advantage of these checks over the ordinary bank-check is very obvious. They have a kind of *generalized* character. They are very convenient for remittance by letter, since they will be cashed by almost any banker, and are cheaper than Post Office orders. They yield a certain revenue to government — a penny apiece. Each check carries its whole history along with it.

The banks keep an account with the Check Bank, but are not obliged to keep a separate account with the purchasers of check books, which is a great relief. Anybody who can write can use these books to advantage, they are safer than so much money, there is no difficulty in making payments in shopping or in paying wages by means of them. The checks are drawn to order and crossed, and are dangerous to meddle with in a fraudulent intent. The Check Bank thus extends the use of checks to a multitude of small transactions, and relieves the other banks from what would otherwise be a great deal of troublesome accounting. The longer these checks remain out before presentation the more profitable to the Check Bank, and their average life has been heretofore about ten days.

Now, if all checks had to be carried separately to a banker for payment, it would take much time and involve much trouble; but by a simple arrangement called a Clearing-House, such time and trouble are spared, and checks are virtually paid off without the intervention of much money by setting them off one against another. The London Bankers' Clearing-House was established in 1775; in 1864, the Bank of England was admitted to it, and since then, the clearing-house itself, and all the bankers and firms using it, have accounts with the Bank of England, and the balances formerly settled by money are now settled by simple bank transfers of account in the books of that great Bank without the use of one penny of money.

The average daily clearings at the London Bank

ers' Clearing-House amount to about £20,000,000, which if paid in gold coin would weigh about 157 tons, and would require about eighty horses to carry it, and if paid in silver would weigh more than 2,500 tons. The annual clearings at that establishment are now about £6,000,000,000, and there are besides many other clearing-houses in Great Britain. The New York clearing-house was established in 1853, and its clearings, though formerly greater, are now just about equal in amount to those of the London establishment.

I will describe, in general, the New York clearings, premising, that the principle is the same, though the details may be different, in all other clearing-houses. Business-men in New York usually pass in to their bankers as a deposit all the checks they have received in the course of a business day. They might, by indorsement, if they chose, use these checks to make their own payments with, but it is now rather the custom in business towns for each man to draw his own check to make payments with, and to pass in the checks he receives to his banker. There are 59 clearing-banks in New York city. Each of these banks sorts out every day the checks it has received drawn on each of the other banks into separate parcels ready for the clearing. Each bank has, therefore, to deliver 58 parcels, which represent the property of that bank, and are a *claim* upon the other banks, and to receive 58 parcels, which represent the property of other banks, and are a claim upon *it*.

Before 10 o'clock in the morning, 59 messengers, having each 58 parcels to deliver, appear at the clearing-house, each reporting at once to the Manager for record the amount of exchange he has brought, which is entered of course as *credit* to his bank, and then all take their positions in order in front of the 59 desks, behind which sit 59 clerks, each representing one of the banks.[1] Each messenger stands opposite the desk of his own bank, with his parcels already arranged in the exact order of the bank-desks before him. Each clerk inside his desk has a sheet containing the names of all the banks arranged in the same order, with the amounts carried out which his messenger has just brought. These are entered in his credit-column. Each messenger carries also a slip ready to be delivered with each parcel to each clerk, on which is entered the amount of exchange he now brings to each bank. The amount brought *to* each bank is *debit* to that bank, just as the amount brought *by* each bank is *credit* to that bank.

At a given signal from the manager, each messenger steps forward to the next desk, delivers his parcel to the clerk behind it, and also the slip that goes with it, which latter the clerk signs with his initials and hands back to the messenger as his voucher for the delivery; and then each advances to the next desk — the whole *cue* of messengers moving in order — at which precisely the same

[1] I witnessed a clearing in May, 1876, and describe the process partly from observation.

things take place as before; and so on, until the circuit of the room is made, and each has reached the starting-point opposite the desk of his own bank, having delivered to each bank the exchange he had for that bank, and having taken a receipt for each delivery. This process takes about ten minutes; at the end of which time each clerk, who had on his sheet to start with the *credit* due his bank, has now in his possession the data to calculate the *debit* of his bank. He enters on his sheet the amounts of exchange delivered to him; and the difference between the total amount *received* and the total amount *brought* by his bank is the balance due to or from the clearing-house as to that bank.

All the clerks then report to the Manager the amounts they have received; and, as they reported on first entering the room the amounts their messengers brought, if the two columns on the Manager's proof-sheet add up alike, no mistake has been made, and the general clearing is over. The clerks are allowed thirty-five minutes after the delivery of the exchanges to enter, report and prove their work. For any errors discovered after that time, fines are imposed, payable by the banks whose clerks have erred. All the banks receive a clearing-house ticket of debit or credit, and the debit ones are required to pay the Manager in legal-tenders before half-past one o'clock; and immediately after that hour the credit banks are paid respectively the sums due to them. The largest sum ever cleared in New York in one day was on Nov. 17, 1868, $206,034,- 920.51; and the smallest sum on Oct. 30, of the panic year 1857, $8,357,394.82.

7. Bills of Exchange. *A bill of exchange is a written instrument designed to secure the payment of a distant debt without the transmission of money.* Thus, suppose A in Boston owes B in New York · $1,000, and another party, C in New York, owes A in Boston a like sum; it is not necessary that A should send the money to B to cancel his debt, and C send the money to A for a like purpose; the two debts by means of a bill of exchange are set off against each other, and both transactions are closed without sending any money from one city to the other. A draws a bill upon C, directing him to pay B $1,000, and sends the bill to B, who, if the bill be drawn on sight, presents it to C for payment; if on time, presents it to C for acceptance, who then pays it at maturity. An acceptance is written upon the face of a bill, as an indorsement is upon its back. Checks are really bills of exchange with some differing legal incidents, and a certified check is an *accepted* bill of exchange, — certification being an acknowledgment of the debt, against which the check is drawn, written on its face. A is called the *drawer* of the bill, C the *drawee* until he has accepted, and then the *acceptor*, and B is the *payee.*

It is not often that the same person, as A, happens to owe to another person in a distant place, as B, exactly the same sum as is owed him in that place by a third person, as C; but by two bills of exchange, one drawn by each creditor on his own debtor, and then set off against the other, the same advantage is gained as if it always happened so. Nearly all these bills come into banks in the way of ordinary business, either for discount or collection, and are adjusted through bank balances. The following is the form of an inland bill of exchange : —

$3,000.   THETFORD, VT., Nov. 29, 1876.

Four months after date pay to the order of Edward G. Smedley three thousand dollars, value received, and charge the same to account of   JOHN BASCOM & Co.

To B. E. PERRY, Boston, Mass.

Smedley indorses on the back, Perry accepts on the face, and this bill is negotiable. Sometimes bills are drawn to the order of "ourselves," in which case the drawers also indorse, and the bill is sold on the joint credit of the drawer and acceptor. Bills may bear an indorsement specifying to whom payment is to be made, or an indorsement in blank so-called, by which is meant that the payee or subsequent holder merely writes his own name upon the bill, which is equivalent to making it payable to bearer. Bills of exchange are either payable at sight, or after an interval fixed in the bill itself; they are either real, or accommodation, bills; and they are either inland, or foreign, bills.

Bills having some time to run before maturity

are usually discounted by bankers, or other money-lenders, that is to say, the payee sells the bill to them, receiving the face less interest for the time it has still to run; and the bill thus serves the purpose of enabling a debt due from one person to become the means of obtaining credit from another person.

What are called *accommodation* bills do not differ in form, or in any other legal respect, from what are called *real* bills. The only difference is, that a real bill is drawn on *an actual debt* owed by the drawee to the drawer, while an accommodation bill is drawn on what the drawee agrees *shall be regarded as a debt* from him to the drawer; in other words, a real bill is drawn on the strength of a *past* transaction, namely, the actual sale of some value by the drawer to the drawee, while an accommodation bill is drawn on the strength of a *future* transaction, namely, the promise of the drawee to act in relation to that bill *as if* he owed the drawer. There has been an unreasoning prejudice against accommodation bills, as if they were a kind of counterfeit coin, and as if the real bill were safer because property has previously *passed* from drawer to drawee. The fact that property has passed is no security for the bill drawn on the debt thereby incurred, because the bill gives no claim to *that* property, which is already beyond reach, but the bill itself is a piece of pure credit based on the good faith of all the names upon it. In point of security there is no distinction at all between real and accommodation bills, since they equally constitute a charge upon the whole estates of the signers; nevertheless, bankers properly prefer to buy real bills, because they thus more directly assist in the transfer of commodities from place to place, and especially because real bills cannot exceed in number the transactions already actually had, while accommodation bills may be multiplied indefinitely for purposes of speculation. *Some* accommodation bills are just as good as any real bills can be; — it depends upon the names, and the kind of business done by the wearers of the names.

Foreign bills of exchange mediate sales between countries, just as inland bills do between different places in the same country, without much transmission of money either way. They are a wonderful sign of civilization. New York dealers are constantly sending goods to London, and London dealers are constantly sending goods to New York; for what they send to London, New York firms draw bills on the parties to whom the goods are consigned; and, similarly, for what they send to New York, London firms draw bills on New York parties. Thus bills on London, that is, on English debtors, can always be had in New York by those who have made purchases in London and wish to remit value to liquidate those purchases; and bills on New York, that is, on American debtors, can always be had in London by those who have made purchases in New York and wish to remit for them.

A class of dealers have sprung up in New York and London, and in all other commercial towns, who find it a profitable business to buy up these bills from those who can draw them, and sell them again to those who wish to remit them. These dealers in foreign bills of exchange are *bankers*, inasmuch as they buy and sell credits; and it is very plain that the law of supply and demand applies to these bills in any place where they are an article of traffic. If more bills than usual are drawn and offered for sale in New York, other things being as before, they will fetch a less price, and *vice versa ;* and my readers can understand very easily what is meant by *the par of international exchanges.*

If all the bills drawn in New York on London are readily bought at their face value (*minus* interest for the time they have to run) by those who wish to make remittances to London, and at the same time bills drawn in London on New York are taken up at the same rate by those making remittances to New York, it shows a substantial equality in the mutual debts of those places, and the exchange is said to be at par. This implies, of course, that there is a well-understood relation between the value of the pound sterling and the dollar, which is, so long as both coinages remain unchanged, $4.8665 to £1. But it rarely happens that exchange between New York and London is exactly at par; and exchange is said to be *in favor* of New York, and *against* London whenever bills on

London will not bring in New York their full **par** value less interest. This is the case oftentimes.

If New York has *sold* more value to London, or to parties (no matter where they live) who allow New York to draw on London for their pay, than London has sold to New York, or to parties (no matter where they live) who must remit the pay from New York, it is plain that more bills on London will be offered in New York than will be readily taken up at full value by those who have remittances to make to London. The competition among the *sellers* of bills will lower their price, since there is not an equal eagerness among the *buyers* of bills ; in other words, the *supply* is greater than the *demand*, and the price goes down of course. New York can pay what debts she has to London easily, for she can buy good bills below par. Exchange is in her *favor*. More value is due to her than from her to London. For the same reason that this is so, bills on New York in London will be above par. London cannot pay the debts she has contracted to New York so easily. Exchange is *against* her. But now notice what follows from this.

Because bills of exchange on New York are now worth more than par in London, say 101, there is a direct encouragement to London parties to send values to New York, because on every cargo sent they can draw bills which can be sold at a premium, that is, above par ; and at the same time, there is a direct discouragement to New York to send more values to London, because the bills drawn on the values sent will only bring, say 99. The place, in whose favor the exchange is, exports with lessened profits to the place against which the exchange has turned ; and the unfortunate party, which has sold less in the past, is stimulated, in very consequence of that, to sell more in the present ; and the fortunate party, which has sold more in the past, is unfortunate in this, that it cannot sell any thing at present for its full value. These simple facts tend powerfully to bring the exchanges back to par again. So every thing tends to right itself in this wondrous world of values.

Here is a magnificently comprehensive law, which vindicates Nature's right to reign in the domain of exchange. If, however, in spite of this law, the exchange continues to be obstinately against a country, it only shows, provided the money of that country be sound, that it has incurred credit-obligations beyond the power of its ordinary exports to cancel, and that there must be an export of gold to pay off the old scores, and a more prudent method of purchasing in the future. Gold goes in this way from one country to another to pay off balances, which ordinary bills can no longer adjust; but, it is important to notice, that if for any reason the difference in the exchanges be sufficient to cover the cost of the transmission of gold, gold will go freely from the country against which the exchanges have turned, and bills will be drawn upon that, as upon common merchandise, and sold at a premium. A decidedly higher rate of discount in the neighboring countries will carry out gold; a decidedly adverse exchange will carry out gold; and other exports will be helped to go out from such a country by means of the premium on the bills drawn upon such exports.

Bills drawn by and upon well-known bankers have naturally a better credit than ordinary commercial bills, the names upon which are less widely known. Accordingly, this business of foreign exchange is falling more and more into the hands of bankers in this way: — Persons sending cargoes of cotton, say to Liverpool, arrange through their bankers to have the proceeds put to their bankers' credit in London, and then the bankers draw bills on London, which will bring a higher price in New York than a mere commercial bill will bring, because a remitter may prefer a bill of higher credit even though it cost him more, since he can buy goods abroad with such a bill with less question than with a commercial bill. Commercial bills are still bought and sold in every commercial town, but bankers' bills are more or less taking their place; and there is a strong tendency to make London the settling-place of the world's transactions by means of bills drawn on and by London bankers, which has come about partly from the commercial prominence of England, partly from excellent banking customs there, but mainly because an immense mass of cheap loanable capital exists there. Interest is at least two per cent less in London than in New York, so that a trader who can get credit there, that is, leave to draw on a banker, virtually borrows capital at London rates of interest, and makes his transactions to that extent more profitable. Instead of first depositing money in London, he gets a credit there, and afterward makes remittances to keep the banker good who accepts and pays his bills.

8. Circular Letters of Credit. These are of great convenience to travellers. They are issued by bankers of world-wide repute to their correspondents in foreign countries, directing each of them to pay to the person named in the letter such sum as may suit his convenience at that time and place, the aggregate of which sums is not to exceed the limit mentioned in the letter itself. As each sum paid is recorded on the letter by the banker paying, there is no danger of overdrawing. To carry such a letter abroad is much better than to carry the money; because, in the first place, money can be had by means of it in all the principal cities of the world in just such sums as are needed; in the second place, persons buying such credit have to pay for no more of it than they actually use; in the third place, the letter is available for no one else than the person named in it, whose signature authenticates it, and so is not liable to be stolen, though it may be lost; and in the fourth place, as respects parties in good credit, the money need not be deposited with the banker at home any faster than it is called for abroad.

9. Cash Credits. This form of credit was invented in Scotland about one hundred and fifty years ago, and, so far as I know, its operations are still confined to that country. The Scottish banks have several peculiarities as compared with those of England and the United States. In the first place, there are but 11 independent banks in all Scotland, but each of these has on the average 78 branches, the one having the fewest has 19 and the one having the most has 125 branches, so that almost every village in the country is provided with banking facilities, and these under circumstances most favorable to the credit of the banks and the profit of the people, because branch banks have all the credit of the central institution to fall back upon and are subject to constant supervision and rectification if in any respect they go astray. This ramification of a single bank into various parts of the country, the smallness of the country itself, and the national characteristic of the Scotch hinted at and encouraged in the lines of Burns, —

" But keek through every ither man
Wi' sharpened, sly inspection,"

are favorable to a minute knowledge of the character and credit of individuals on the part of any bank.

In the second place, the Scottish banks, but not the English, are allowed to issue £1 notes, an: these are in universal use among the people, and the banks that sell Cash Credits pay out for this purpose their own notes exclusively. In the third place, such is the organization of the Scotch banks, and such has always been their excellent management, that many of them have at all times a surplus of credit to sell, that is, when they have discounted all the good paper offered, they still have resources for further operations in credit.

Under these circumstances they have fully developed the system of Cash Credits, which allows any man of good character, who has a reasonable prospect of succeeding in business, and who can find two or three friends of good standing to vouch in general for his accounts, to open an account with the bank without any previous deposit, to draw out and pay in on that account just as if he had deposits, and to be charged interest only *on the balance to his debit.* As this interest is less than the discount would be for an account of equal size, cash credits are less profitable to the banks than the discounting of paper, but more profitable than to let any of their funds lie idle; and at the same time, the system affords help to every deserving young man who needs it. Multitudes of Scotchmen have risen by means of so slight a stepping-stone as this to the high places of opulence.

The banks usually advance in this way but a moderate sum, say from £100 to £1,000, but as this is not a dead loan, but a living account constantly operated upon by paying in and drawing out, instances are given of operations to the amount of £50,000 in a single week on the strength of a cash credit of £1,000. The persons who guarantee a young man's account are called *cautioners* in the Scotch law, and are of course interested in his success, are ready to assist him with their counsel, keep a watchful eye on his business proceedings, have the right to inspect his bank account at all times, and to stop it at any time if any thing is wrong; and it scarcely needs to be added, that, under all these circumstances taken together, the national custom of cash credits has been a great conservator of character, and a quick stimulator of prosperity, in Scotland.

These nine are the principal forms of the instruments of credit; and we will now notice that credits are practically extinguished in three ways; — first, by a payment of coin-money, which puts a commodity in the place of the credit, and of course extinguishes the right to demand ; second, by renewal, that is, taking a new credit in lieu of the old one, as when I accept a check in payment of a debt ; and third, and chiefly, by set-off, as in book-accounts and at the clearing-house, because a mutual release from debt is a mutual payment of debt. Credit, in most cases, is like a circle, which returns perpetually into itself.

The advantages of credit have been, perhaps, sufficiently indicated already. They may be classified under four general heads : — First, *credit usually passes existing capital from hands which are less to hands which are more able to use it pro-*

ductively. Those best able to make capital tell are generally those most desirous to obtain it, and frequently those best able to offer good security for it. Credit is the channel through which capi- tal goes from the hands of the idle, the aged, those indisposed and those incompetent to use it productively, into competently productive hands. Joint-stock companies gather up the driblets of unoccupied capital here and there, and, combining them, enter upon paths of profitable production, which individual enterprise cannot tread. Sav- ings-banks receive the surplus earnings of the poor, and, paying a fair interest on each deposit, loan out the aggregate at a higher rate on choice securities, thus stimulating frugality in a wide circle of depositors, and also aiding production by opportune loans to the best class of borrowers. Sound life-insurance companies illustrate the bene- fits of credit in a gratifying light, and, by elevat- ing and widening the views of men, tend to make them better producers and better citizens. Banks, as well in their capital stock, as in their deposits and discounts, operate to put capital where it will do the most good.

Second, *credit affords amazing facilities for ad- justing the accounts of the world's commerce.* Bills of exchange both inland and foreign, checks, the clearing-house, bankers' drafts, and travellers' credits, all facilitate settlements. The great prin- ciple of settlement is SET-OFF, or a mutual release from debts; but also, the creation of one debt is often at the same moment the extinction of an-other:

Third, *credit dispenses with the use of a great deal of expensive metallic money.* Some metallic money there must always be, in order to furnish the denominations of value, in order to afford the basis of credit, and in order to settle up the bal-ances of credit-exchanges; but credit can take the place of money to an extent never yet real-ized, even in Scotland; and this use and extension of credit are economizing of expense; less coin is needful ; London settlements, for example, are made first at the clearing-house, and then the bal-ances cleared at the Bank of England without any money at all.

Fourth, *credit creates a new capital.* It cannot do this indefinitely, but it does it actually. Besides all the commodities in the world, and all the personal services ready to be exchanged, there is a body of credits with which *purchases* can be made. Besides the past, and the present, the future can be made to a limited degree to pay tribute to exchanges.

On the other hand, there are some disadvan-tages connected with the use of credit. Some-times by means of credit, particularly book-accounts, capital steals out of the hands of the enterprising and productive citizen into the hands of indolent and unproductive consumers. This is a loss not only to the dealer but also to the community, inasmuch as bad debts in the accounts

of some customers have to be made up for in part
by more onerous terms in the accounts of other
customers. Long credits are not to be commended except as given to governments, certain railroads, and possibly some other parties, for whom
the future is not likely to have reverses in store
For, it must always be remembered, that there are
more uncertainties connected with credits than
with material commodities and personal services,
since the future is more indeterminable than the
past and present. In a different sense from that
in which he has used them, we may quote the
lines of the good Whittier ; —

" We know not what the future hath
Of marvel or surprise."

Also, credits may be used in such manner as to
bring about commercial crises. It is still a disputed point, whether the use of pure credits, not
to speak now of credit-money, tends to raise the
scale of general prices. Whether it does so or
not depends on the further question, whether the
demand for things offered for sale is more intensified by credit facilities in buying them than their
supply is increased by credit facilities in producing them. We may be absolutely sure that the
law of supply and demand governs all prices.
Demand is the desire to purchase coupled with the
power to purchase. Credit affords such facilities
for buying, that it is certain more is bought by
almost everybody than would be bought under

an absolute system of cash payments. It is also certain that salable things of every kind are brought more easily and abundantly to the market through the facilities credit gives to production.

Whether demand or supply be the more stimulated by credit is a delicate and difficult question, and on its solution depends the inquiry whether general prices are raised by credit; but however those questions may be decided, it is pretty clear that commercial crises have their rise in disordered credits, and that the collapse is caused either by the failure of certain parties to meet their matured credit-paper with immediate settlement, or by an apprehension of such failure. In times of confidence and prosperity various forms of credit-paper are multiplied; in times of over-confidence and speculation the volume of such paper is unduly increased, and the character of some of it insufficiently scrutinized; then come the beginnings of distrust; then follows a loss of confidence; credit is much less freely given than before; some parties whose debts are maturing find it impossible to provide an acceptable set-off, or payments in cash; their failure may precipitate the failure of others their creditors, at any rate, it causes consternation and a further suspension of credit; next comes the general crash, unless some central power, like the Bank of England, can offer unbounded credit to all solvent parties; and then succeeds a period of stagnation and distress. Such crises, more or less intensified however by the action of *credit*.

money, swept over this country in 1837, again in 1857, and again in 1873.

We conclude, then, that Credit is good; but it requires general caution and strong control to keep it from becoming evil.

We may throw into the following summary the substance of the discussions in this chapter: —

1. *Credits are* RIGHTS *bought and sold just like commodities and services, and therefore claim an equal place with these in Political Economy.*

2. *Credits accordingly round out in a wondrous way the* THREEFOLD *world of values.*

3. *Economics and morals touch each other in credits, which have their foundation in human* CHARACTER.

4. *Credits put even the* FUTURE *under contribution for productive purposes, and consequently must take a share in its uncertainties.*

5. *Credits minimize money, utilize* SET-OFF, *and maximize production.*

6. *Bankers buy and sell credits, and thus become* BENEFACTORS.

7. *Credits are* LIABLE *to abuse, always involve some losses, often bring on commercial crises, and sometimes pile up national debts.*

CHAPTER VI.

TAXATION.

WE have now reached the last stage in our journey. The end of it is already within view. If parts of the road have seemed dry and dusty to my fellow-travellers, the direction of it at least has been straight forward over hill and dale, and points of view have certainly been gained here and there displaying the wonderful nature of man, and the still more wonderful providence of God. I still bespeak the patience of those who have gone with me thus far, both because the journey is now near its completion, and especially because this last stretch of it promises the most instructive prospects of all. ·

It might seem at first sight as if Taxation were not properly a topic of Political Economy, inasmuch as that is a field of voluntary action, while it is scarcely voluntary with the individual citizen or subject whether he pay taxes or not. But, on a closer view, it becomes apparent, that the people do really tax themselves, either directly or indirectly; that they organize governments primarily for the security of person and property; that the origin and increase of property depend upon the exercise of the rights of exchange, which government is instituted in part to make secure; that taxes are really a return for services rendered, and may be justified on the strict principles of exchange ; that government, while it has other important functions, renders, by its laws, courts, and officers, by the force which it is at all times ready to exert in behalf of any citizen or the whole society when threatened with evil in person or property, services on the principle of the division of labor, one set of agents devoting them·selves to that work ; and that the practical rules of taxation at any rate, whether the fundamental reasons for it or not, must be found within the purview of our science.

We inquire, accordingly, into the SOURCE, out of which taxes must be paid ; into the MODES, in accordance with which taxes are actually raised ; and into the guiding PRINCIPLES, under which all taxes ought to be levied.

It is very clear, in the first place, that all taxes have to be paid out of the *gains of exchanges.* Indeed, there is no other possible source out of which they can be paid. Taxes are collected in money ; and the only way, gifts and plunder aside, both of which are out of the question, by which any man gets money to pay his taxes with, is through exchange of some sort or other. Everybody must pay his taxes out of income ; the sources of income are only three, namely, wages, profits, and rents ; and each of these is a result of exchanges. Even the retired merchant, who lives on the interest of his money, and pays his taxes out of interest, must at least loan out his money

to get the interest, — which is an exchange. La
borers pay their taxes out of earnings, capitalists
theirs out of profits, real-estate holders theirs out
of rents, — all of them consequently out of exchanges.

It is, therefore, alike for the interest of the
government as tax-gatherer, and for the interest
of the people as tax-payers, that exchanges should
be free. As the only motive to make exchanges
is the gains to be derived from them, and as taxes
can only be paid out of these gains, it is very foolish as well as unjust for a government to prohibit
exchanges, or to try to make them more onerous
than they naturally are. The nation whose internal and external exchanges are the freest is,
other things being equal, necessarily the most
prosperous, and pays its taxes the easiest, since
the reservoir out of which taxes are drawn becomes
in this way the largest, and the ratio of taxes to
the whole gains of exchanges the smallest. In
other words, the interests of government, which
must be maintained by taxation, and the interests
of the people, who can only thrive by exchanges,
are identical.

In the second place, the modes in which governments practically levy their taxes are two,
namely, *direct* and *indirect*. A direct tax is levied
on the very persons who are expected themselves
to pay it; an indirect tax is demanded from one
person in the expectation that he will pay it pro-
visionally, but will make himself good by means

of a higher price which he in turn will demand of the next purchaser of the article taxed. Thus an income tax is a direct tax, while duties on imported goods are indirect taxes. Both alike come out of the gains of exchanges, and are so much subtracted from what those gains would otherwise be; but the differences between them after all justify the distinction drawn, and will justify us in studying each mode somewhat carefully. Let us begin with direct taxes.

From the nature of the case, direct taxes must be either on INCOME or EXPENDITURE. These are personal to the individual, and taxes on them must be borne by him, and cannot be thrown off upon others in the same way as indirect taxes may be. As the difficulty of a tax on a person's whole expenditure is much greater than one on his whole income, inasmuch as the items are far more numerous and diffused, it is never attempted to levy taxes on one's entire expenditure, but only on some special forms of expenditure, such as horses, carriages, watches, plate, and so on, kept for personal use. The United States have repeatedly levied such taxes as these, but they have been of short duration, and, as such taxes do not reach all persons will any fair degree of equality, they are so far forth objectionable. There is a better way to tax than to tax expenditures in any form.

But if any tax on expenditures is selected, I am much inclined to think with Mr. Mill, that a house-tax, levied on the occupier, and not on the owner unless he be at the same time the occupier, is the best form of such a tax. Taking society at large, the house a man lives in and its furniture are probably the best index attainable of the size of his general expenditures. The house and its con·tents are open to observation and current remaik; they are that on which persons rely more perhaps than on any thing else external for their consideration in society and general station in life; the tax can be assessed with very little trouble on the part either of the assessor or of the occupier; and even a domiciliary visit is scarcely required, as the house may speak for itself and its contents. On the other hand, the tax would not reach at all that comparatively large class of persons who do not keep house; nor would it reach with any fairness two other classes, the comparatively rich who care nothing about style, and the comparatively poor who frequently affect style. On the whole, and for good reasons, the nations are looking away from taxes on expenditures.

It is not so, however, with taxes on income. For more than thirty years the English have found their income tax to be the most uniform, unfailing, expansive and manageable of all their fiscal expedients. Their rate has varied at different times from fourpence to sixteen-pence to the pound of income. 1 1 1857, this tax alone realized $80,255,000 to the English exchequer. The Germans have had as yet but a short experience with an income tax, but they are now successfully using it as one of their means of revenue. The late national income tax was new in this country, and for certain reasons not inherent in the nature of the tax became unpopular in influential quarters, and was discontinued after a few years' trial; but it was productive while it lasted, yielding, in 1866, $60,894,135, and would have been much more so, had it been popularly regarded as a permanent and proper tax.

The beauty of an income tax is its simplicity and its harmony with the fundamental ideas of property and of taxation itself. The sources of income, as we have seen, are only three; a tolerable method of book-keeping will enable any man to determine what his aggregate income of the year has been; it is only a question of net receipts; and if all other taxes were abolished, and it were settled that an income tax should be the policy of the nation, state, or municipality, it would make no difference when the money was earned, when the profits really accrued, or when the rents became actually due, the receipt of the income within the year would mark the time of its proper taxation.

Besides, as all taxes must come from the *gains* of exchanges, it would seem reasonable that each man's taxes should be in exact proportion to the *sum* of his gains by exchanges. I do not think that there can be any other just rule of taxation. It is sometimes said, that each man should be taxed according to his *property ;* but when we come to analyze this remark, it amounts to what has just now been said. What is property? The old

Roman Law said, and said rightly, *Property is any thing which can be bought and sold.* The very substance of property is the power and right to render services in exchange; the test of property is a sale; that which will bring nothing when exposed for sale either never was, or at least is not now, *property;* the right of the government to tax anybody, consequently, depends on the question whether he has something to sell; or has actually sold something; and the *amount* of the tax would seem to be determined by the amount of the *sales,* just as the ability *to pay the tax* certainly hinges on the fact and the amount of the sales.

The farm, the foundry, the mill, the railroad, the real estate of every name; personal property of every kind; and personal acquirements and efforts of all descriptions, best appear, for the purposes of taxation, *through the gains realized by means of them.* If, for any reason, any of these forms of property should become unproductive, taxes should cease to be derived from them; indeed, *must* cease to be derived from them, because their owners can no longer pay taxes by virtue of them. If it be objected, as it has been, that lands, for example, presently unproductive, might be held untaxed under this principle for the sake of a prospective rise of price, I would reply, that that is no objection, that when the lands are sold, or rented, or otherwise made productive, the owner should be taxed on that revenue, that it will be time enough then, especially as men do not like to hold unproductive forms of property. Quick property alone is able to pay taxes, and, therefore, property should be taxed only so far as it is quick.

There is an illusion about land and other real estate that needs to be dissipated before men will understand clearly the whole matter of taxation. All property has its *limits* as well as its *birth* in human services exchanged; without constant watchfulness and foresight, without constant *efforts* in improvements and repairs, every form of real estate will deteriorate and become unproductive. Land even in Great Britain, where land is scarce, is worth only about 25 years' rent; and without the exercise of intelligence and will, every form of property ceases to exist. Therefore it is right to trace property for the purpose of taxation to the person of its owners, and to make the revenue they derive from it the basis of the claim that they contribute to the support of the state, and the size of the revenue they derive from it the gauge of those contributions.

It may also be objected, that, under this principle of an exclusive income tax, wages, the result of personal and professional exertion, would be taxed just the same as profits and rents, the result of previously accumulated property. That consequence would certainly follow; and I cannot see why it ought not to follow. Can anybody give a solid reason why wages should not be taxed as high as rents? It might be said, perhaps, that a professional man earning a large income, on which taxes are paid the same as on a similar income of a land-proprietor, dying, leaves to his children no further means of support, while the land-proprietor, dying, does leave such means. I admit that this is so; but then, the income from that land continues to pay taxes, while that professional income does not! Other members of the profession will do the business which the former one would have done had he lived, and they may be made to pay taxes on the income from it. What a man transmits to his children, whether a great name or a great estate, has nothing to do, as I take it, with the amount of taxes that he ought to pay while he lives. It seems to me, accordingly, that the kind of activity by means of which a man realizes his gains, has nothing to do with the question of his taxes; as he must pay his taxes *out of* these gains, why should he not pay taxes *in proportion* to these gains, from whatever source derived?

As government is instituted and supported, in part, for the protection of property, and as property in its ultimate analysis *is the right of rendering services for a return*, it is plain that a demand for taxes from individuals proportionate to the aggregate of such services of theirs is in harmony with the ground principles of taxation. A universal and exclusive income tax would be just such a demand. Besides this, such a tax has a grand advantage over all other forms of taxation in that it has no tendency *to disturb prices*. Were there no taxation except on incomes, and were the incomes rightly rendered, the prices of every thing bought and sold would be just as if there were no taxes at all! Taxation would then be like the atmosphere, pressing equally on all points and consciously on none.

It is through *tricks wrought on prices* that the greatest injustice has been done and suffered in this country in times past; the depreciated currency, for example, raises some prices and not others, and some prices before others, and thus distributes its mischiefs unequally; the "protective" tariff-taxes play fantastic tricks with prices, raising some and lowering others, thus working monstrous injustice on a great scale; and almost all forms of taxation become unequal and unjust through their diverse action on prices. But a universal income tax, properly levied and fully responded to by the payers, would have no influence at all upon prices, could by no possibility work essential injustice, and would be certain to be very productive.

One incidental advantage of such a tax in such a country as this would be, that all men would be obliged to keep regular accounts, more orderly methods of business would prevail, each man would know better where he himself stood and whom of others it would be safe to trust, failures would be less frequent and widespread, and every thing financial would be more known and aboveboard.

A second incidental advantage of an exclusive

income tax, and one too of great moment, especially in a country organized as ours is, in which
taxes have to be paid, first to the local municipality, second to the state, and third to the nation,
would be, that the local government might ascertain the incomes once for all, the state and nation
afterwards collecting merely an additional *per
centum* for themselves; or better still by amica-
ble arrangement, neither party yielding its inherent right to tax, one set of officials might ascertain
and collect the tax for all three governments at
one and the same time.   The vast economy of this
simple plan is manifest enough ; and it is also manifest enough that official jealousies as between the
governments would oppose its adoption.

One objection to an income tax has been the
publicity resulting from it.   This is no objection
at all, inasmuch as every man who pays taxes
would seem to have a *right to know* that his neighbors are contributing to support the government
pro rata with himself.   In bearing up the great
burden of government all citizens are copartners,
and in this view each has a right to demand a
look into the books of the rest.   It is only by
publicity and openness of method and result, that
suspicions of unfairness and injustice in taxation
can be kept at rest among the citizens.

A second objection has been commonly urged,
that men will not give in a true return of their
income.   It is true, that many men will not of
their own free impulse make a true return, but

they can be made to do so, as the forms are per-
fected, as fraudulent returns are promptly pun-
ished, and as the memory and conscience of the
payers are quickened by the action of a healthful
public opinion brought to bear through the annual
publication of the list of their returns. Men are
not usually so isolated from each other, the various methods of rendering services for a return are
not so secret, as that a man's neighbors do not
know pretty well the general amount of his income. Then there is the additional security of a
solemn oath, of a fear of detection and punish-
ment, of a desire to maintain a good mercantile
credit, and a wish to stand well with one's class.
At the very worst, it might be said, that evasions
and fraud accompany also all other forms of taxation.

An income tax has not yet had a fair trial in
this country; special reasons made the late law
obnoxious; it was enacted as a temporary expedient only, and not as a national experiment; but I
am thoroughly convinced that if the system were
permanently established in lieu of all others, the
difficulties under it would grow less and less every
year, it would prove amply productive and elastic
for the varying wants of the governments, and
would subject the governments themselves to the
constant and healthful supervision of the tax-
payers. It may be long before we shall ever come
to this; but the truth remains, nevertheless, that
an income tax is the justest of all possible taxes.

We come now to indirect taxes. All of these are in effect, and most of them are in form also, taxes on sales. The only way, in fact, in which any person, from whom a tax is demanded and by whom it is paid, can throw off that tax upon some-body else, is either to sell the taxed article out-right for a higher price on account of the tax, or to make some other exchanges in connection with it, the terms of which are more onerous to the other party by reason of the tax. A tax on soda fountains, for example, may be reimbursed to the payer either by the resale of the fountain itself, or by a higher price charged to the drinkers of the beverage, by which the tax is distributed over many persons and much time. The taxes, by means of stamps, on bank-checks, liquors, and tobacco, and on railroad, insurance, and gas com-panies, levied by the present United States inter-nal revenue law, are indirect taxes, whereby the government gets in a lump what is afterwards dis-tributed over many subordinate exchanges.

One advantage of indirect taxes is, that men pay them as a part of the price of the goods they buy, without thinking perhaps that it is a tax they are paying, and consequently without any of the re-pugnance that is felt towards a tax-gatherer who comes with an unwelcome demand. But, on the whole, it is doubtless better both for the govern-ment and for the people that men should know . when they are paying taxes and how much *taxes* they pay; for, it is a countervailing disadvantage

of an indirect tax, that the price of the commodi
ty is usually enhanced to an extent much beyond
the amount of the tax, partly because the tax is a
cover under which dealers may put in an unreasonable demand, and partly because the tax, having
to be advanced over and over again by intermediate. dealers, profits accumulate as an element of
the price.

Tariff-taxes are the most important taxes of this
class. Our people paid to government in customs-
duties in the year ended June 30, 1876, $148,071,-
985, and the year before, $157,167,722. They
paid in internal revenue to the national government during the same years respectively $116,700,-
732, and $110,007,494. These were all indirect
taxes; and the ultimate buyers of the things thus
taxed paid a great deal more in consequence of
the tax than the government received from it.
The net revenue of the national government from
all sources, of which these two are the chief, was
in 1870 just one-third more than in 1876, namely,
$411,255,748.

In our third chapter on Commerce, it was laid
down, that tariff-taxes, in order to be productive
and not unjust, must be levied in accordance with
three principles, namely, first, on articles mainly
or wholly imported from abroad, and not also produced at home; second, on as few articles as will
produce the needed revenue; and third, at such
low rates as shall not greatly lessen the importation of the articles taxed. When levied in accord-

ance with these principles, tariff-taxes are a tolera- ble means of revenue, especially if different kinds of taxes are adopted as between the local, state, and national governments. If the municipalities tax mainly real estate, and the states tax mainly corporations, a rude result of justice may be reached, if the nation taxes mainly imports which do not come into competition with native products. But I have already given reasons for believing that an income tax might be substituted for all these with great advantage to both governments and people. At any rate, the tariff-taxes at present levied in this country violate each of these three principles, and are as wrong in purpose as they are disastrous in practice.

For example, tea and coffee are not produced in this country at all, and are almost universally used, and therefore are just the articles to bear a tariff-tax. The average net imports of coffee into the United States for the eight years 1872–79 were 310,908,438 pounds, and the average price of this 15.5 cents a pound; if this average importation had borne a duty of 3 cents a pound, which was the rate when the duty was removed in 1872, the treasury of the United States would have realized $9,327,253.14 a year from this one source; the ultimate consumers of the coffee would have paid something more than this sum in consequence of the tax, because the tax would have been advanced two or three times over before the coffee reached their hands; but it is evident that the tax would have raised the price of nothing but the coffee, and substantially all the people paid would have gone direct to the treasury. But, unfortunately, there is no tax at all on coffee, — excellent in all respects as such a tax would be, — because certain protectionists combined to repeal it in order to *keep* on the statute-book "protective" taxes tenfold more onerous. It was a sop to Cerberus. The total annual production of coffee throughout the world is just about 1,000,000,000 pounds; and of this the people of Holland consume about 18 pounds *per capita*, of Belgium 9 pounds, of Norway 8½ pounds, of the United States 8 pounds, of France 4 pounds, of Germany 3 pounds, and of England 1 pound, *per capita*.

For a good many years the importation of tea' into this country just about kept pace with the population, at the rate of one pound for each inhabitant. Of late the consumption of tea has been increasing *per capita*, and is now approaching 1½ pounds apiece. The average net imports of tea for the eight years, 1872-79, were 60,071,875 pounds, and the average wholesale price of this 31.5 cents per pound. If this had borne a duty of 15 cents a pound, which was the rate when the tea-duty was abolished in 1872, the treasury would have realized $9,010,781.25 a year from this source, without sensibly burdening the people beyond the burden of the tax itself. This abolition was an-other purely protectionist measure, and another sop to the triple-headed guardian of the nether world.

The treasury actually lost in those eight years, by the repeal of these two simple and unobjectionable duties, $146,704,275.12. Indeed, tea and coffee together may easily be made to bring into the treasury $25,000,000 a year: four cents a pound on coffee and twenty cents on tea would be only reasonable duties, and would raise that sum; these articles are in universal consumption, and, if there are to be tariff-taxes at all, these are the things to bear them.

The consumption of cane-sugar in the United States in the calendar year of 1879 was 743,000 tons, — nearly 9 per cent more than in 1878, — and about 45,000 tons besides were boiled out of molasses. Add to this the maple-sugar consumed, and the likelihood is, that each man, woman, and child in the country uses on the average nearly 40 pounds of sugar a year. The consumption of sugar in Great Britain is larger that this *per capita:* on an average of 27 recent years that consumption was 43.82 pounds, and of tea during the same time 3.37 pounds. Now, a tariff-tax on sugar is not so simple a matter as one on tea or coffee, because some cane and other sugars are made in the country itself, and the price of *these* will be enhanced by a tariff-tax on the imported sugar, and because crude sugars in many forms are imported to be refined and, as it were, re-manufactured here; still, sugar is such a universal necessity of life, and the part grown here so small relatively to the whole consumption, that a tariff-tax on it is entirely proper, if there be any tariff at all. An average of three cents a pound on the entire amount used will bring in $50,000,000 a year. If domestic sugar should ever come to be a considerable part of the whole consumption, then an excise on that part, corresponding to the tariff-tax on the rest, would prevent any injustice otherwise flowing from the tax.

According to our consul at Lyons, there were 18,000,000 pounds of silk produced in the world in 1879, and its value $83,000,000. Some of this silk is imported into this country, and may well be subject in all its forms to tariff-taxes for revenue; but care should be taken in this, as in every thing else, that an excise supplement the tariff whenever considerable amounts of domestic goods are raised in price by the latter. That enhancement of price should go to the treasury, and not elsewhere! These four, with wines, liquors, tobaccos, fruits, and perhaps a few articles more, might well constitute the entire list of tariff-taxed articles. The British tariff is precisely of this character, and realizes regularly a little over $100,000,000 a year. Aside from our national debt, which is now being rapidly paid off, a revenue of $100,000,000 from the tariff, and $100,000,000 from internal taxes and other miscellaneous sources, is ample for the legitimate uses of the United States. A larger revenue breeds unconstitutional, extravagant, and corrupt national expenditures.

When tariff-taxes are laid, not for revenue, but

t) raise the price of home products, some curious results are exhibited. For instance, take blankets in 1875. The duty on imported blankets was from 85 to 95 *per centum*, equivalent to 20 cents a pound *extra* to the price charged by foreigners. We consumed 70,000,000 lbs. of blankets in 1875, and the price of the whole consumption was largely enhanced by this duty, indeed this enhancement was the sole motive for putting such duty on, while the revenue collected from blankets imported in that year was a paltry $8,451.22. If we suppose, for the sake of the illustration, that the home blankets were raised in price quite up to the price of the foreign with the duty added, although as a matter of fact they were *not* raised quite so high, then the people paid for blankets $14,000,000 in consequence of a tariff-tax in order that the treasury might receive $8,451.22 out of it ! Was there ever a tax more shrewdly devised to make the people pay *much* in order that the treasury may get *a little?*

All the bunting that was used in this country for flags in the decade 1870–80 was doubled in price by a tariff-tax, which amounted to $5.70 gold per piece of twenty square yards. The ruling price of the domestic bunting was just about $10 gold per piece, while the old price before the duty was put on was from $5 to $5.50 gold per piece. The duty was 20 cents per square yard, and 33 per cent of value additional.

For the two fiscal years 1873 and 1874, the

average duty actually paid on imported *cottons* was 36 *per centum* of their value; on *glass* and its manufactures, 46 *per centum;* on *iron and steel* and their manufactures, 31.50 *per centum;* on other *metals* and their manufactures, 31 *per centum;* on *paper and books*, 25.50 *per centum;* and on *wool* and its manufactures, 54.50 *per centum.*

The duties on hay-knives, reaping-hooks, scythes and sickles, were, in the year of grace 1880, 45 per cent; on shovels and spades, if of iron 35, and if of steel 45, per cent; on anvils, blacksmiths' hammers and sledges, 2½ cents per pound, — all to make the farmers happy and prosperous, and to encourage the interests of American labor! If *taxes* could make a people prosperous, we should be prosperous indeed; if complicated burdens could make labor thrive, then American labor would long ago have been beyond the need of artificial help. But suppose, on the other hand, that *all taxes of every name* could be abolished to-morrow, that governments could live on air, that all tariffs and tax-gatherers should go by the board together, — would not that be a wonderful relief all round? Would anybody suffer from such a state of things? Would American labor pine and die for lack of a chance *to pay taxes?* Would opportunities to buy and sell and get gain be lessened or destroyed by the sudden disappearance of the tax-gatherers?

Certainly, governments cannot live on air, and therefore taxes will always be necessary, but they

will also always be a necessary *evil ;* and no cun-
ning manipulations in tariffs, no sleight-of-hand
tricks in taxes, no fallacious promises to the igno-
rant classes, can transform a negative into a positive, — a minus sign into the plus sign, — or enrich
the whole by depleting the pockets of a part.

I append a few principles applicable to taxation
in all forms and at all times.

1. Taxes should be *simple.* The payers should
be able to understand the whole process by which
they are to be taxed, and be able to calculate beforehand about what the government will demand
from them as their contribution to the public
burdens. Every thing in taxation should be open
and clear. To conceal, to complicate, to play fast
and loose, is bad enough anywhere, and too bad in
taxation. To combine, as our tariff does, *specific*
and *ad valorem* duties upon the same article, vio-
lates this sound rule. It makes it difficult for the
importer to know what his tax will be. It grows
an abundant crop of misunderstandings, bicker-
ings, frauds, and corruptions at the custom-house.

Specific duties, that is, taxes by the pound,
yard, gallon, and so on, are better than *ad valorem*
duties, that is, taxes upon the supposed value, because they are simpler and more calculable. To
combine the two on the same article is a device
of " protection," is in the interest of concealment,
and is a godsend to informers. Almost all nations
have been of late years simplifying their systems
of taxation. Great Britain has taken the lead in

this. The United States have simplified their internal-revenue system, while the tariff, though somewhat simpler than it was, is still the home of twists and turns. Some of the states, and notably Pennsylvania, have lately improved their state tax-systems; and attention has been drawn to the defects of municipal taxation by the startling frauds of the late government of New York City. Much remains to be learned, and still more to be done, by the nation, states, and local governments, in the interest of a simple, definite and just taxation.

2. Taxes should be *low*. A high tax not infrequently stops exchanges in the taxed articles altogether, and of course the tax then realizes nothing to the government. As the only motive to an exchange is the gain of it, the exchange ceases whenever the tax cuts so deeply into the gain as to leave little margin to the exchangers. The greater the gain left to the parties after the tax is taken out, the more numerous will the exchanges become, and the greater the number of times will the tax fall into the coffers of the government. In most articles, consumption increases from a lowered price in a greater ratio than the diminution of the rate of tax; so that the interests of the consumers and of the revenue are identical. On certain articles of luxury and ostentation, high taxes may properly enough be laid, because their incidence will hardly tend to diminish consumption, and it would be scarcely to be regretted if

it did. Fashion is abashed whenever her fancies become too common; and a high tax sometimes works in harmony with fashion, and becomes productive when and because comparatively few are called on to pay it. The rich, however, are more evenly reached through an income tax, than through any taxes on expenditures no matter how shrewdly levied.

A splendid illustration of the general principle that traffic increases as charges diminish is furnished by the railroads. In the ten years 1870–79 the Lake Shore and Michigan Southern Railroad lowered its charge for moving one ton of freight one mile from $1.50 to $.64, and the number of tons moved that distance mounted up from 574,-035,571 to 1,733,423,440; that is, charges being reduced 57 per cent, traffic increased 202 per cent, and earnings increased 22 per cent. In the eleven years, 1869–79, the New-York Central and Hudson-River Railroad decreased its charge per ton from $2.38 to $.79, that is, 67 per cent; and the tons moved went up from 589,362,849 to 2,295,827,387, that is, 289 per cent, and the earnings increased 30 per cent.[1] The Boston and Albany Railroad and Pennsylvania Railroad show similar though less striking results. The history of the Atlantic cables illustrates equally well this fundamental principle of trade and taxation, — each lowering of the charge per word for transmission has been followed by a sudden and large increase in the number of words transmitted.

[1] Edward Atkinson to Merchants' Club of Boston.

3. Taxes should be *economical*. That is to say, the tax-money should be kept out of the pockets of the people as short a time as possible, disbursement following quick upon collection. It is poor policy to gather taxes at the beginning of the year which will not be disbursed till the end of the year. Let the people use their money till it is wanted at the treasury; and if the taxes do not then come in as fast as they are wanted, it is better to issue what are called in England exchequer bills, and in this country certificates of indebtedness, to be redeemed at the end of the year from the proceeds of the taxes, than to let the people's money lie idle in the treasury.

4. Taxes should relate to *property* and not to *person*. I do not see how a poll tax can be justified to any man's reason. It stands, at any rate, upon different ground from all other taxes, and is to be defended, if it can be defended at all, by a different set of reasons from those applicable to other taxes. A man who pays a poll tax must make some exchanges in order to enable himself to pay it, and why should not the tax be conditioned on the exchanges, as all other taxes are, rather than on the poll, the possession of which does not enable a man to pay taxes at all? It is usually said, that poll taxes are paid to government for the protection of one's person, and property taxes for the protection of one's property: is, then, the government at liberty *to fail to protect* the person of one who pays no poll tax? Are not the

persons of all citizens or subjects equally sacred to the law, whether they pay poll taxes, or not? That, therefore, is no sound reason for a poll tax. The whole truth seems to me to be, that the right to tax on the part of the government grows out of the whole service rendered by government to the individual, and that, as the return service (or tax) is connected with and limited by the exchanges which the individual makes under the eye of government, the tax itself should be proportioned as nearly as possible to the amount of those exchanges, and should be justified simply on the ground of them.

5. Taxes should not disturb *prices*. Taxes are an element which may be made to play, — which have been made to play, — fantastic tricks with prices. What has become famous under the name of "Protection" is nothing in the world but a shrewd scheme to raise certain prices by means of certain *taxes*. Taxes are too serious and sacred a matter to be made a cat's paw of in this indirect manner for an unworthy purpose. Taxes, like an exclusive income-tax, which affect no prices, are obviously the best of all; taxes, which affect prices less than other taxes, are better than those taxes; while taxes, like protective tariff-taxes, which are *designed* to disturb prices, are of necessity the very worst of all.

6. Taxes should be *considerate towards the poor*. If the necessities of the government require it, it has the right, in accordance with the principles

that have now been unfolded, to demand of all persons. who are capable of making exchanges and who do make them, something in the form of taxes. But it is every way better, when possible, that people of very small incomes should be ex-empted from taxation altogether; because, in the present age of the world, the well-to-do citizens of every country are able to bear without too great difficulty the legitimate burdens of their govern-ment; and because nothing tests better the degree of civilization which a nation has reached than the care and solicitude it displays for the welfare of its poorer citizens.

The principal propositions of this chapter may be summarized thus:—

1. *Taxes are in effect voluntary on the part of the payers, and are a return* SERVICE *for services rendered.*

2. *The only source of taxes are the* GAINS *of exchanges.*

3. *The freest possible exchanges are alike the interest of* GOVERNMENTS *and peoples.*

4. *Direct taxes are better than indirect, and an* INCOME-TAX *the best of direct taxes.*

5. TARIFF-TAXES *are only tolerable on a few such articles as tea and coffee.*

6. LOW *rates in taxation work like low charges in transportation.*

7. *Those taxes are always the best which disturb current* PRICES *the least.*

INDEX.

A.

B.

C.

www.ingramcontent.com/pod-product-compliance
Lightning Source LLC
Chambersburg PA
CBHW030909270326
41929CB00008B/623